Language Classification by Numbers

Language Classification by Numbers

April McMahon
and
Robert McMahon

OXFORD
UNIVERSITY PRESS

OXFORD
UNIVERSITY PRESS

Great Clarendon Street, Oxford OX2 6DP

Oxford University Press is a department of the University of Oxford.
It furthers the University's objective of excellence in research, scholarship,
and education by publishing worldwide in

Oxford New York

Auckland Cape Town Dar es Salaam Hong Kong Karachi
Kuala Lumpur Madrid Melbourne Mexico City Nairobi
New Delhi Shanghai Taipei Toronto

With offices in

Argentina Austria Brazil Chile Czech Republic France Greece
Guatemala Hungary Italy Japan Poland Portugal Singapore
South Korea Switzerland Thailand Turkey Ukraine Vietnam

Oxford is a registered trade mark of Oxford University Press
in the UK and in certain other countries

Published in the United States
by Oxford University Press Inc., New York

© April McMahon and Robert McMahon 2005

The moral rights of the authors have been asserted
Database right Oxford University Press (maker)

First published 2005

British Library Cataloguing in Publication Data

Data available

Library of Congress Cataloguing in Publication Data

Data available

Typeset by SPI Publisher Services, Pondicherry, India
Printed in Great Britain
on acid-free paper by
Ashford Colour Press, Gosport, Hampshire

ISBN 0-19-927901-2   978-0-19-927901-2
ISBN 0-19-927902-0 (pbk.)   978-0-19-927902-9 (pbk.)

1 3 5 7 9 10 8 6 4 2

For our sisters

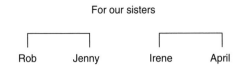

Rob   Jenny   Irene   April

Preface

The title of this book should really be expanded in good eighteenth-century fashion, with an added coda 'in which the authors suggest that using quantitative methods to test hypotheses and represent results may be a useful addition to comparative historical linguistics'. Our editor would gently and tactfully suggest that this might be a bit long to fit on the cover, but it is worth noting here that the force of that extra long would-be title holds for the entire content of this book. What we are *not* doing in our discussions and proposals below is trying to replace current historical-linguistic methodology with computer programs, or careful, nuanced and linguistically aware analysis of data by facile counting and enumeration. We are not proposing short cuts; we are not entirely sure we believe in them. What we are suggesting is that it would be good for historical linguists, and even better for relations between historical linguists and other historical disciplines like genetics and archaeology, to incorporate some testing, simulation, and computational model-building in their work, in a way which has proved productive and interesting in corpus linguistics and sociolinguistics.

The methods and models we will be discussing are not all new; they are certainly not all ours; and they are by no means the whole story. We will stress throughout that these techniques are an addition to the historical linguist's tool kit, not a replacement for the historical linguist. Our suggestion that this is 'language classification by numbers' might, in fact, be improved by a change in the preposition: we are really advocating language classification **with** numbers, that is with quantitative methods and some statistical testing, among other approaches. The 'by numbers' part here, however, is intended to be slightly reminiscent of those painting kits those of us who are not very artistic (for the record, that's April and not Rob) used to be given for Christmas in the hope that it might trigger some latent talent (it didn't). The point of those kits is that they are precisely a starting point: they provide a framework, and some explicit guidance, but when they are completed they still do not give a full, completed, and satisfactory picture. Further work needs to be done, melding the colours into one another, and interpreting the result. In exactly the same way, our quantitative approaches are meant to provide an outline, a suggested classification, which then requires interpretation and filling out using linguistic expertise. But the framework itself, if it can be agreed and used, provides a helpful starting point for addressing historical-linguistic questions which have been notoriously recalcitrant; and, as we shall see, we can also use quantitative techniques to support hypotheses which historical linguists have formulated already, to aid their presentation to and acceptance by colleagues in other, more numerically minded disciplines.

The involvement of two authors in a book seems to at least double the number of people who have to be thanked; but this task is a pleasure. First, we gratefully acknowledge the financial support of the Arts and Humanities Research Board for the 'Quantitative Methods in Language Classification' project underlying the book (grant AN6720/APN 12536). Our co-workers on the project, Paul Heggarty and Natalia Slaska, have been deeply involved in the research reported here, and have given their time freely to discuss issues and read drafts of this book; we are enormously grateful for their input, expertise, and collegiality. We thank the Department of English Language and Linguistics at the University of Sheffield, which hosted the project from 2001 to 2004, and in particular Andrew Linn, Joan Beal, Richard Steadman-Jones, Jayne Carroll, Claire Cowie, Emma Bradley, and Jackie Elkington, who provided help, support, and ears at crucial moments. Also in Sheffield, Rob thanks all the members of the North Trent Molecular Genetics Laboratory, and especially Ann Dalton, Steve Evans, and Richard Kirk, who took a friendly interest in what he was doing with the other 50% of his time. Sheila Embleton, Don Ringe, Tandy Warnow, Patrick Sims-Williams, Russell Gray, Quentin Atkinson, Hans-Jürgen Bandelt, Peter Forster, Colin Renfrew, and David Bryant have participated in many discussions of our work and theirs at conferences and electronically, and have cheerfully provided data, programs, pre-publication papers, ideas, and helpful criticism, much improving the proposals made here, and leaving us optimistic that there can be a real community of scholars addressing the vital questions of population histories. We also thank the various audiences at meetings and invited talks who have listened to our ideas and provided suggestions and encouragement; and in particular, though it would be invidious to pick out any individuals, we are grateful to colleagues outside historical linguistics who have strengthened our own conviction that there is a place for quantitative work in language classification, and that geneticists, archaeologists, computer modellers, and other colleagues are interested in its outcomes and potential. We also thank our OUP editor John Davey for his patience and enthusiasm (not necessarily in that order); and our children, Aidan, Fergus, and Flora, for their forbearance and generally good-humoured tolerance of our periodic preoccupation with what the computer was doing rather than what they were. Finally, we dedicate this book to our sisters, Irene and Jenny, with love and in the recognition that family trees also have some real-world relevance and value.

April McMahon
Rob McMahon

Contents

List of Figures

List of Tables

1

How Do Linguists Classify Languages?

1. 1 Classification and Language Families

In this book we shall be considering a range of methods which can be used in the comparison of languages (and indeed dialects or other varieties). However, classification is not just comparison, but comparison with a particular goal in view—the goal being the discernment of meaningful resemblances in the data, which in turn may allow us to identify those languages which descend from a single common ancestor, and to recover the history which has produced that divergence. Resemblances do, in some cases, have other causes; and although in the chapters that follow we shall concentrate on grouping languages into families, in Chapter 8 we return to the issue of comparison more broadly.

It must be confessed that classification in and of itself does not immediately sound particularly gripping, a problem of perspective which is common to classifiers in other disciplines, and which clearly rankles with Luria, Gould, and Singer (1981: 661):

Taxonomy, the science of classifying and ordering organisms, is often caricatured by people who don't understand it as a dull, mindless field that has no purpose beyond giving names to species in incomprehensible Latin. Professional taxonomists have never had such a narrow conception of their activity. They have always felt that the order expressed by similarities and dissimilarities among organisms reflects the causes of organic diversity and that a proper description of this order would reveal its cause. The quest of the best taxonomists has always been for a 'natural' system, one that reflects the causes of order, not just an artificial arrangement for efficient pigeonholing.

Not all of this description fits comparative linguistics (for one thing, historical linguists are more likely to be analysing the 'incomprehensible Latin' than inventing names in it), but there are key similarities. One is the misapprehension that classifying just means inventing boxes and shovelling entities into them; and the other is the absolute conviction among those doing the classifying that their enterprise is in fact an essential and explanatory one. Harrison (2003: 214), for instance, sets out 'the goals of comparative historical linguistics' as in (1), and is adamant that ' "True" historical linguists view the third goal as the real prize, the ultimate aim of the exercise.'

> (1) The goals of comparative historical linguistics (after Harrison 2003):
>   (*a*) to identify instances of genetic relatedness amongst languages;
>   (*b*) to explore the history of individual languages;
>   (*c*) to develop a theory of linguistic change.

Our own goals are more limited, since they are essentially restricted to the exploration of Harrison's point (*a*). On the other hand, without having a clear idea of how we are to 'identify instances of genetic relatedness among languages', which admittedly interacts with point (*b*), there is no way of progressing to point (*c*). Developing repeatable and reliable methods for diagnosing genetic linguistic relationships, then, ultimately equips us to go far beyond classification itself, and provides a basis for theorizing about language change.

How do linguists currently classify languages? Before starting to approach the question of methodology, we have to make a decision on perspective: our work will crucially adopt a historical view of relatedness. If we are simply looking at similarities between languages now, today, or at some fixed point in the past, and therefore taking a synchronic view, we may well end up classifying languages typologically. In that case, we note whether or not they share certain structural features, without necessarily worrying too much about where those features came from. They might be areal features, which have been borrowed by a number of languages from another with which they have been in contact. They might be accidental resemblances, which have developed because there just are not very many ways of doing certain linguistic things: taking one example, if a language has definite articles, they must either come before the noun, as in French *le loup* ('the wolf'), or after the noun, as in Romanian *lup-ul* (also meaning

'the wolf'), or indeed both before and after. However, taking a diachronic, historical perspective means we are keen to classify according
to the source of the features, not just the fact that resemblances can be
observed. This means it is a priority to distinguish those features which
signal common ancestry from those which have arisen for other reasons,
notably chance or borrowing. Again, there is a biological analogue here,
since biologists initially classified species according to their physical,
phenotypic features; but priorities, and our understanding of the underlying systems, have changed, and now classification typically proceeds by
prioritizing genealogical affinities, which signal common ancestry.

In comparative historical linguistics, then, we are interested in prioritizing features which indicate common ancestry, and descent through
time with gradual divergence from that common source. We want to
identify valid genetic groupings of languages which are more closely
related to one another than to any other language outside that grouping:
'genetic' here does not mean there is any necessary connection with
human biology (though we return to some mooted correlations in Chapter 5), but that we are dealing with family relationships. Once we arrive at
these groupings, they are conventionally shown in family trees, of the
kind familiar from representations of relationships between biological
species, or human individuals, as in Figure 1.1.

What the tree in Figure 1.1 tells us is that the languages under the
topmost node, the Germanic languages, form a valid genetic grouping.

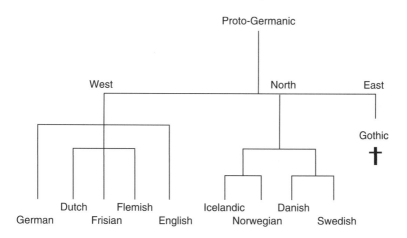

Fig. 1.1 Germanic family tree

They may be related as a whole to other languages or groups (and indeed we know this is the case—Germanic is only one subgroup of the much larger Indo-European family), but no single Germanic language is related more closely to any language outside the family than it is to the others within it. The tree also shows that these Germanic languages fall into subgroups, which are even more closely related, and shared a common ancestor even more recently. Finally, the node at the top of the tree has been labelled as 'Proto-Germanic', the hypothetical common ancestor for the group as a whole. Proto-languages like this are typically not attested, since they are usually assumed to have been spoken too early to be recorded in writing. They are therefore prehistoric systems, and just as we can reconstruct aspects of prehistoric human societies or prehistoric species like dinosaurs or woolly mammoths, so part of the comparative-linguistic enterprise involves reconstructing the most likely characteristics of these ancestral languages. In turn, small, relatively recent families like Germanic can be included in larger and older families like Indo-European, for which a partial tree, including all proposed subgroups but not all languages within these, is given in Figure 1.2.

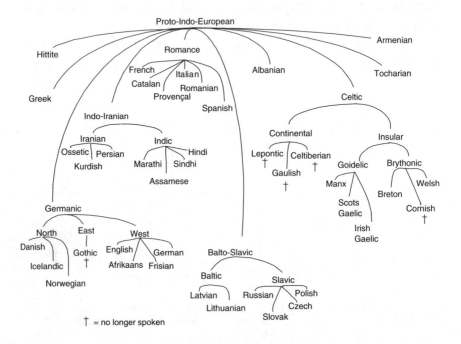

Fig. 1.2 Indo-European family tree

1. 2 The Comparative Method

1. 2. 1 An Outline of the Method

The last section provided an outline anatomy of a linguistic family tree; but it is still not clear how these trees are produced. Various methods for classifying languages exist: all have some drawbacks, and some are extremely controversial, as we shall see in Section 1.3 below, when we turn to Greenberg's method (1987) of mass comparison. However, there is one method which is typically seen as the gold standard by comparative historical linguists, and which is intrinsically bound up with the construction of the Indo-European tree in Figure 1.2, though it has also been applied to other language groupings worldwide. This method, which has been under development for more than a hundred years, is known simply as the 'comparative method', and is described by Harrison (2003: 213) as 'the *sine qua non* of linguistic prehistory', and 'the only tool available to us for determining genetic relatedness amongst languages, in the absence of written records'. Only a brief introduction can be provided here, but much more comprehensive summaries and discussions can be found in Hoenigswald (1960), Durie and Ross (1986), Fox (1995), and chapters 1–4 of Joseph and Janda (2003).

The comparative method is primarily a method for reversing linguistic history, and therefore has two indivisible parts: the demonstration of linguistic relatedness, and the reconstruction of a hypothetical common ancestral system. It has not, however, classically been applied to some random collection of languages to see whether they are likely to be related or not. Instead, there is an initial stage of working out whether certain languages are likely to be related, and in the development of the method on Indo-European this initially involved the observation of morphological similarities. For example, English and its sisters in the Germanic family tend to have a mini-paradigm of the *good-better-best* type, which sets them apart even from their Indo-European relatives, let alone the other languages of the world. French, for example, from the fellow Indo-European Romance subgroup, also has suppletion here, with *bon* not showing any clear formal resemblance to the comparative *meilleur* and superlative *le meilleur*; but it does not have the Germanic pattern of initial [g] in the basic form and [b] in the comparative and superlative. At the higher, Indo-European level, many languages are linked by having a three-way distinction in the gender system for nouns, conventionally labelled masculine, feminine, and neuter, just as Old English did, though the inflectional markings keeping the three genders apart have disappeared during the recorded history of the language. As Nichols (1996) shows, morphological affinities of this kind are important, not just because they exist in certain languages and not in others, but because the probability of their occurrence by chance in a range of languages is very low. Though we need not go into the detail of the calculations here, she suggests that the probability of finding an Indo-European gender system in a language chosen at random is less than one in a million (1996: 51).

It is worth taking a slight detour at this point to establish that Nichols's point does not exclude languages which lack inflectional morphology: as she notes (ibid. 63),

there are various circumstances under which groupings and reconstructions of isolating languages may be said to be consistent with the comparative method. One such situation is where the family is sufficiently shallow that relatedness is self-evident (e.g. Tai, Chinese) or has a written history that makes its relatedness evident (Chinese). Sometimes an isolating group fits into a deeper family that has more morphology and whose relatedness has been established in part on the evidence of that morphology, as Chinese fits into Sino-Tibetan or Vietnamese into Austro-Asiatic or Kwa into Niger-Congo.

It is also possible to use structured sets of lexemes, such as a system of numerals, though the whole set would need to be present in the entire series of languages; or to use features like tone, since 'where tone correspondences are regular the tones may be regarded as an arbitrary lexical classificatory device (rather like the gender or declensional and conjugational classes of Indo-European) that incorporates some paradigmatic grammatical organization into the lexicon' (ibid. 64).

These preliminary comparisons, then, establish that there is prima facie evidence for relatedness, and that it is worth pursuing the possibility in more detail. 'Once relatedness is assumed, then the labor-intensive process of working out the correspondences and cognate sets begins . . . This work ultimately yields a detailed picture of the branching structure of the family tree, and it often brings into the family additional languages that did not figure in the initial assumption of relatedness' (ibid. 41). The most important aspect of the next stage is that it does not involve collecting likely-looking bits of evidence piecemeal, since this might allow us to build a hypothesis of relatedness on chance resemblances or loans. Accidents do happen, and there are some well-known and striking chance resemblances between languages which do not appear to be related: for instance, both English and Persian have the word [bæd] meaning 'bad'; Italian [dɔnna] 'lady, woman' closely resembles Japanese [ɒnna] with the same meaning; and *aska* means 'ask' in the Jaqaru language spoken in Peru. Chance is a weak hypothesis, and can typically be disproved straightforwardly in most lexical cases, since similarities will generally extend well beyond individual words. The solution, then, is to look for regular and repeated similarities, such as those in (2), rather than one-off resemblances.

(2) Indo-European correspondences (partly after Durie and Ross 1996: 6):

Ancient Greek	Sanskrit	Gothic	Modern German	English
pod-	*pad-*	*fōt-*	*Fuss*	*foot*
pénte	*pañča*	*fimf*	*fünf*	*five*
ed-	*ad-*	*it-*	*ess-*	*eat*

As Durie and Ross suggest, it is pushing our concept of chance to unreasonable lengths to assume that it can account for these extremely regular correspondences of initial [p-] in Greek and Sanskrit as against [f-] in Germanic, or final [-d] in Greek and Sanskrit as against [-t] in Gothic and English and [-s] in German, which recur quite predictably in many more sets of words. These repeated similarities of form and meaning are the basis of the comparative method, and are also helpful in ruling out another possible explanation, namely borrowing. Although speakers may borrow many words, especially from more prestigious neighbours, they are not so likely to borrow basic vocabulary of the sort shown in (2), generally opting instead for religious, cultural, or technological vocabulary. In addition, loans are often adopted with certain non-native sounds, and will commonly fail to fit into the regular correspondence sets found in native vocabulary, so that repeated similarities like those in (2) are stronger evidence than absolute identity of sound and meaning. Borrowings can, however, be difficult to trace, and remain a serious problem for comparative historical linguistics; and we return to this issue in Chapters 2–4 below.

The existence of regular, repeated correspondences, then, suggests that the words in which they are found are cognates, or differentiated reflexes of the same item from the proto-language. This leads to two further essential characteristics of the comparative method.

First: 'When historical linguists talk about the "comparative method", what they usually have in mind is not just a method but also an associated theory' (Durie and Ross 1996: 3). This theory is the regularity hypothesis put forward in the so-called neogrammarian manifesto of Osthoff and Brugmann (1878), whose central claim is that sound change takes place regularly, affecting all the eligible words with the appropriate sound in the appropriate context, and affecting them all in the same way. What this means is that a sound change should not just select some examples of initial [p-] or final [-d] at random: it should alter all of them, and cause the same change in each case. This regularity lies behind the patterns we observe in (2), which are repeated throughout the lexicon: the same correspondences can be seen in 'father' with Greek and Sanskrit initial [p-] but Germanic [f-] in German *Vater* and English *father*, or in the final consonants of English *hot* versus German *heiss*. Of course, accepting the regularity hypothesis does not mean that we are necessarily committed to every aspect of the neogrammarian view of sound change: we might in particular not wish to argue now that changes affect all eligible lexical items simultaneously. We are at liberty to adopt more recent research, leading to a more speaker-centred, sociolinguistically informed view of change (Labov 1994, 2001) and incorporating lexical diffusion (Wang 1969; Chen and Wang 1975), without losing the regularity hypothesis and hence the comparative method. This is because, simplifying radically for present purposes, a change which keeps on diffusing for long enough will give an eventual outcome virtually indistinguishable from a change which happened all at once. The 'virtually' indicates that diffusing changes may sometimes run out of steam before they have affected absolutely all the candidate forms, so that there may be a few remaining exceptions—though these can in themselves be valuable in providing clues to the change having happened, and to what it has done.

The second key characteristic of the comparative method which follows from the identification of cognates and the acceptance of the regularity hypothesis is our ability to reverse regular changes and hence reconstruct the most plausible shape of the common ancestral form in each case. If changes were sporadic, and their patterns partial at best, we could not hope to reverse them; but regularity allows us to do exactly that, in combination with our general knowledge (based on a combination of phonetics, phonology, change in progress, and typology) of which changes in which directions are most common and natural. For example, to take (2) above, we find recurrent correspondences of [p-] in Greek and Sanskrit (and indeed also in Latin), with [f-] in Germanic. We know from surveys of a whole range of languages (see, for instance, Foulkes 1993) that [p-] very commonly changes into [f-], and indeed stops commonly turn into fricatives more generally. However, it is very rare for [f]- to turn into [p-], if it is possible at all: Foulkes finds only two examples, and both are controversial. We likewise know that stop sounds regularly devoice cross-linguistically at the ends of words, making it more likely that the stem-final sound in the 'foot' and 'eat' words was originally voiced [-d] rather than voiceless [-t]. Within Germanic, our already established generalization that stops tend to become fricatives, not vice versa, covers the correspondence of [-t] in English and Gothic with [-s] in German. By these and other similar processes we therefore reconstruct Proto-Indo-European *pod-/ped- 'foot', *penk^{w}e 'five', *ed- 'eat'. This process of reconstruction simultaneously provides us with the likely ancestral forms, the probable course of sound changes from the common ancestor through the subgroups, and criteria for placing languages within those subgroups. Although Durie and Ross (1996: 6–7) give these steps as sequential in their summary of the comparative method, reproduced in (3), they acknowledge that there is often recursion between the stages.

(3) Steps in the comparative method (Durie and Ross 1996: 6–7):
   (*a*) Determine on the strength of diagnostic evidence that a set of languages are genetically related; that is, that they constitute a 'family'.
   (*b*) Collect putative cognate sets for the family (both morphological paradigms and lexical items).
   (*c*) Work out the sound correspondences from the cognate sets, putting 'irregular' cognate sets on one side.
   (*d*) Reconstruct the proto-language of the family as follows:
      (i) Reconstruct the protophonology from the sound correspondences worked out in (*c*), using conventional wisdom regarding the directions of sound changes.
      (ii) Reconstruct protomorphemes (both morphological paradigms and lexical items) from the cognate sets collected in (*b*), using the protophonology reconstructed in (*d*) (*i*).
   (*e*) Establish innovations (phonological, lexical, semantic, morphological, morphosyntactic) shared by groups of languages within the family relative to the reconstructed proto-language.

(*f*) Tabulate the innovations established in (*e*) to arrive at an internal classification of the family: a 'family tree'.

(*g*) Construct an etymological dictionary, tracing borrowings, semantic change, and so forth, for the lexicon of the family (or of one language of the family).

1. 2. 2 Validating the Comparative Method

There are, inevitably, some limitations of the comparative method, to which we turn in the next section. However, there is one very considerable point in its favour: we know it works. Linguists do not always have proof positive that their methods give the right results, and of course since language is human behaviour, and humans are prone to behaving in unpredictable and downright odd ways on occasion, we cannot guarantee that a method which succeeds in some circumstances will not encounter difficulties in others. However, it is worth providing two cases where careful application of the comparative method has provided verifiable results.

As noted above, proto-languages are by definition relatively elderly, and will typically have been spoken at a time before they could be preserved in writing. Occasionally, however, we find direct or indirect evidence for a proto-language, and perhaps the most celebrated case of this kind involves Latin. Latin is generally taken to be the ancestor of the Romance group of languages, which includes French, Italian, Spanish, Catalan, Sardinian, and Romanian, among others. Of course, much of the Latin which has been preserved (leaving aside the odd lucky break like the somewhat more colloquial graffiti at Pompeii) is in rather high style, and it is reasonable to assume at least a stylistic gap between our records and the 'vulgar' spoken Latin of the average Roman citizen. But if Latin is not itself Proto-Romance, we might think of it as closely related to a smartened-up, Sunday-best version.

Hall (1950, 1960, 1976) reports on his coordination of a group of Romance scholars who convened to reconstruct Proto-Romance from their knowledge of the daughter languages: this exercise produced a translation of part of *Animal Farm* into Proto-Romance, and a short excerpt can be seen in (4).

(4) Hall (1960)—Proto-Romance

U⌃nus kértus ómo abé⌃bat u⌃na bélla uí⌃lla, kon u⌃na kása, múlta térra et múltas bésṭias. Máịs nó⌃n érat bónus illi ómo, ánṭiis érat múlto málus.

Sémper mále traktábat illas béstias, battéˆbat illas, nek dábat illéis (ad) sátis kíbu nek ákua. Ille béstie nóˆn érant konténte. Uoléˆbant káusas melióˆres.

'A certain man had a beautiful farm, with a house, much land, and many animals. But the man was not good; on the contrary, he was very bad. He always treated the animals badly, used to beat them, nor did he give them enough food or water. The animals were not happy. They wanted better things.'

Anyone reading the Proto-Romance reconstruction with the smallest knowledge of Latin will see clear affinities between the two, regardless of minor transcriptional decisions (marking stress, using <k> for more usual Latin <c>). There are obvious Latin-vocabulary items in the excerpt and elsewhere in the longer text, including *villa* 'farm, house', *vita* 'life', *bene* 'well', *dormire* 'sleep', and *terra* 'earth'; and the passage culminates in the fabulous 'Ómnes béstie súnt ekuáles, máis alikúˆne béstie súnt plúˆs ekuáles kue áltre' (ibid. 204) ('All animals are equal, but some animals are more equal than others' (ibid. 205)). Hall and his colleagues find that their reconstruction incorporates the effects of some known changes within Latin, but not others, so that /ei/ has become /i/ (as it did by around 150 BC) and /æ/ has become /e/ (a change usually dated to the first century AD). However, there is no sign in the reconstructed Proto-Romance text of the later changes of /e/ to /i/ and /u/ to /o/, which seem to have taken place in the first to second centuries AD. This allows Hall to date Proto-Romance, which he sees as a daughter of Old Latin and a sister of Classical Latin: he claims that the passage in (4) 'would have been at least five-sixths comprehensible, and perhaps even more so, to a Roman of ca. 50 B.C.' (ibid).

However, the Proto-Romance reconstructions are perhaps most interesting in their mismatches with Classical Latin. Hall argues that there is no evidence from the surviving daughter languages to allow reconstruction of either an /ns/ cluster, or a final /m/ in polysyllabic words, so that these are not included in the Proto-Romance text, even though we know they did appear in Latin: thus, we find reconstructed **omine* for attested Latin *hominem* ('man', accusative singular), and **mesa* for *mensam* ('table', accusative singular). However, there is confirmation from a variety of sources to suggest that exactly those reconstructed forms were in regular use in spoken Latin. For example, the *Appendix Probi*, which was compiled in the third to fourth centuries AD and advises Latin users of the forms they should not use (Baehrens 1922), includes

instructions like 'mensa, NON mesa', while Hall (1960) notes the existence of a tomb inscription which features on adjacent lines two different
variants of 'this tomb', *sepulchru istum* and *sepulchrum istu*. The apparent
breakdown of agreement here suggests that the −*m* no longer corresponds to anything in speech, though it is retained, at least part of the time,
in the (typically more conservative) spelling.

This attempt at reconstruction is not entirely uncontroversial: it was,
for example, carried out by Romance scholars, and you do not become a
Romance specialist by being completely unfamiliar with Latin, raising
questions over the independence of the enterprise. A second illustration
of the success of the comparative method is therefore in order, and this
involves the labiovelar sounds of Proto-Indo-European (PIE).

A series of three labiovelar stops (which we shall transcribe as voiceless
aspirated, plain voiceless, and voiced, though readers familiar with the
glottalic hypothesis will know that there are other possibilities; see Hopper 1973, Gamkrelidze and Ivanov 1995) is typically reconstructed for
Proto-Indo-European. The reflexes of these labiovelars $*/k^{wh} k^w g^w/$ seem
in most daughter languages to reflect the operation of normal sound
changes—so, as shown in (5), we typically find that the reconstructed
voiceless $*/k^w/$ has regularly developed to Latin $/k^w/$, to Old English /hw/
(where both the labial and velar elements are retained, but factored out
into separate sounds), and to Sanskrit /k/ or /s/ depending on the context
(but either way, losing the labial element). However, what we find in
Greek is enough to make us question the reconstruction of the labiovelars
completely. We do not find a single reflex of PIE $*/k^w/$; we do not even
find different but closely related reflexes determined in a clear and understandable way by the phonetic context. We find either /p/ before back
vowels, or /t/ before front vowels, and no evidence at all from even the
earliest stages of Greek that these were ever the same thing.

(5) | Greek | Latin | Sanskrit | |
|---|---|---|---|
| tettares | quattuor | catur | 'four' |
| -te | -que | ca | 'and' |
| hippos | equus | asvas | 'horse' |

However, evidence for exactly that has subsequently come from an
unexpected quarter. In the late nineteenth and early twentieth century the
archaeologist Sir Arthur Evans discovered a series of clay tablets in
Knossos, on Crete. He associated these tablets with the early Bronze

Age Minoan civilization, and found that they included three different writing systems. The earliest, from about 2000 BC, have a rudimentary, pictorial script. The second batch, from about 1750–1450 BC, are written in what is now known as Linear A: this is a version of the earlier script, reduced to outline form, and remains undeciphered. The third and most recent set of tablets, from 1450–1200 BC, are also represented in several locations on the Greek mainland where, fortunately for posterity, they had been baked and hence preserved in palaces destroyed by fire. It is on these tablets that the writing system known as Linear B was found.

The decipherment of Linear B is a linguistic detective story, made all the more complex because there were no bilingual texts to aid the process, and nobody knew either the script or the language. (A much fuller version can be read in Chadwick 1990.) The first steps towards decipherment were taken by Alice Kober in the 1940s, but the process was completed by the Mycenaean scholar John Chadwick, and his perhaps unlikely collaborator the British architect Michael Ventris. At the age of fourteen Ventris apparently heard a talk by Sir Arthur Evans on the mystery of Linear B and resolved to decipher the script—a vow which perhaps should have been taken seriously as he had, according to Chadwick, been reading on Egyptology, in German, since the age of seven. The decipherment was additionally complex since it turned out that Linear B was a syllabary, providing one symbol for each syllable, rather than one for each sound, as in an alphabetic system, or one for each meaning, as in a logographic system like Chinese. In a syllabary, because the symbol for each syllable is holistic, we would not expect the symbols for *say*, *see*, and *sew* to share any property just because they have the same initial spoken consonant: each will be written completely independently. It follows that decipherment is considerably more taxing in such cases; Ventris was successful primarily because he based his work on cryptography or code-breaking, working out a grid of signs he suspected of sharing a consonant or vowel, and then trying out the decipherment on tablets which seemed likely to contain placenames. When the technique began reliably to allow decipherment of placenames near Knossos, Ventris and Chadwick turned to other tablets, and began, to their considerable surprise, to decipher nouns which looked remarkably like Greek. The one possibility which had not been seriously suggested was that Linear B might have been used to write Greek, which is known from quite early in an alphabetic script, especially because the Minoan civilization was generally regarded as non-Greek. It is true that there is not a particularly good match between Linear B and the Greek sound system: each symbol represents a whole syllable, made up of a consonant and a vowel, so that a Greek syllable with a cluster of consonants has to be represented as CV-CV, as in *ti-ri-po* for /tripos/ 'tripod'. Final consonants also often have to be omitted, so we find *o-no* for /onos/ 'donkey'. It seems likely that the early Mycenaean Greek speakers adopted the Linear A writing system, which may have been developed for a language typologically very different from Greek, and used it for Greek as best they could, on the principle that any writing system is better than none. It is not particularly surprising, however, that it fell out of use, to be replaced by the more flexible alphabetic system borrowed from the Phoenicians.

However much the mismatches between Linear B and spoken Greek may have frustrated its early users, Ventris and Chadwick's decipherment provides us with very clear evidence in favour of the Proto-Indo-European labiovelars. Crucially, we find a single set of syllabic symbols in all the cases where we would reconstruct PIE $*/k^w/$—recall that these, oddly, have later Greek /p/ or /t/. Although we do not have a segment-by-segment spelling system for Mycenaean Greek, and therefore cannot prove that the mystery segment at the beginnings of these syllables is indeed a labiovelar, we know that the symbols are not the ones used in syllables which have /p/, /t/, or /k/—the initial consonant must therefore be something else, and the labiovelar is a strong contender. The conventional transliterations for these Linear B forms, with <q>, are shown in (6), providing at least a measure of confirmation of certain results from the comparative method. The later Greek results may be surprising, but at least we have evidence that the /p/ and /t/ in these contexts go back to a single segment in the Mycenaean period, leaving us with a slightly bizarre set of changes to contend with in the history of Greek, but strengthening the case for the PIE labiovelars.

(6)
Greek	Latin	Sanskrit	Linear B	
tettares	quattuor	catur	qetr-	'four'
-te	-que	ca	-qe	'and'
hippos	equus	asvas	i-qo	'horse'

1. 2. 3 Some Limitations of the Comparative Method

The results in the last section, along with the remarkable insights achieved over the past century and more into the history of a range of languages and their reconstructed ancestors, must be seen as successes, and as partial validation of the comparative method. Nonetheless, like any method seeking to reach back into prehistory, the method is limited in what it can achieve.

First, not all linguistic material is suitable as input to the comparative method. There are issues of the linguistic levels on which the method operates: there have certainly been attempts to reconstruct syntax, for example, but they are notably more problematic than phonological or morphological reconstruction, partly because we know less about what is natural in syntactic change, which axiomatically becomes harder to reverse (Watkins 1976; Lightfoot 1983; Campbell 2004: 297–306). Leaving aside this issue, however, we must be careful to exclude certain types of lexical items from comparison, particularly onomatopoetic forms and nursery words. This exclusion reflects the fact that the comparative method relies not only on regularity of change, but also on arbitrariness, to combat chance similarities. If certain words are non-arbitrarily linked, they are likely to share features for reasons other than common ancestry, and this will interfere with our results. As Campbell (2003: 272) notes: 'Ono-matopoetic forms may be similar because the different languages have independently approximated the sounds of nature, and they must be eliminated'. Swadesh (1954: 313) suggests omitting anything that means ' "blow, breathe, suck, laugh" and the like, that is all words which are known to lean toward sound imitation' (Campbell 2003: 272), and Camp-bell suggests a range of others, such as ' "cough", "sneeze", "break/cut/chop/split" ... "crow" (and many bird names in general) ... "snore", "spit", "whistle" ' (ibid. 273), though he also notes that 'Judgments of what is onomatopoetic are subjective' (ibid. 272). As for nursery words, these again show non-arbitrary similarities of sound, especially initial sounds, cross-linguistically, and there is general agreement that they should be omitted: these are typically terms for immediate family members, especially 'mama' and 'papa', but also grandparents, siblings, 'aunt', and 'uncle'.

Omissions of this kind require some screening of the data, but they are not serious enough to stop a method in its tracks. Perhaps more serious is the question of idealization, a recurrent one in linguistics generally: how much can we reconstruct, and how close do our results come to the actual phonetic reality of the proto-language? Inevitably, our approximation to a full system, and to the details of that system, must be only partial: for instance, no known language is dialect free, and yet we reconstruct to an apex, a single node at each stage, giving the impression of a uniform system. Hall (1960: 205) hotly contests the allegation of proto-language uniformity, arguing that:

> Of course there were alternative forms in Proto-Romance for some of those used in the text: thus, some speakers would unquestionably have said /ipsa u͜íˎlla/ or /u͜íˎlla illa/ or /u͜iˎlla ipsa/ for 'the farm'; some might have said /érat nekessáriu/ or /besoˎniábat/ 'it is necessary' instead of /estopéˎbat/ . . . Some of the features of the text inevitably belong to slightly different strata (social, regional or temporal) from others

However, even if we are in a position to reconstruct these different alternatives, what makes variation meaningful for both linguists and language users is knowing who uses the different variants, and under what circumstances: and these socio-historical conditions are beyond our reach.

As for the phonetic realism of proto-languages, this is one of several cases where comparative linguists seem to be prone, sometimes to the detriment of progress in the discipline, to setting up apparently diametric oppositions which turn out to be nothing of the kind: we shall meet two more below, in the controversies between 'lumpers' and 'splitters', and the wave versus the tree model. It is possible to find claims that reconstructions are purely formulaic cover terms for sets of correspondences: Lass (1993) cites Zawadowski, who perhaps takes this furthest in setting up numbers for correspondence classes, rather than using phonetic symbols. However, as Lass (ibid. 169) also notes, 'Protosegments must be assumed to have some kind of phonetic content if their reflexes are to be intelligible.' So, if Zawadowski sets up *6 as the cover term for one correspondence class, and *7 for another, and we observe that all the reflexes descending from *6 are labial, and all those coming from *7 are alveolar, we already know something about the most likely phonetic, or at least more abstract phonological, content of the protosegments. That is, 'the reconstructing historian is making claims about substance whether he thinks he is or not' (ibid.).

The conclusion here seems to be that proto-languages (another observation due to Lass (ibid.)) are like icebergs: you get a glimpse of one part, but you know a lot more is concealed under the water. However, we can strive to apply the comparative method as best we can, prioritizing certain types of evidence and setting others aside, and making reasoned but not extreme hypotheses about phonetic quality: we cannot recover every detail, but we can try to make our reconstructions as realistic as possible. There is, however, one really serious difficulty for both the comparative method and the family trees which it generates, and this involves language contact. First, contact-induced changes cannot be shown in family trees, which are composite pictures of only those changes involving diversification from the proto-language. Trees consequently give only a partial picture, and indeed Schleicher's family-tree model, put forward in 1862, was quickly followed by Schmidt's wave model (1872), which shows the spread of particular linguistic features over a geographical area. Again, this is not really a question of which model we should choose, as Rankin (2003: 186) observes:

much ink has been spilled... wondering which theory, the family tree (*Stamm-baum*) or the supposedly competing wave theory (*Wellentheorie*) is 'true'. Both are true. But they are oversimplified graphic representations of different and very complex things, and it seems hyperbole to call them theories in the first place. One emphasizes temporal development and arrangement, the other contact and spatial arrangement, and each attempts to summarize on a single page either a stack of comparative grammars or a stack of dialect atlases.

More problematically, if trees and tree-construction methods are based on evidence which necessarily excludes borrowings, we have to be very sure we can factor out those loans. Pulgram (1958) uses an improbable but effective nonsense reconstruction for Proto-Romance to illustrate his point that we may over-reconstruct by not recognizing borrowings. He observes that since all the Romance daughter languages have cognate forms for French *prêtre* 'minister', *évêque* 'bishop', the Romans must have been Christians, while the Romance equivalents for French *bière*, *tabac, café* 'evok[e] a picture of Caesar's soldiers guzzling beer and smoking cigars in sidewalk cafés' (ibid. 147). The example might be exaggerated for effect, but the problem is a real one, and the development of methodologies to deal with borrowing will be a recurrent theme throughout the book.

Finally, it is often claimed that the comparative method is intrinsically limited in the time depth over which it can operate; we return to this issue in Chapter 7, which deals specifically with dating. This is, of course, an issue of balance: as Harrison (2003: 230) puts it, 'Time is both parent and adversary to the comparative method: without change through time, there is nothing to compare; with enough change over enough time, comparison yields nothing.' Indeed, the underlying question is not one of time per se, but of the magnitude of change: again, Harrison (ibid.) expresses this extremely clearly:

The effect of time has nothing whatsoever to do with any putative upper limit on the comparative method. It has to do with the availability of evidence. The more time, the more change, the more lexical replacement, the fewer cognates: end of story. The limit is a practical (and statistical) one, not a temporal one.

None of these problems is sufficient to rule out the use of the comparative method: indeed, they may be beneficial in keeping linguists aware of the possible limitations and conscious of how the method should best be used. Removing onomatopoetic forms and nursery words reduces the likelihood of accidental resemblance. Knowing the structures of the languages under comparison guards against the inclusion of 'false friends', where we find resemblance but crucially not recurrent correspondences: thus, Greek *theos* and Latin *deus*, both meaning 'god', are not cognate, since this is the only case where those initial sounds match—the usual correspondences are *d* : *d* (Latin *duo*, Greek *duo* 'two'), or *f* : *th* (Latin *foris* : Greek *thuros* 'outside'). Depth of knowledge conversely encourages the inclusion of true correspondences which nonetheless appear immediately lacking in plausibility; one of the best known is the strikingly odd but regular correspondence of Latin *du*- with Armenian *erk*-, both derived from Proto-Indo-European *dw- (PIE *dwow, 'two', *dwaro 'long'; Armenian *erku, erkar*). We must acknowledge that family trees cannot tell the whole story, but equally that they do capture one important aspect of linguistic history; this does not mean we should castigate or reject the tree model for not incorporating contact, which it was never designed to do in the first place. We have to accept that there are limitations of applicability in domain and in the extent of change over which we can reconstruct; and that those reconstructions will necessarily be partial and idealized. These limitations are counterbalanced by evidence that the comparative method can produce convincing results; but, equally, those results can only be obtained if the method is applied rigorously, by linguists who know the languages they are comparing extremely well. This might seem to reduce the scope for automatizing the comparative method, and for testing, confirming, or extending its findings. In turn, this has opened the way for alternative methods which seem easier to apply; and in the next section we turn to the best known of these, Greenberg's mass, or multilateral, comparison.

1. 3 Mass Comparison

In the last section we spent a considerable amount of space outlining the comparative method, since it involves a complex series of steps and procedures. There is no 'rule book' for the comparative method (though it is sometimes suggested that Hoenigswald (1960) can be seen as an attempt at producing one), but it is tried and tested, and it was necessary for us to consider each element of the process, as well as some of the evidence showing the method can succeed. When we turn to Greenberg's mass comparison (1987), we find that it has been the subject of considerable media attention (Morell 1990; Ross 1991; Wright 1991, for example), which might suggest it requires at least equal elucidation here. However, what we cannot do is to discuss details of the method itself, since it is so straightforward and non-technical that in the eyes of many historical linguists it scarcely qualifies as a method at all. As Wright (1991: 55) puts it, 'First, forget all this stuff about rules of phonological correspondence. Second, forget all this stuff about reconstructing proto-languages. Third, write down words from a lot of different languages, look at them, and wait for similarities to leap out.'

Mass comparison, then, differs from the classical comparative method in not requiring regular correspondences to be established, and in excluding the proto-language reconstructions which provide both a test and a confirmation of those correspondences. The priority, instead, is to consider lexical and grammatical elements from as many languages as possible: a comparison of these will result in 'the grouping of languages into a certain number of obviously valid genetic units' (Ruhlen 1991: 120).

This summary raises several substantial questions. We cannot deal with all the repercussions here, but interested readers can find a detailed rebuttal of mass comparison in McMahon and McMahon (1995) and references given there. We concentrate here on the questions of whether or not mass comparison and comparative method are really separate methods, of what Greenberg means by 'comparison', and of the reliability of mass comparison.

It is tempting to speculate that the litres of ink spilt over mass comparison would have reduced to mere blots if Greenberg had not attempted to present it as an independent method in its own right. Everyone in historical linguistics accepts that some kind of inspection method is a necessary precursor to the comparative method: we have to take a look, form a hypothesis—and then, crucially, test it. Initially, this is what Greenberg and Ruhlen (Greenberg's greatest supporter) seem to think too.

Ruhlen argues that biological classification has always begun by inspection, and that the difficulty in accepting Greenberg's approach is essentially one of nomenclature: 'Greenberg's attachment of a new name to this process has led some to believe he is employing a new and unreliable method. In fact, he is simply starting the only way one can' (1991: 383). Similarly, Greenberg (1987: 3) suggests that 'my remarks are not intended as an attack on the validity of comparative linguistics or on the importance of undertaking reconstruction. Rather, the discussion is meant constructively as a way of taking first steps where the comparative method has not been applied for want of an assured basis in valid genetic classification.' However, Greenberg almost immediately contradicts himself, arguing that 'Basically what I am denying is that there really are two separate steps' (ibid. 7)—in other words, 'if there are grounds for making a hypothesis, there are automatically grounds for accepting it: the "proof" stage represented by the comparative method is therefore strictly unnecessary' (McMahon and McMahon 1995: 176–7). This separation of the two methods, and indeed rejection of the comparative method, seems also to follow from Ruhlen's reference to 'the mistaken belief that reconstruction and sound correspondences play a crucial role in linguistic taxonomy' (1994: 6); and Greenberg himself promises that 'the notion that regular sound correspondences can fittingly be called demonstrative ... will be shown ... to be illusory' (1987: 2). If this is the case, then we must address the detail of mass comparison, since we cannot guarantee that it will be used solely as input to the later application of the comparative method.

What, then, is involved in the actual application of mass comparison? In fact, it turns out that this question is very difficult to answer. The main, and most controversial, application of the method has been in the analysis of native languages of the Americas (Greenberg 1987), and here Greenberg proposes three genetic groupings: of Eskimo-Aleut in the furthest north, Na-Dene mainly in Canada and down the west coast, and Amerind over the whole of the rest of the continent. Of these, Amerind is the locus of most controversy, as a major superfamily of over 500 languages and 11 substocks.

Greenberg's approach centred on his collection of notebooks, in which he kept transcriptions, from a wide range of sources, of a large number of lexical and grammatical items. If enough data from enough languages are considered together, he argues, then languages will automatically fall into groups. However, we might anticipate a difference of opinion over whether volume of evidence is more important than quality. Greenberg's mass comparison (which Campbell and Mithun (1979a) call the 'laundry-list' approach) generates a vast amount of data, but the intrinsic problem is whether we can determine that in any given case we are really comparing like with like. The comparative method includes two independent checks of comparability: first, we must establish that correspondences are recurrent (which helps us rule out one-off fortuitous resemblances); and then we must also be able to reconstruct a most likely common ancestral form, showing that the daughters have developed by plausible sound changes (which helps to rule out borrowings and particularly wild long-range comparisons: see Sect. 1.4 below). However, there seem to be no such checks and balances in the case of mass comparison, where what counts as a match, in either phonetic or semantic terms, is what Greenberg says counts as a match. There is a significant literature demonstrating that criteria for determining matching in mass comparison are almost entirely lacking (Campbell 1988; Matisoff 1990; McMahon and McMahon 1995): for example, Goddard (1987: 657) suggests that 'similarity in meaning may encompass entire semantic fields or long word-association strings', such as Greenberg's Amerind etymology 'back$_1$', which includes forms meaning 'back, wing, shoulder, hand, buttocks, behind'. Turning to phonetic similarity, Goddard (ibid.) points out that in multilateral comparison 'Acceptable similarity in shape is often a match of only a single consonant', as in the forms *$mye{:}w$ 'road' and ma from the Amerind etymology 'go$_1$', and *-sit-'foot' compared with $ʔas$ and si in the etymology 'foot$_2$'. Campbell (1988: 600) likewise observes that many of Greenberg's candidates for phonetic similarity are very short:

while monosyllabic CV or VC forms may represent true cognates, they are so short that the similarity could easily be due to chance. And if only one or two segments of longer forms are matched, with no explicit proposal to account for the unmatched segments, then chance becomes a strong possibility. It is important to account for the whole word, not just for some arbitrarily segmented part of it. A match of only one or two segments will not be persuasive.

As Campbell suggests, it is vital that we should be able to distinguish between the results of any valid method and chance; and in the total absence of criteria for deciding what counts as a real or meaningful resemblance this is impossible to guarantee. We shall see demonstrations in the next chapter that the results of mass comparison are in fact indistinguishable from chance. This also invalidates Greenberg's further assertion that a major advantage of mass comparison is the sheer quantity of languages compared: as we shall see, increasing the number of languages is only likely to increase the reliability of the results obtained if we also insist that the supposedly common features are required to occur in more of the languages. If we do not make this requirement, then we simply increase the likelihood of finding chance similarities, and in the absence of clear and agreed criteria for determining what is a match we may then misclassify these chance resemblances as indicators of common origin. As Wright (1991: 58) puts it, Greenberg 'doesn't spell out criteria for deciding when two words correspond closely enough to qualify as a match. Greenberg himself may not need such pedantry; his intuitive sense for linguistic affinity is the subject of some renown. But other linguists may. And science is supposed to be a game anyone can play.'

It seems, then, that mass comparison is not strictly repeatable, and is therefore not amenable to testing. The method is very good at finding patterns, but no good at all at telling us whether those patterns mean anything. Greenberg's counter-argument here is that the patterns must be meaningful simply because the data are so plentiful: and on the face of it the numbers do look persuasive, with 107 grammatical features and 281 etymologies making up the case for Amerind. It is, of course, important that Greenberg's comparisons include both lexical and grammatical items, since this seems to hold out the hope of bringing mass comparison closer to the comparative method: as we saw in Section 1.2 above, initial work on Indo-European was strongly focused on morphology. However, 'It is safe to say that the number of grammatical items provided by Greenberg as evidence for *Amerind* is in fact far lower than 107' (Adelaar

1989: 250). In fact, the grammatical features tend to link only small numbers of the actual languages and substocks, as shown in (7).

(7) Grammatical features linking two or more Amerind substocks in Greenberg (1987) (reproduced from McMahon and McMahon 1995: 210)

No. of substocks	No. of features
2	22
3	8
4	9
5	0
6	5
7	1
8	0
9	0
10	1
11	2

As (7) indicates, only two of Greenberg's grammatical features recur in all 11 substocks, and these are first-person $-n$ and second-person $-m$, which on any criteria must count as short forms, and are also extremely frequent worldwide (Matisoff 1990, Nichols 1996). A staggering 59 of the total 107 are only found within individual substocks, giving no evidence at all for higher-order groupings.

Much of the case, then, must rest on lexical data, and here we encounter two problems. First, there is another numerical argument: of Greenberg's initially impressive 281 etymologies, more than half only link 2 or 3 of the 11 substocks (and none link all 11). The average number of lexical matches per pair of substocks is only 27 (McMahon and McMahon 1995: 211). Recall also that the criteria for matching are unclear, so that these alleged matches may be only the 'phono-semantic lookalikes' Matisoff (1990: 109–10) identifies for Proto-Sino-Tibetan and Amerind, hastening to add that he does not see these groups as related. As Matisoff continues, 'sober-minded scholars have shrunk from megalocomparisons not because they are so difficult, but because they are so easy'.

Although Greenberg claims to be using both lexical and grammatical data in establishing Amerind, we have seen that the weight of evidence rests firmly on the lexical material. Lexical lookalikes have been the foundation for many claims of distant relatedness, as noted by Trask (1996: 223), who gives a list of supposed cognates which have been proposed in attempts to connect Basque and Caucasian. Basque is a regular target for the tidiers-up of the linguistic world, who seem offended by the existence of isolates and are often desperately keen to scoop them up into some family or another; and, as Campbell (2003: 263) suggests, 'excessive zeal for long-range relationships can lead to methodological excesses'. Its association with long-range comparison, including attempts to reconstruct elements of 'Proto-World' (see Bengtson and Ruhlen 1994), has also done Greenberg's method no favours in terms of its acceptance in mainstream comparative linguistics. Trask observes that two of the Basque items are actually glossed with the wrong meanings, and another only has the given meaning 'in one very doubtful source', though 'It is completely out of order to cite forms or meanings which are severely localized or attested only in sources of questionable reliability when such forms and meanings conflict with the bulk of the evidence available' (Trask 1996: 223). For instance, Basque *maño* is glossed as 'masculine', but actually means '(little) mule'; this problem arises because Spanish *macho* has been used in a bilingual dictionary, and means both 'mule' and 'masculine'. Furthermore, Trask (ibid.) continues:

the alleged Basque *abets 'voice', *beri 'this same', *kala 'castle' ... do not exist at all: these are either blunders resulting from misunderstanding the secondary sources used or sheer fantasies on the part of the people drawing the comparisons ... The point of all this is that the people who drew these comparisons did not know anything about Basque. They contented themselves with extracting items incomprehendingly from bilingual dictionaries and other secondary sources, not all of them reliable sources of information, and as a result they made a spectacular series of blunders

One might expect that Greenberg, whose reputation in historical linguistics is significant, would simply not have made errors of this magnitude. But he did. McMahon and McMahon (1995: 183–5) list a range of error types in his data, ranging from the inclusion of false cognates, through the listing of non-existent forms, to the attribution of forms to the wrong languages (some of which are also non-existent). Ruhlen (1994: 121) suggests that etymologies should not be dismissed 'for ... reasons ... as trivial as the misidentification of a language'; though, as McMahon and McMahon (1995: 186) remark, 'presumably we are to conclude from this that it would do no harm to collect data from Hungarian, mislabel it Italian, and build, on the basis of the transitivity of genetic linguistic relationship, to which Greenberg is firmly committed, a composite group from Romance and Finno-Ugric'.

Turning to a more specific example, Goddard (1987: 656) reviews the 142 etymologies in Greenberg (1987) which include data from Algonquian, and argues that 'Errors in the Algonquian data alone invalidate 93 of these equations.' In 34 cases the forms cited by Greenberg are actually unrelated; 21 involve isolated forms, often from Blackfoot, which cannot be reconstructed for Proto-Algonquian; 10 are wrongly analysed or segmented; in 8 the phonology is wrong; in 7 the reconstruction cannot be supported; and 2 do not come from an Algonquian language at all (McMahon and McMahon 1995: 185). Goddard (1987: 656) considers that the remaining 49 etymologies are much more likely to be due to chance than to support wider relationships including Algonquian.

Perhaps the most astonishing aspect of mass comparison, however, is Greenberg's attitude to errors of this kind, which, far from leaving him covered in shame and embarrassment, do not appear to trouble him at all. His claim is that mass comparison 'is so powerful that it will give reliable results even with the poorest of materials. Incorrect material should have merely a randomizing effect' (Greenberg 1987: 29). The problem is that although errors may cancel each other out in some circumstances, they will simply compound in others, a fact captured succinctly in Matisoff's (1990: 110) comment 'garbage in, garbage out'. Again, this is clearly relevant to the question of whether the supposed matches identified by the supposed method are real or fictitious; and this again takes us back to the question of whether the results of mass comparison are distinguishable in principle from chance. We return to this question, and frame a wholly negative answer, in Chapter 3.

Here we find another of those intrinsically unhelpful apparent oppositions beloved of historical linguists, this time setting 'lumpers' against 'splitters'. Greenberg sets up mass comparison in opposition to the splitting tendency he sees as dominating American linguistics over most of the twentieth century, whereby adherents of the comparative method attempt to fragment Native American languages into an unfeasibly large number of small genetic groupings, with no prospect for higher-level classification. This he attributes (1987: 4) to classical comparativists' caution, deriving from their belief that making a false grouping is worse than missing a true one, whereas Greenberg sees the errors of omission and commission as equally serious. Conversely, Campbell and Mithun (1979a: 37) hold that 'Although the past is characterized by much "lumping" and the present by ready "splitting", the crucial difference lies in the demands for supporting evidence.' In other words, those practising the comparative method are intrinsically cautious in the absence of decisive, recurrent similarities and plausible reconstructions; and this caution may well be warranted in view of the errors commonly found in long-range comparisons based on second-hand lexical evidence. However, as Campbell and Mithun note, failing to group languages now leaves the option open for the future, while grouping in error may establish an unsubstantiable family which is then fed into further comparisons, multiplying errors elsewhere in the projected family tree. So-called 'splitters' are not necessarily totally opposed to higher-level classification: they simply await evidence which seems better than chance. That does not seem to us such a bad strategy.

1. 4 Why Historical Linguists Need Quantitative Methods

The previous section might seem to suggest that all historical linguists need is patience. However, waiting in the hope that better evidence will simply emerge is not an option, since evidence in linguistics, as in many other disciplines, cannot simply be lifted directly off the shelf: it also has to be analysed. It is with this stage of analysis that the problem currently lies, since we have more than one possible way to approach the classification of languages into families, and we face serious difficulties in evaluating them. Consequently, patience is necessary but not sufficient: we must remember the exhortation to 'Pray to God, sailor, but row for the shore.'

The current difficulty comparativists face is our inability to test and demonstrate family relationships, so that these can either be proved beyond reasonable doubt, or refuted. If we cannot tell good results from bad ones in a formal and repeatable way, we cannot hope to distinguish good methods from bad ones either. The comparative method is central to comparative linguistics; but it is based primarily on case law, and typically taught in association with its application to a particular family. Hoenigswald (1960) does give steps and principles which responsible historical linguists will usually follow; but the relative informality of the method, and the lack of testability beyond the checks built into the method itself, mean we have to rely on the experience and integrity of individual prac- titioners to do so. This brings the comparative method uncomfortably close to mass comparison, where accepting results means believing impli- citly in the linguistic intuitions of the method's inventor. Both methods rely on an individual linguist's knowledge of a particular language group, but this makes both inevitably subject, at least potentially, to interference from individual linguists' opinions. If we cannot guarantee getting the same results from the same data considered by different linguists, we jeopardize the essential scientific criterion of repeatability. Although we feel as a scholarly community that we can rely on comparative method more than mass comparison, justifying that preference is difficult, partly because the criteria for deciding what counts as 'the same' are not worked through formally in either case. This is like playing Snap without deciding in advance what counts as the same—do we want identity, as in pictorial versions for younger children, or are we matching by number, suit, or both? Not working this through in advance inevitably leads to chaos and tears before bedtime. The tears before bedtime of comparative linguistics have led to some intemperate language in the literature, and a fair amount of press coverage, over the last decade or so.

In our view, the solution is to seek to formalize our methods, and to add a quantitative dimension, in the interests of confirming or ruling out particular results (and, by extension, the methods which have produced them). There are other areas of linguistics which have benefited consid- erably from the inclusion of a quantitative perspective, including notably sociolinguistics; likewise, corpus-based approaches have produced in- sights into language change which could not be achieved on the basis of smaller quantities of data collected piecemeal and analysed with the naked eye. If we are seeking an insight into trends, then computational methods can be of considerable help. They may also assist us in answering two other outstanding questions.

First, although we might be able to group languages into a family with a certain measure of security, using the comparative method for instance, subgrouping is still a matter of considerable unclarity, since the method as it stands does not allow for the quantification of degrees of relatedness. When we see two languages at 'the same level' in a family tree, should this be interpreted as meaning they have changed by approximately the same amount since the immediately higher node, or since their common ancestor? At the moment, there is no way of representing branch lengths in trees or measuring similarity in an agreed and meaningful way; and this may require the development of new, additional methods of comparison.

Second, historical linguists may share a general sense, for the most part, that the comparative method is proven and promising, and that mass comparison is neither, but their arguments have been detailed and specific, and their evaluation has not transmitted itself to colleagues in other historical disciplines. Thus, archaeologists and geneticists tend naturally to favour mass comparison, since it is presented as a method providing measurable results, over a potentially unlimited time depth, and is moreover straightforward to apply. The comparative method, on the other hand, is sometimes presented as a mystery into which one can only be initiated after years of philological training; moreover, it is suggested that numbers are anathema to its practitioners, and that it is intrinsically limited to a period of perhaps 8,000–10,000 years, bringing it nowhere near the evolutionary time which interests geneticists. Cavalli-Sforza (2000: 137–8), for instance, speaks out in support of Greenberg's work, and clearly sees other comparativists as simply old-fashioned, unwilling to accept big ideas, and as 'disallowing reliable measurements'. Geneticists and archaeologists will inevitably continue to accept what they see as bold hypotheses, unless we can convince them that the bold hypotheses are unsound hypotheses, based on unsound methods. To do this we need to speak the language of prehistorians, and that language consists partly of numbers.

This does not mean that we are seeking to replace historical linguists, with their deep knowledge of individual languages and groupings, by sleek, humming computers and programs which smooth out all the bumps (wherein reside most of the linguistically interesting aspects of the languages we are comparing). However, we can aspire to combining the two in a way which might allow us to argue convincingly against the methodological lunatic fringe. We can try to come up with ways of testing and supporting our good methods and results, and of testing and rejecting bad ones.

This is the first of the three aims of this book. The second involves the development of new methods which can supplement the comparative method in situations where it cannot realistically be applied, and which are based on a range of levels of the grammar: if we have a number of independent methods, they may support each other, and perhaps increase the time depth over which we can operate. As Nichols (1996: 65) notes, linking our second and third objectives:

What linguistics needs now are heuristic measures that will be valid in situations where comparativists cannot expect to have reliable intuitions, measures that will detect relatedness at time depths at which face-value individual-identifying evidence has disappeared and the standard comparative method cannot apply. And since any such heuristic is likely to be improved if it can take into account the evidence offered by archeology, human biology, and other fields, it is important that communication be improved between historical linguists and other human prehistorians.

As well as allowing us to work in an interdisciplinary way, we can hope that the development of quantitative techniques will allow us to evaluate claims of congruence between historical-linguistic data and those from archaeology and genetics. Pursuing these proposed correlations is our third aim.

In short, in the following seven chapters we aim to develop testability for existing methods, and to pioneer new ones. We hope to assist historical linguists in demonstrating that their partly intuitive conclusions are the right ones, and to develop methods to assist in cases where the linguistic evidence is unclear, and no amount of linguistic knowledge can provide more than a tentative hypothesis. Comparative linguists have to get better at hypothesis testing for our own sakes, but also because it will help us in interactions with colleagues from other disciplines. We also need to be able to show, particularly for such interdisciplinary purposes, the difference between a promising or even proven method and a seriously flawed one. Finally, in our scientific opinion, blank slates do not exist; where they appear to, they tend to reflect a wilful rejection of earlier spadework and at least partial hypotheses. We have no intention of going it alone in this way in what follows, but will be staying close to the linguistic ground at least initially, in testing, evaluating, and extending two well-worn comparative-linguistic methods. These are approaches based on meaning lists in Chapter 2 and the comparative method in Chapter 3.

2

Lexicostatistics

2. 1 Comparing Like with Like

The essential first step in the development of any quantitative method is identifying something to measure. If we want to use a quantitative technique to establish whether languages are likely to be related, or whether they fall into the same subgroup, or how similar two languages are relative to a third language, we need to decide what we are going to count; and to ensure that we are comparing like with like, the something we are counting has to be the same across all the languages we are comparing. Indeed, to make the method as flexible as possible we need that something to be the same in all the languages we might ever want to compare. In comparative linguistics this is a tall order.

Our first thought might be to turn to sociolinguistics, where quantitative methods have enjoyed such success, and adopt the strategies developed there. However, sociolinguistic studies tend to operate within a single speech community (Patrick 2002), where speakers share the same norms of behaviour and attitude, and the same variable elements of linguistic structure. It is possible, therefore, to isolate a set of variables and to study the circumstances, both linguistic and non-linguistic, under which the different variants emerge. For example, we might consider a phonological variable (t), with variants [t], used mainly by women, and glottal stop [ʔ], mainly used by men. We might find a syntactic variable (negation), with multiple negation (*I didn't do nothing*) favoured by lower-class speakers, and single negative markers (*I didn't do anything*) the dominant variant for middle-class speakers; or a lexical variable, where the meaning (be sick) might be expressed by *vomit* for older speakers and *throw up* for younger ones. These examples are simplistic, since typically a range of interacting factors of sex, class, age, level of education, ethnicity, and more will affect the variant we find, making the quantitative approach of counting variants and correlating them with non-linguistic factors both complex and enlightening. However, they do show the types of variables with which sociolinguists frequently work.

For historical linguists, however, determining variables is not so straightforward, because we are not dealing with individual speech communities or even languages, but the range of possible variation within human language in general. If we want to develop a quantitative approach to phonetics (and we return to such a possibility in Chapter 8), what are we to measure? There are many different sounds in the world's languages, but some are restricted to a small number of languages, like the click sounds, which are mainly found in Southern Africa. Others are much more widespread, like the voiceless labial plosive [p]: but how are we to compare this in a system like Hawaiian, where it is one of 8 consonants, with the situation in Georgian, where it is one consonant among 80 (Ladefoged and Maddieson 1996)? Turning to morphosyntax, are we to compare the categories of subject, object, and so on (leaving aside as another question those languages where such categories might not be relevant) regardless of the strategies languages use to signal them—which might involve adding agreement markers like affixes, or putting them in a specific position in the sentence, or using a separate word along with the noun? Or should we consider the strategies themselves, asking whether we are dealing with a language which has inflectional morphology or one lacking it, one with fixed word order against another where anything goes?

All these are open questions, and not unanswerable in principle, though the answers might be many and varied (see again Ch. 8 below, and Heggarty forthcoming). However, the earliest and best-known quantitative method in comparative linguistics did not seek to develop comparisons in either phonetics or morphosyntax, but instead focused on vocabulary. This may seem surprising, since intuitively the lexicon might seem the most highly and unpredictably variable part of the grammar: we know that words acquire new meanings between generations (*gay, wicked, cool*), and that one word can be replaced by another (*wireless, radio*) within a short time-span. We also know that the same area of meaning can be covered by a single word in one language, like *brown* in English, but two or more words in another, like *brun* and *marron* in French. Some languages have a word for a particular concept, while others have to paraphrase or borrow, as English has borrowed *Schaden-freude* from German, and a whole host of languages spoken in cultures which did not formerly have helicopters, pacemakers, or e-mail have borrowed the words for those newly introduced ideas from English.

Although vocabulary might seem inherently unstable, and meaning amorphous and not amenable to universal segmentation, the method of lexicostatistics assumes that there are certain concepts for which every human language is highly likely to have a word, because all humans are highly likely to have to talk about them. Moreover, these concepts are so ubiquitous that the words will be frequent, and therefore probably learned early. The hypothesis is also that they will therefore be relatively resistant to linguistic change, and especially to cross-cultural replacement. Words for such deeply ingrained and universally relevant human experiences might consequently be good candidates for cross-linguistic quantitative comparison, and we explore this lexicostatistical approach in the next section.

2. 2 Classical Lexicostatistics

The development of classical lexicostatistics is inextricably linked with the name of Morris Swadesh, though in fact Embleton's historical survey (1986, 2000) makes the point that work of this kind predates Swadesh, with associated methods used, for example, by Sapir (1916), Kroeber and Chrétien (1937), and Ross (1950). We define lexicostatistics here as the use of standard meaning lists to assess degrees of relatedness among languages. However, lexicostatistics in this sense has frequently been confused with one application of the method, glottochronology, which seeks to date the splits of sister languages from their common ancestor. Indeed, Fox (1995: 279–80), in the only textbook devoted exclusively to linguistic reconstruction, notes that 'Though potentially different in scope, these two terms are used virtually synonymously by most scholars, as they designate what is, in effect, a single method'. Campbell (1998: 177) seems to support the distinction in principle, though suggesting that it is not often observed in practice:

glottochronology is defined as a method with the goal of assigning a date to the split-up of some language into daughter languages, whereas lexicostatistics is... the statistical manipulation of lexical material for historical inferences (not necessarily associated with dates). Lexicostatistics in this sense is broader. However, in actual practice, this distinction is almost never made; both names are used interchangeably.

On the other hand, Joseph and Janda (2003: 173) are careful to differentiate lexicostatistics from glottochronology, while Embleton (2000: 160 n. 3) actively argues for differentiation: 'Some authors, particularly in the 1960s, use the terms glottochronology and lexicostatistics interchangeably... This leads to confusion—and often debate at cross-purposes—over the goals or achievements of the particular method used in a particular piece of research.' It is easy to see how this confusion has arisen, since Swadesh (1952, 1955) focuses his discussion closely on dating. However, our view is that lexicostatistics is a prerequisite to glottochronology, which is an application and extension of that method. We return to glottochronology in Chapter 7, in a specific discussion of dating, but for the moment exclude the potential application to calculating time since divergence from our evaluation of lexicostatistics. This is not to say that no questions have been raised over the assumptions of lexicostatistics, but rather that glottochronology makes more assumptions, and those it makes are more problematic. Identifying lexicostatistics with glottochronology, and rejecting both on the basis of problems specific to the latter, runs the risk of throwing out the meaning-list baby with the time-depth bathwater.

We use the term 'meaning list' rather than the more common 'word list' because the latter is potentially ambiguous. Lexicostatistics operates not by comparing words in different languages but by setting up an agreed test list where each slot is a meaning and then comparing the items that occupy the same slot cross-linguistically. So, in a lexicostatistical analysis of English and German we might take the meaning 'two' as one item in the list, and would then be comparing *two* with *zwei*. We obtain a score across the whole list by scoring 1 for each case where the two items are cognate, and 0 for each case where they are not. The prior application of the comparative method tells us that *two* and *zwei* are cognate: we know the <w> in the English spelling used to be pronounced in Old English, as it still is in some dialects, such as Scots [twɔ:] or [twe:], and there is a regular correspondence of initial [t] in English with [ts] in German, seen also in *tide* versus *Zeit*, or *ten* versus *zehn*. The idea is that the total scores for meaning-list comparisons over different pairs of languages can tell us how closely related those languages are, therefore helping us with questions of subgrouping. For this reason, it is vital to include only the most common, colloquial items, not searching for cognates at all costs: thus, a slot for 'dog' must be filled by English *dog*, even though a knowledge of German *Hund* might make it terribly tempting to dig around in the more specialized vocabulary and put in *hound* instead. As Swadesh notes, 'There is a certain danger of subjectivism in filling out the test lists for given languages and in scoring cognates between a pair of lists' (1955: 129), and it is this subjectivism we must guard against in applying lexicostatistics.

The next question is how we determine the composition of the meaning list. To allow maximum comparability across languages, and to guard against accidental resemblances and borrowing, such lists do not include whatever random items the experimenter fancies: as Campbell (1998: 177–8) tells us, the most basic assumption of lexicostatistics is that 'there exists a *basic* or *core vocabulary* which is universal and relatively culture-free, and thus is less subject to replacement than other kinds of vocabulary'. Trask (1996: 23) defines these basic meanings as:

chiefly the items of very high frequency which we would expect to find in every language: pronouns, lower numerals, kinship terms, names of body parts, simple verbs like *go, be, have, want, see, eat*, and *die*, widespread colour terms like *black, white*, and *red*, simple adjectives like *big, small, good, bad*, and *old*, names of natural phenomena like *sun, moon, star, fire, rain, river, snow, day*, and *night*, grammatical words like *when, here, and, if*, and *this*, and a few others.

It is not clear exactly how the items for the list were selected; Swadesh (1952: 455) tells us only that 'It was not difficult to form a list of about two hundred relatively stable lexical items, consisting of body parts, numerals, certain objects of nature, simple universal activities.' Swadesh (ibid. 457) does note that 'Suitable items for a test list must be universal and non-cultural. That is, they must refer to things found anywhere in the world and familiar to every member of a society, not merely to specialists or learned people.'

It is important to stress here that classical lexicostatistical comparisons are not based on superficial similarity; this would make it indistinguishable from mass comparison, though the use of a fixed list might in fact confer an advantage on lexicostatistics here. What is counted is not the number of similar items between two lists, but the number which can safely be assumed to be cognate. It follows that prior application of the comparative method is necessary for this method to work most reliably, or at least that a certain amount of initial effort has to go into looking beyond the lists themselves to assess whether the identified similarities extend into regular and recurrent correspondences. Trask (1996: 362) argues this point particularly strongly, contending that 'lexicostatistics... can be applied only *after* the languages of interest have been shown to be related and *after* cognate words have been securely identified'. He is strongly opposed to applications of lexicostatistics which seek to establish relatedness, such as the work of Tovar et al. (1961), who compare lists from Basque and a range of other languages including Caucasian and Berber. Their figures include 10% 'cognates' for Basque and Berber, and 7.5% for Basque and Kartvelian. However, as Trask (1996: 362) rightly observes, this is an overextension of the method, since:

all that these pretty numbers represent is the proportion of arbitrary resemblances between the languages by which the authors are prepared to be impressed. Such work constitutes an abuse of lexicostatistics: guesswork wrapped up in numbers expressed to any number of decimal places is still guesswork, and it should not be presented as anything better. ...

As we shall see recurrently through this book, mathematical models and methods are not a substitute for careful and reasoned linguistic investigations, though that has not prevented attempts to use them in this way. What quantitative approaches can do is to validate the results of purely linguistic methods: moreover, if our quantitative approaches are complementary to the linguistic ones, and produce highly correlated results, we might gain confidence to adopt the quantitative approach alone in cases where our tried and tested linguistic methods simply cannot work, whether for lack of data or because of some intrinsic unclarity in the situation. We do not start, however, from the assumption that the linguistic methods can be nudged aside in every case.

Another key consideration in applying and evaluating lexicostatistics involves the number of slots in the test list. According to Campbell (1998: 179), Swadesh started with 500 items, but then progressively reduced the list length, so that the most commonly used lists now include 100 or 200 meanings. Swadesh himself observes that he opted for 215 items in early lists, but recommends the omission of 15 items, including 'brother', 'sister', several numbers larger than five, 'to cook', and 'to dance', which are 'unsatisfactory for many language groups' (1952: 455). Subsequently, Swadesh (1955: 124) suggests a further reduction to 100 items: 'defects in the old list were repeatedly made evident. The only solution appears to be a drastic weeding out of the list, in the realization that quality is at least as important as quantity'.

The rationale for these reductions, leading to the 100-item list, is provided in Swadesh (1955). First, a number of items are excluded because they are thought not to be culture neutral; these include 'ice', 'snow', 'freeze', 'snake', 'sea'; numerals above two; and some natural objects like 'salt', which is commonly traded (ibid. 125). Certain activity meanings, like 'cut', 'pull', 'dig', and 'squeeze', are removed because they cannot reliably be matched in all languages, and also 'belong to a distinctly lower level of stability than the bulk of our test items' (ibid.). Similarly, Swadesh (ibid.) rejects 'interlingually ambiguous and unstable object words' including 'leg', 'back', 'guts'. For example, 'The leg includes the foot, ankle, calf, shin, knee, thigh. Many languages have a single word for foot and leg. Others make a distinction between the lower and upper leg. Little wonder therefore that *leg* turns out to be one of the least stable items on the list' (ibid.). Furthermore, Swadesh argues that synonymous items like 'wife' and 'woman' must be rejected because if a language has the same item for both meanings then either both will be cognate or neither will be; crucially, the two slots in the list are therefore not independent. For this reason the 100-item list excludes 'wife', and similarly 'river', 'lake', 'sea' because of 'water'; 'far' because of 'long'; 'short', 'thin', and 'near' because of 'small'; 'dust' because of 'earth'; 'fog' because of 'cloud'; 'leg' because of 'foot'; 'they' and 'he' because of 'that'. Swadesh notes that there are still some possible cases of duplication (ibid. 125–6), such as 'water'/'rain', 'skin'/'bark', 'big'/'long', 'how'/'what', 'who'/'what', 'this'/'that' (and here his practice seems rather inconsistent, since he has removed 'short' but not 'long'). He suggests as an alternative that (ibid. 126):

Another approach to the problem of potential duplication would be to leave the cases in but to mark them specifically, so that they may be scored only when the compared languages do not involve duplication. This would enable us to add some otherwise excellent test items—including *lip* (tending somewhat to duplicate *mouth* or to be expressed as a compound *mouth-skin*) and *arm*, in addition to some of those already mentioned—but would complicate the scoring by virtue of the need to check each comparison for synonyms.

In the computer age, however, this added complexity scarcely registers as an objection, and would seem clearly to confer an advantage in terms of improving accuracy, as discussed further in the next section.

Swadesh further proposes the removal of cases which may have shared or identical roots, such as 'this'/'that', 'who'/'what'/'when'/'where'/'how', 'kill'/'die', 'I'/'we', 'thou'/'ye': 'the revised list therefore drops *when, where, how, ye* but it keeps the rest of the words as minor risks. When a language has two equivalents for *we*, inclusive and exclusive, the former is to be used because it is less likely to repeat the root of the first person singular' (ibid.). He also excludes imitative words, like 'blow' which tends to have labials or sibilants and rounded vowels, and also 'breathe', 'laugh', 'puke', 'scratch', 'laugh', 'cry', along with nursery words like 'papa', 'mama'. A few items are removed because they are 'too bound up with peculiarities of language morphology' (ibid.); these include 'if', 'because', 'and', 'at', and 'in'. The eventual 100-item Swadesh list includes 93 meanings from the earlier 200-item list, with an additional 7 new meanings. The 200-item list is shown in (1) below, with the items found in the 100-meaning list marked with an asterisk, and the extra 7 meanings in bold at the end. We return in Chapter 4 to the question of the optimal length of list, and to a statistical comparison of the 200- and 100-meaning options.

(1) Swadesh 200-meaning list (items in 100-meaning list marked with *)

all*	blood*	dirty	father
and	blow	dog*	fear
animal	bone*	drink*	feather*
ashes*	breathe	dry*	few
at	burn*	dull (blunt)	fight
back	child	dust	fire*
bad	cloud*	ear*	fish*
bark*	cold*	earth*	five
because	come*	eat*	float
belly*	count	egg*	flow
big*	cut	eye*	flower
bird*	day	fall	fly*
bite*	die*	far	fog
black*	dig	fat (grease)*	foot*

four	many*	sharp	tie
freeze	meat*	short	tongue*
fruit	mother	sing	tooth*
give*	mountain*	sit*	tree*
good*	mouth*	skin*	turn
grass	name*	sky	two*
green*	narrow	sleep*	vomit
guts	near	small*	walk*
hair*	neck*	smell	warm*
hand*	new*	smoke*	wash
he	night*	smooth	water*
head*	nose*	snake	we*
hear*	not*	snow	wet
heart*	old	some	what*
heavy	one*	spit	when
here	other	split	where
hit	person*	squeeze	white*
hold (take)	play	stab (pierce)	who*
how	pull	stand*	wide
hunt	push	star*	wife
husband	rain*	stick	wind
I*	red*	stone*	wing
ice	right (true)	straight	wipe
if	right (side)	suck	with
in	river	sun*	woman*
kill*	road*	swell	woods
know*	root*	swim*	worm
lake	rope	tail*	ye
laugh	rotten	that*	year
leaf*	rub	there	yellow*
left (side)	salt	they	**breast***
leg	sand*	thick	**claw***
lie*	say*	thin	**full***
live	scratch	think	**horn***
liver*	sea	this*	**knee***
long*	see*	thou*	**moon***
louse*	seed*	three	**round***
man*	sew	throw	

2. 3 Objections to Lexicostatistics

A range of objections to lexicostatistics have been raised in the literature; in fact, Swadesh's own work prefigured the majority of these. First, Teeter (1963) argues against the use of any method focusing only on the vocabulary—anyone doing this 'has mistaken the dictionary for the language'. As we shall see in the next chapter, there have been moves to include morphological and phonological items in more recent quantitative approaches, notably in Ringe et al.'s computational-cladistics project (2002). In any case, the best lexicostatistical work is careful to build on the findings of the comparative method, and thus considers recurrent correspondences to decide on cognacy judgements; strictly, lexicostatistics is therefore not simply a lexical method but also a phonological one. It is worth noting, though, that there will be some cases where the methods comparative linguists can apply will be limited by the availability of data. This is particularly true of endangerment situations, where speakers may be few and elderly. Such situations are increasingly common: Nettle and Romaine (2000: 5) cite a 1962 survey suggesting that of the estimated 300 languages spoken in the territory of the present-day USA in 1492 only 175 were still spoken; moreover, only 6 of these then had more than 10,000 speakers, with 51 having fewer than 10 speakers. Dorian (1978) notes that 'semi-speakers', who use the minority language only in specific situations and may be restricted in their supply of interlocutors, are also typically lacking in confidence, fearing errors and omissions in their production. In such cases we may have to rely on lists of basic, frequently occurring vocabulary and very little else, so that it is clearly worth testing methods based on such restricted evidence. If we assess lexicostatistical approaches and find that they are workable and reliable for languages where we have a known history and plentiful evidence, we will then have a valuable resource that may be applicable to more poorly attested systems.

However, even if we are sympathetic in principle to the idea of a lexically based means of comparison, we must question whether the proposed list is the most appropriate one. Lexicostatistics, as we have seen, relies absolutely on the identification of universal, basic meanings; but Hoijer (1956) argues that no list can ever be culturally neutral. Swadesh (1952: 457) himself notes this problem, and suggests some possible solutions:

they must be easily identifiable broad concepts, which can be matched with simple items in most languages. Of course, it would be impossible to devise a list which works perfectly for all languages, and it must be expected that difficult questions will sometimes arise. This can, however, be very simply met by omitting the troublesome item when necessary. The rules for filling in the list for each language may be stated as follows: (a) Try to find one simple equivalent for each item by disregarding specialized and bound forms and the less common of two equivalents. (b) Use a single word or element rather than a phrase, even though the meaning may be broader than that of the test item. (c) Where it is impossible to find a single equivalent, omit the form.

We can break this general problem of non-universality down into several different subtypes. First, there is no set procedure for deciding which of several translation equivalents to include: the idea is that we should include the most basic equivalent, used in normal conversation, but this does not always give us enough guidance. (Gudschinsky (1956) suggests tossing a coin, but, as we saw in the discussion of mass comparison in Chapter 1, assuming randomness as a solution, with errors cancelling each other out, is not an ideal way to proceed either.) Examples of what Embleton (2000: 149) calls 'the problem of "multiple synonyms"' are common in the literature, so the problem is not a marginal one; it can be illustrated with English *little* and *small*, which could easily occupy the same slot in the Swadesh list. Campbell (1998: 181) notes that Navajo has no single word for 'water', but separate items for 'stagnant water in a pool', 'drinking water', and 'rain water'. Which of these would be more basic? Similarly, K'ichean (Mayan) languages may have more than one 'burn' word, with *k'at* 'burn accidentally', coexisting with *-por* 'burn on purpose'; and likewise there are commonly three items covering the meaning 'eat': *-waʔ* 'eat bread-like things', *-tix* 'eat meat', and *-lo* 'eat fruit-like things' (ibid.). In Cuzco Quechua (Paul Heggarty, personal communication), the adjective 'old' applied to a man is *machu*, but for a woman it is *paya*. Which of these is more basic? Worse still, simply discarding one of these items might rob us of data which help us assess how closely related languages are; and indeed this is even more highly relevant if we are making comparisons between dialects, where we need as much high-resolution data as we can find. For instance, in Quechua there are two different roots for the numeral 'four', *tawa* and *trusku*. Some dialects have one, and some have the other; but in a third set of dialects both co-occur, giving us a means of classification. Exactly these apparently problematic, intermediate cases can provide us with valuable data if we are interested in assessing degrees of similarity; but they can work against the requirement for a single item in each slot on each list.

Conversely, languages may have one word covering more than one meaning on the list; and a number of these many-to-one matches recur cross-linguistically. Campbell (ibid. 182) notes that ' "man" and ... "person" are homonymous in many languages. Many languages do not distinguish ... "bark" from ... "skin" or ... "feather" from ... "hair", where "bark" is just "tree skin" and "feather" is just "bird hair" '. This gives rise to what Kessler (2001) calls 'the shared roots problem': if 'bark' is 'tree skin', and the 'bark' slot and the 'skin' slot therefore have the same root, then the items in the list are not fully independent, compromising the statistical robustness of the results. In a sense, this problem reflects a typological bias in the original construction of the list: European languages typically use many different lexical roots to express differences of meaning. However, a method requiring us to collect and compare roots is less compatible with the structures of languages elsewhere in the world, such as those in the Andes, which often have polysynthetic structures, relying on a much smaller number of roots but a large number of derivational suffixes. Swadesh observes that 'die' and 'kill' may be expressed with a single root and an optional causative marker, though he still includes both in the 100-meaning list. However, Heggarty et al. (2003) note that in Ecuadorian Quechua, for instance, the problem of shared roots is much more general, with the same root in 'mouth' and 'tongue', 'skin' and 'bark', 'river' and 'water', 'big' and 'long', and elsewhere.

Embleton (2000: 149) notes two further difficulties in establishing compatibility between lists. First, there may be no equivalent at all for a particular meaning slot, and of course this becomes more likely with a longer list, because longer lists almost inevitably include more culturally restricted meanings. Embleton (ibid.) does not see this as a particularly major difficulty: 'Normally this is best dealt with just as a statistician would with any missing data, namely as a blank'. More importantly, she asks, 'How should one deal with "partial cognation"? For example, in the Romance languages, the word for "heart" is sometimes cognate to *cœur* and sometimes cognate to *corazón* ... Proposed solutions include always counting these as positive, always counting these as negative, or some sort of fractional scoring system' (ibid.). Swadesh (1955: 122) already left the door open to greater flexibility in scoring and list comparison: 'Ordinarily only one equivalent is taken for each test item, more than one only when there is no way of choosing among the common equivalents.' Heggarty (forthcoming) suggests some ways of incorporating these more complex matching calculations and allowing both one-to-many and many-to-one matchings between items and slots, and this is pursued in Chapter 6 below.

However, including more complex matching systems for a standard list is not the only option: 'A contrary suggestion has been to develop variants of the test list for different large areas of the world. This would require great care both in the selection of the local items and in deter- mining variations in the retention rates connected with each list' (Swadesh 1955: 124). The second of these objections disappears immedi- ately if we reject glottochronology, or see it at best as a secondary application of lexicostatistics: the concentration on a single rate of change for the most basic vocabulary, and the supposed universality of the resulting calculations, is the main motive for retaining a rigidly structured single list, and if we do not assume a set rate of change or intend to calculate time depths we immediately gain more freedom in the shapes our lists can take. The other reason for requiring an absolutely fixed, universal list would involve the use of lexicostatistics to propose macro- families, or even to reconstruct Proto-World. Our view is that if adopting multiple lists stops that kind of application we are all for multiple lists.

Of course, this does not mean that anything goes: it is vital that the list should be at least substantially the same for groups of languages we might reasonably wish to compare, and indeed we might wish to require substi- tutions to fall into the same general area of meaning, with one body-part meaning or kinship term being replaced, as far as possible, with another. One option would be to retain a core list, with different sets of optional extra meanings depending, for example, on geographical area; or certain items in the core list could be substituted by a more locally relevant meaning for particular areas. For example, 'cow' and 'lamb' are not species native to the Andes, and where words for these exist in Quechua and other indigenous languages they are invariably borrowed from Span- ish. Heggarty et al. (2003) suggest that these should be replaced by 'llama'; variation in this slot reveals local affinities between dialects and languages which the common Spanish loans for 'cow' would obscure completely. Various modified lists of this kind have been proposed, though their adoption does not always imply that the linguists concerned are fully committed to lexicostatistics, let alone glottochronology, in general: Matisoff (2000: 335) notes that 'It has been repeatedly observed that the standard Swadesh lists are culturally and grammatically inappropriate for many linguistic areas of the world, full of over- and under-differentiations. I have attempted to mitigate these problems somewhat by compiling a 200-word list more appropriate for Southeast Asia, though this is comparable to applying a bandaid to a gangrenous foot.' Matisoff's CALMSEA list (for 'Culturally and Linguistically Meaningful for Southeast Asia') is closely based on the Swadesh 200-meaning list: the meanings excluded from the Swadesh list include 'back', 'knee', 'leg', while new meanings include 'arrow', 'bamboo', 'boil'/'cook' 'brain', 'finger/toe', 'frog', 'monkey', 'peas/beans', 'penis', 'plantain'/'banana', and 'village'. Modified Swadesh lists have also been proposed for use in Australia (O'Grady 1960; Alpher and Nash 1999); some excluded Swadesh meanings are 'all', 'bird', 'cold', 'mountain', 'night', and 'red', while meanings specific to the list include 'armpit', 'down', 'forehead', 'north', and specifically for the 'top end' of Australia, 'goanna' and 'mangrove'. Black (n.d.) proposes a number of additional meanings for the subclassification of Australian languages: these include 'spearthrower', 'boomerang', 'possum', 'pelican', 'dream', and 'hole'. Again, this suggests that longer and/or more locally specific lists may be useful for particular purposes, notably subgrouping and dialect comparison.

There is a final, further problem with any lexicostatistical comparison, and this involves borrowing, which has been alluded to but not properly confronted in the discussion above. Clearly, in a comparison of languages 1 and 2, if a slot in language 1 is filled with a loan, and if that loan comes from language 2 or a relative of language 2, then we may counterfactually interpret the similarity of the items in that slot as indicating common ancestry. The same problem will arise if languages 1 and 2 have both borrowed extensively from a common external source. This problem is alleviated if the comparative method has already been applied, distinguishing real, recurrent correspondences from loans. However, in cases where loans are particularly hard to spot (as is often the case for old loans, or borrowings within a family), or where the comparative method cannot be applied fully because of a paucity of data, interference from loans can be very real.

2. 4 Testing Methods

Borrowing represents such a major problem for any method of discerning and constructing families that it will be considered in much more detail in the next two chapters. However, even leaving borrowing aside there have been calls to dispense with lexicostatistics altogether, on the basis of the other problems discussed above. For example, Lunt (1964*a*: 251), in an intemperate editorial comment on Dyen (1964), suggests that:

There is no point in continuing. The lexicostaticians [*sic*] crippled by an untenable basic assumption, plagued by the unrealistic need to set plusses [*sic*] or minuses as answers to questions that do not admit an unqualified yes or no, seek refuge in a simplistic manipulation of numbers. But since the numbers do not derive from any linguistic reality, the fancy formulas and elaborate tables are meaningless— simplicism has become simple-mindedness. It is regrettable that so much time and effort has been consumed in such idle delusion.

Dixon (1997: 35–6) similarly argues against the basis of lexicostatistics:

Swadesh (1951) put forward a magical formula for establishing 'genetic' relation- ships. There would no longer be any need to spend decades compiling grammars and dictionaries, then looking for systematic correspondences and working on reconstruction. One simply gathered a specified 100- (or perhaps 200-) word list of core vocabulary in each of a number of languages and compared them, noting—by inspection—how many items appeared to be cognate... Like all short cuts, this didn't work. It was based on illicit assumptions... There were (for some people) a few mad, happy years of 100-word list comparison before lexicostatistics was decisively discredited.

There are several assumptions we can unpick here. If we accept Dixon's view, then lexicostatistics is equivalent to mass comparison, but over a set list. However, we have seen that there are strong arguments for increasing the flexibility of test lists, and of the comparisons we can make between them, to allow partial matches between slots, for instance. We have also seen that it is preferable, wherever possible, to apply lexicostatistics after the comparative method, since our judgements of whether two items match are crucially based on assumed cognacy, not on whether the items simply resemble one another. In this sense, lexicostatistics does not seek to prove genetic relatedness, but to provide an indication of degree of re- latedness which in turn can be fed into other possible applications.

Dixon also makes a point more clearly related to borrowing, arguing that 'There is no universal principle that core vocabulary . . . is less likely to be borrowed than non-core items. This does appear to hold for the languages of Europe . . . and of many other parts of the world. But it does not apply everywhere, and cannot be taken as an axiom, a partial basis for the postulation of genetic relatedness' (ibid. 10). In particular, Dixon argues this does not hold for Australia, where he sees affinities between languages as far more likely to reflect a long-standing contact relationship than family membership. Models of the lexicostatistical kind, with their assumptions about basic vocabulary, borrowability, and so on, are there to be tested; and if it turns out that Dixon is correct, and there is no basis for those assumptions among Australian languages, then we have learned something and can refine our method either by modifying the assumptions or restricting its applicability. We do not, however, think that throwing out the method is the right reaction. Indeed, we shall briefly consider some Australian data in Chapter 6 below.

On the other hand, there are great advantages in adopting a mathematical approach when we assess a model in this way, and these are summarized concisely and clearly by Embleton (2000: 143): 'The usual advantages of mathematical techniques are 'objectivity' (including replicability), speed, and ability to handle large volumes of data.' Lexicostatistics may, in essence, be a rather simple mathematical model, but a mathematical model it is nonetheless; and Embleton (ibid. 150) notes that there have been attempts to improve it (see Van der Merwe 1966, Sankoff 1973): 'More parameters were added to the model (e.g. to account for 'drift'), replacement rates were allowed to vary from meaning to meaning, multiple synonyms for test-list items were allowed, all increasing accuracy when tested on "known" cases.' Some of these innovations echo those argued for in Section 2.3 above, and there are moves afoot elsewhere to test and refine the assumptions of the model. For example, next to no attention has been devoted in the literature to any consideration of how the items filling the slots in a test list are actually collected, and it has to be assumed (in part from the errors we find) that sometimes the collection involves a linguist and a bilingual dictionary rather than any real informants at all. Slaska (in preparation) is considering the variation which can arise in lists when they are collected from monolingual speakers (by elicitation techniques based on pictures, actions, and so on) as opposed to bilingual speakers (who are asked to translate an English list). Slaska is also investigating the variation within these groups, and assessing the likely motivations for such variation from a sociolinguistic perspective.

Developments of this kind are likely to increase our understanding of the model, and of the possible pitfalls in its application, but they may also increase the complexity of processing its results. The more refined a model becomes, the more parameters of possible variation (and possible interference, not necessarily intentional, by the experimenter) it acquires. It follows that more complex models need computational, quantitative treatment even more than simple ones, and that criteria of replicability and robustness become more important as the parameters involved increase. Lexicostatistics, in other words, is not only a quantitative method; it must be tested by quantitative means, and applied in a controlled way to different situations, so that we can assess where and why it is applicable, and where and why it gives problematic results. Embleton (2000: 155) suggests that historical linguists may be resistant to this kind of quantitative investigation because:

first, the typical training of a historical linguist will not involve anything remotely close to mathematics, so mathematics is something quite alien, possibly even to be feared; and second, an erroneous but prevalent view that things scientific (like mathematical methods) are supposed to be objective, infallible, mechanistic, generate incontrovertible proofs, etc., so that once you feed the data into the black-box, the answer comes out the other end (and concomitantly, if an answer known to be wrong comes out the other end, you throw out the black-box). ...

It is not hard to find comments in the literature testifying to Embleton's view that quantitative approaches are alien to historical linguists, and Ross (1950: 59) provides an excellent example:

In comparison to old and established techniques, numerical methods must surely always be either inefficient or supererogatory. That is to say, on the one hand, if no solution to a problem of this kind can be reached with the old methods then I would not trust a numerical solution, and on the other hand, if a solution can be reached with the old methods, then a numerical solution is unnecessary.

Much more recently, as we shall see in Chapter 5, Gray and Jordan (2000) have been drawing family trees for Austronesian languages, using a program adopted from biology. Cysouw (2000) stresses that their work is not free-standing:

The authors are very keen to proclaim that their quantitative methods, which are taken from biology . . . are important, or even better than the methods used by linguists . . . The authors used 'an efficient computer algorithm' on the unpublished data from Blust's Austronesian Comparative Dictionary to build a language-tree of the Austronesian languages. As far as I can see, nothing new results from their analyses. There is a rather nice congruence between their tree and the tree as I knew it from the literature . . . The method is a nice addition to historical linguistics, but there is nothing really new. So, it seems to be possible to publish an article in *Nature* just by using the right computer program and forget that many years of research has been performed in linguistics to be able to perform these analyses.

On the contrary, our view is that producing familiar trees from familiar data still constitutes a step forward: the trees *are* in fact different, not in shape, but in statistical robustness and assured viability. It is clear that this role of quantification is not always appreciated by other linguists; but it is vital that we should be able to test quantitative approaches, whether to comparing meaning lists or to drawing family trees, to show their results over known data are sufficiently sensible and familiar to make it worthwhile extending them in the future, to cases which cannot be resolved by the application of more traditional linguistic methods. Of course we must not forget that prior linguistic analysis is necessarily involved; these programs are only ever as good as the data and analysis that underlie them, and it is a priority to ensure that those are sound and robust. However, we agree with Kroeber and Chrétien (1937: 85), who believe that statistical analysis may 'validate and correct insight, or, where insight judgments are in conflict, help to decide between them. In short, it increases objectivity, sharpens findings, and sometimes forces new problems.'

As well as new problems, we can anticipate that the application of computational techniques to cognacy scores or family trees will also show relationships and patterns which might be suspected but cannot be demonstrated by non-quantificational methods. We know this is a reasonable expectation because this is precisely the result that has emerged from the application of quantitative techniques in sociolinguistics and in corpus studies. Just counting and accumulating numbers in corpus work is not, of course, the point—this would be empty quantification. But observing the patterns which we can build following that stage of counting allows us to interpret our numbers, seen in the light of what we know of internal and external history, as evidence for or against particular hypotheses. As we shall see in the next chapter, aspects of the comparative method are amenable to computational testing; but this does not remove the need for linguistic judgements, or rule out any differences of interpretation and opinion. Stochastic or probabilistic methods are particularly suitable for human behaviour, which is stochastic itself, and no such method can provide absolute proof (hence the inappropriateness, as Embleton (2000: 155) observes, of any unthinking faith in a scientific 'black box'). Since we know that in many cases we will still be left weighing the options, it follows that we will never be dealing with opposing probabilities of 0 and 1. In turn, this introduces an element of liberation in dealing with intrinsically messy linguistic data: although it is important to make sure the data are as clean and the judgements as objective as possible, it blessedly doesn't matter if we have to leave the odd gap or a peculiarity or two creep in, because we have to evaluate the results each time, not just swallow them whole. Having said that, there will be methods which simply do not lend themselves to quantification, and we may decide this is a reflection on those methods. While, as we shall see, we can develop computational approaches to meaning-list comparisons, and to aspects of the comparative method, including the generation and testing of family trees, it seems highly unlikely that any program could be designed to confirm Greenberg's results for Amerind, (1987), precisely because his criteria are unclear, and programming depends crucially on explicitness.

In the chapters that follow we adopt the research strategy set out by Embleton (1986: 3) and discussed in McMahon and McMahon (2003). Although this strategy derives from work in applied mathematics, Embleton suggests that it might fruitfully be employed in developing and testing quantitative methodologies in linguistics too. The three steps central to this strategy are shown in (2).

(2) Embleton (1986: 3)—steps in quantitative analysis:

   (i)   to devise a procedure, based on theoretical grounds, on a particular model, or on past experience...

   (ii) to verify the procedure by applying it to some data where there already exists a large body of linguistic opinion for comparison, often Indo-European data...This may lead to revision of the procedure of stage (i), or at the extreme to its total abandonment;

(iii) to apply the procedure to data where linguistic opinions have not yet been produced, have not yet been firmly established, or perhaps are even in conflict. In practice, this usually means application to non-Indo-European data. . . .

In the spirit of Embleton's three-way division, the first stage of our investigations in this book should involve the testing and automatization of existing approaches to language comparison and classification. It follows that one important goal of the book is to explore ways of confirming what we feel we already know, but by different, repeatable, and statistically testable means. We have therefore chosen to focus on new approaches to two well-worn tools of language classification, namely meaning lists and family trees; and for the most part, in keeping with the implied chronology of (2), we shall report results from the reanalysis of relatively clear cases; as Embleton notes, this generally means Indo-European. In Chapters 5 and 6, however, we report on exploratory extensions of the methods under discussion to unclear, and typically non-Indo-European, cases. We turn first, however, to an attempt to computerize aspects of the comparative method.

3

Tree-based Quantitative Approaches: Computational Cladistics

3. 1 Probability-based Approaches

3. 1. 1 Real and Apparent Patterns

Before turning to attempts to construct and evaluate linguistic family trees, which will be the main topic of this chapter and the next, we return briefly to lexicostatistics, and to disturbing similarities of this method with mass comparison. In the chapters that follow we will be using elements of lexicostatistics, for instance in generating trees based on cognacy scores over standard Swadesh-type lists. We have also said that, in common with many comparative historical linguists, we regard mass comparison as inherently problematic, and as crucially compromised by a lack of rigour in determining what can count as a phonetic or semantic match. However, there remain areas of overlap between the two methods, since both are predominantly lexically based, and involve the comparison of lists. True, those lists are set in lexicostatistics, while there is no basic vocabulary criterion in mass comparison; lexicostatistics also tends to be applied step by step, in a series of pairwise comparisons between languages, whereas in mass comparison the more lists, the merrier. But, at least at first glance, these differences do not decisively favour lexicostatistics. For one thing, we made a series of suggestions in Chapter 2 for a slackening of the constraints on the composition of test lists, so that many-to-one or one-to-many matches between items and meanings might be allowed, and culture-specific meanings might be included in locally variable lists. Worse still, Greenberg (1987: 27) clearly sees the simultaneous comparison of multiple lists as strongly advantageous: 'To inspect languages pairwise, or at a half-guess, is a different thing from a multilateral comparison undertaken with a consciousness of the types of resemblances that are likely to bespeak common origin.' Moreover, Greenberg argues that mass comparison is free from the restrictions of time depth (see Ch. 7 below) which affect lexicostatistics and the comparative method, since 'there is no theoretical limit to the depth at which classification can be carried out when the number of languages examined is large' (ibid. 28–9). It would appear that mass comparison and lexicostatistics emerge as approximately equal on the issue of list composition, with mass comparison edging ahead on the number of lists to be compared.

This would seem an excellent initial test case for the applicability of quantitative methods. We have already seen that lexicostatistics is closely connected with the comparative method, since it requires judgements of whether items on different lists are cognate. Mass comparison, on the other hand, operates either prior to the comparative method or instead of it. We can therefore have confidence in lexicostatistical scores to the extent that we have confidence in the comparative method, and especially in its ability to distinguish common ancestry, as signalled by regular, recurrent correspondences, from chance or borrowing. Evidence was presented in Chapter 1 for the reliability of certain results of the comparative method, and we turn to computer modelling of aspects of the method in Section 3.2 below, and to the vexed question of borrowing thereafter. It is not clear, however, that the results of mass comparison can in principle be distinguished from chance; and if they cannot then we can have no confidence in the method.

However, this is not only a problem for mass comparison. As we saw in Chapter 2, classical lexicostatistics relies on the determination of cognates by rigorous prior linguistic analysis; this will usually involve prior application of the comparative method. When we claim two items are cognate within lexicostatistics, we therefore mean that they occupy the same semantic slot in our more-or-less basic meaning lists; that they are phonetically similar, within the parameters of known or reconstructed sound change; and that we have demonstrated their likely descent from a single, common ancestral form. An obvious problem then arises in applying lexicostatistics where the histories of the languages compared are poorly known; or indeed in possible applications of the method in determining whether those languages are related at all. For instance, Trask (1996: 347–8) relates two proposed etymologies for the Basque word *gorotz* 'animal dung': one school of thought sees an apparent phonetic match with reconstructed North Caucasian **k'urč'V* 'dung' and Burushaski ɣ*urAš* 'dung', feeding this into a long-range, macro-family comparison. The opposing suggestion involves borrowing of Old Spanish *croça* [krotsa] 'yellow', with a perhaps slightly contrived but plausible series of subsequent semantic shifts, and the additional observation that earlier Basque lacked initial /k/, which it is known to substitute with /g/ in other loans. In fact, the apparent resemblance might also be due to sheer chance. The problem is that as we move further back in time the evidence available to decide between competing hypotheses of this kind becomes more tenuous, so that we must fall back on statistical approaches.

In *any* scientific approach there is a clear need to demonstrate that the results one finds, and holds up as meaningful and important, can in fact be distinguished from apparent patterns resulting from chance. This is generally achieved by applying probability theory, and establishing the likelihood of finding these same results by chance: the more unlikely that possibility is, the more confidence we have in our results. There have been various attempts to develop probability-based models to assess the validity of claimed cross-linguistic matches. What is required is a method sensitive enough to detect relationships that we know from the comparative method to be correct though distant, and robust enough to reject connections that we believe to be the result of chance resemblance. Only when we have developed and tested such a method can we then begin to use it to establish unknown relationships, and to assess more controversial methods like mass comparison. Nonetheless, we must accept that those statistical methods are precisely that: statistical. They can tell us about the balance of probabilities, and help us assess the overall likelihood of proposals; but they will not provide conclusive proof when applied to individual examples. In using statistical, probability-based methods we will inevitably get it wrong a proportion of the time, either by misclassifying true cognates as unrelated because of unusually convoluted or bizarre sound changes, or by classifying chance lookalikes as true cognates. These are tests of the big picture, not of whether individual items are really cognate or not.

3. 1. 2 Probability for Beginners

Before proceeding we must consider exactly what a statistical test involves, with apologies to those readers who imbibed probability theory with their mothers' milk. We can start by looking at a simple example of coin tossing. If you were asked to say what would be the outcome of tossing a coin 10 times you might suggest 5 heads and 5 tails. If we then tossed a coin 10 times and it landed 'head up' in 9 out of the 10 tosses, would you accuse us of weighting the coin in favour of landing on one side? The language-comparison analogue is a situation where you count a number of apparent matches between languages (our version of 'heads', the outcomes) and again you are asked whether this number could result from chance alone or from the influence of some other factor. In both cases there are two possible approaches. Where the distribution of underlying probability is known, a theoretically expected number of outcomes can be determined and the observed test result compared to the theoretical values to give a probability (p) of obtaining that test result. In practice, the standard cut-offs used are $p = 0.05$ and $p = 0.01$; that is, if the test result or an even higher number could be predicted in fewer than 5% or 1% of trials by chance alone then the null hypothesis of chance resemblance is 'rejected' at the 5% or 1% level respectively. This does not of course prove the alternate hypothesis, nor does it absolutely rule out chance as an explanation, since at the 5% level around 1 in 20 random sets of trials will by definition give a result which looks like our test result.

To return to the coin-tossing experiment, our null hypothesis is that we have tossed 9/10 heads simply by chance. Making the assumptions that each toss of the coin is independent of the others, and that the coin is balanced, the predicted outcome of a head on the first toss is 0.5. The possibility of a head on the second toss is also 0.5, because the events are independent. So the probability of exactly 9 heads in a row followed by 1 tail is $(0.5)^9 \times 0.5 = 0.00097$.

However, there are 10 different ways in which we can achieve 9 heads—for example, we could have the 1 tail first, followed by 9 heads. When looking at a particular outcome it is important not to calculate the absolute chance probability of that outcome alone after the event—in a coin-toss experiment of 1,000 tosses the chance of exactly 500 heads is small (and the chance of getting 500 heads in a row is vanishingly small), but the chances of approximately the same number of heads and tails is large. There is a general mathematical formula for such problems where there are two possible outcomes on each trial (heads OR tails for the coin toss, matched OR not matched in the meaning list), called the binomial equation, shown in (1) below.

(1) probability (p) of a series of events $= (N!/r!(N-r)!)p^r (1-p)^{N-r}$

In the case of our coin-toss experiment this is a trivial calculation, but the equation can be used to calculate the probability of any sequence of events in N independent trials in which two possible outcomes can be expected in each trial with probabilities p and $(1-p)$ respectively. Setting the number of trials (N) = 10 and the number of observed positive outcomes (r) = 9 (heads), with each head having an individual probability of occurrence $p = 0.5$, the binomial equation predicts a probability of 0.00977 for 9 heads in any sequence from 10 trials. This is part of the story; but we are really interested not in this value alone, but rather in the possibility of obtaining *at least* 9 heads in any order from the 10 tosses (that is, the probability of 9 heads *and* the probability of more than 9 heads). So we have to recalculate the binomial for 10 heads and then add the two results, for 9 and 10 heads, together, giving a composite probability of $0.00977 + 0.00098 = 0.01074$. Thus, the probability of getting 9 or more heads out of 10 tosses of an unbiased coin is p = 0.01074, and we can expect this in slightly more than one trial in a hundred, by sheer chance. This is an unlikely event, but not impossible. If in our calculations we insist on the 1% level of probability, we would always have to say that getting 9 heads from 10 coin tosses could have been the result of chance. If we allow for the 5% level, we will interpret the same result as being significant, and will exclude chance as the most likely determining factor.

Alternatively, we can approach the problem using simulation. In the case of coin tossing one could simply start with an unbiased coin and repeat the series of 10 tosses 100 or 1,000 or 10,000 times, recording the number of heads on each iteration. Simple inspection would then reveal the proportion of times that 9 or 10 heads turned up by chance. These two approaches would be expected to give very similar outcomes because the underlying distribution of probability on each coin toss is known: a uniform random variable of probability 0.5 for a head and 0.5 for a tail. However, this is also a useful method in cases where the distribution of underlying probabilities is not known; in the case of simulation, it is possible to change the underlying assumptions, such as the probability of

0.5 for a head or a tail, to see just what happens when these are reset and the simulation rerun.

3. 1. 3 Probability and Language Comparison

3. 1. 3. 1 Setting the Scene

If we are to extend these probability calculations to language comparison, we first need to work out how we establish the statistical likelihood of any given number of matches between words in compared lists. In order to do so, we must crucially have some linguistic content for the notion of matching. That is to say, we cannot simply test the probability of two forms being cognate *in toto*: we need to put some item-specific content on that notion, by assessing, in the ideal case, how likely it is that a form consisting of a labial nasal followed by a low back vowel followed by a voiceless alveolar stop could be cognate with a form consisting of a voiced velar stop followed by a high front rounded vowel followed by a voiceless alveolar fricative followed by a voiceless alveolar stop. In fact, this is exceptionally complicated, since it requires us, strictly speaking, to put definite numbers on similarities between sounds of different kinds, and to quantify the likelihood of one changing into another. We also need to know the average number of timing slots per word in each language, the variances of these estimates, the number of phonemes in each system, and the frequency distribution of each phoneme across timing slots. And we need to know these things for all the words in the language, not just the ones in the list under direct comparison, to do the job properly. We return to this peculiarly horrible and recalcitrant set of problems in Chapter 8, but for the moment will focus on various partial probability-based models which represent different simplifications of the real-world situation.

Before describing and evaluating these models, however, we should note that the probability-based approaches contribute to our evaluation of methods for language comparison without even being used. Just formulating the question of how we are to measure and assess the probability of chance similarity takes us one step forward, because it rules out mass comparison altogether. Above all, when we subject our results to probabilistic testing we must ensure that the establishment of 'similarity' is based on clear and unambiguous criteria. If we do not specify criteria, then we cannot calculate probabilities, because we do not know what the search space is from which we choose our matches. A total of 5 matches from 10 comparisons might look impressive; but if it turned out that we had found 5 matches from 10 million comparisons we might not be so pleased; and leaving the criteria for matching open, leaves the door open to this kind of undisciplined picking and choosing too. It is true that there are no explicit criteria for the comparative method either, in the sense that we cannot write rules that say 'a labial nasal will never in any circumstances match a high front vowel'. However, there are checks and balances in terms of the reconstructions carried out as part of the method; and we do know a good deal about the likely types and directions of sound change, which are fed into an assessment of the plausibility of cognacy judgements. In a sense, this makes the comparative method an excellent candidate for probability-based testing, since it is based on (admittedly rather intuitive) probability distributions itself.

In lexicostatistics it is easier to see where to begin to apply statistical testing, although the nature of linguistic data does not make this straightforward. The first problem lies in the comparability of meaning; to mitigate the difficulties inherent in such comparisons we assume a fixed set of slots (as in a standard Swadesh list) and a set and invariable meaning for each slot. Although this is a gross simplification, glossing over problems of semantic ambiguity, and one-to-many and many-to-one matches, it is helpful in the development of an initial model. If we accept that semantic matches follow automatically from the structure of our lists, then comparison within each meaning represents a single trial of phonetic matching between a pair of languages, with two outcomes: a match or not a match. (See Chapter 8 for discussion of more sophisticated phonetic matching techniques.) Assuming that each trial is independent of all the others (that is, the word present in a particular slot in a language is not affected by the word in any other meaning slot in the list), then the probability of obtaining a particular set of matches across the list is the product of the chances of a match at each individual slot in the list, as in the coin-tossing illustration in 3.1.2 above. The problem then becomes merely one of determining how likely it is that similar forms of words appear in each of the meaning slots by chance alone. Unfortunately, as usual, this is easier said than done, for the reasons given earlier, since a complete picture of relevant probabilities would require a complete knowledge of all phonological constraints on human languages, both universal and language-specific. In the absence of omniscience, we must again assess simplified, partial models.

3. 1. 3. 2 Initial Consonant Comparison and χ^2 (Chi-Square) Calculations

One simplification, introduced by Ross (1950) and pursued in Ringe (1992, 1996), involves matching only the first segment in each slot of a meaning list. If we consider only English, and only a standard Swadesh 200-item list, we find that the two most frequent initial consonants are /s/ and /f/, which turn up in 33 and 18 words respectively (data from Kessler 2001). So, the English-specific frequency of these two initial sounds for this list is estimated as 33/200 = 0.165 for /s/ and 18/200 = 0.09 for /f/. In German, initial /ʃ/ and /f/ appear in 25 (0.125) and 22 (0.115) of the 200 items respectively. If we compare the two lists meaning by meaning it is noticeable that several words in English that begin with an /s/ have an initial /ʃ/ in German; but how many such matches can we expect by chance alone?

Ross (1950) began from the classical Saussurean assumption of arbitrariness, suggesting that since there is little non-conventional relationship between form and meaning the expected occurrence of an initial /ʃ/ in a German word and an /s/ in a corresponding English word with the same meaning would be merely the product of the occurrence of initial /ʃ/ in German and initial /s/ in English. The language-specific frequencies of these two initial sounds are 0.165 (English /s/) and 0.125 (German /ʃ/), so the expected frequency of that pairing is the product of these two frequencies, or 0.0206 for English and German. In a 200-word list, chance would therefore predict an average of 0.0206 × 200 or 4.12 words with an /s/–/ʃ/ pairing. In fact, as shown in Table 3.1, a total of 12 meanings have this particular sound correspondence in the Swadesh 200-item lists, many more than the 4.12 of our chance calculation. The numbers in the body of Table 3.1 represent the observed phoneme matches between German and English compared meaning by meaning: for instance, 8 words start with

Table 3.1 *Observed* initial-segment matches in the Swadesh 200-meaning list

English	German			
	/ʃ/	/f/	Other phonemes	Row totals
/s/	12	0	21	33
/f/	0	14	4	18
Other phonemes	13	8	128	149
Column totals	25	22	153	200

/f/ in German and some segment other than /s/ or /f/ in English, while 14
start with /f/ in both English and German (data after Kessler 2001).

For some linguists this would be enough, and the excess of observed
over expected numbers would be taken as proof of relationship between
the languages. Indeed, the comparative method involves the gradual
accumulation of many such matches until chance becomes a very unlikely
explanation, though without quantifying the degree of certainty at any
point. But how can we be sure that our observed number of 12 matches
for English /s/ and German /ʃ/ is really big enough, relative to the predicted
4.12 matches, to justify our conclusion of relatedness? What kind of excess
of observation over prediction *is* enough? What makes matters worse is
the fact that our predicted 4.12 matches is not an absolute value: the
number of chance matches in any actual comparison could be more or
fewer, since any prediction carries with it a range of acceptable outcomes
around the stated mean. In other words, we might find an actual value of
2, or of 6, corresponding perfectly properly to our predicted 4.12 matches;
but how are we to know what that acceptable range of values is?

We urgently need a statistical test to indicate the degree of confidence
any proposed connection should inspire. Ross's approach (1950) extends
the comparison illustrated above for English /s/ and German /ʃ/ to a full
comparison of all initial segments in any two languages over any set list.
The outcome is an extended version of Table 3.1 above, containing data
on all observed correspondences. Ross noted that this type of table can be
tested for significance using a χ^2 (Chi-square) statistic. The exact mathematical justification of χ^2 is not relevant here, but a more detailed
treatment of the theoretical aspects of statistical testing of meaning lists
can be found in Kessler (2001: chs. 1–3).

The application of χ^2 involves two stages. First, we need a calculation
of the expected number of word-initial-segment matches for each pairing
in our two languages, as shown in Table 3.2. The expected number of
chance matches for any pair of initial segments can be determined by
multiplying their frequencies in the two languages together, and, in turn,
these frequencies are found in the row and column totals of Table 3.1. For
example, the pairing of /f/–/f/ has a probability of 18/200 × 22/200 =
0.0099, so we would expect 1.98 matches. Each cell in Table 3.2 therefore
has an expected value E = (row total × column total)/200.

The second stage in χ^2 testing calculates a χ^2 value for each cell of Table
3.2: essentially, we take the difference between the values in Tables 3.1 and

Table 3.2 *Expected* number of word-initial-segment matches

English	German			
	/ʃ/	/f/	Other phonemes	Row totals
/s/	4.125	3.63	25.245	33
/f/	2.25	1.98	13.77	18
Other phonemes	18.625	16.39	113.985	149
Column totals	25	22	153	200

3.2, or between the observed and expected value, square that number to allow big differences to weigh more heavily than small ones, and scale each resulting value by the number expected in that cell. Our worked example is shown in Table 3.3: each cell contains two values, the x^2 calculation on the left, and the (observed-expected) value in brackets on the right. The overall x^2 value for this table is then calculated by adding up all the cells to give a single number, which can be compared to statistical lists showing the probability of obtaining a particular x^2 for tables of a particular size. Conventionally, the particular list of x^2 values to be consulted is determined by a calculation of 'degrees of freedom', which is the number of rows minus 1, multiplied by the number of columns minus 1. Since Table 3.3 has 3 rows and 3 columns, the appropriate x^2 values are those published for 4 degrees of freedom (since 3 rows minus 1 is 2, and 3 columns minus 1 is 2, and 2×2 is 4): these values are approximately $x^2 = 9$ for the 5% probability level and $x^2 = 13$ for the 1% probability level.

Adding up all the individual x^2 values in Table 3.3 gives a total x^2 of 112.6. It does not take a mathematical genius to see that this value considerably exceeds both 9 and 13, the prescribed values for a table with 4 degrees of freedom at the 5% and 1% levels respectively. If the null hypothesis is that repeated sound recurrences between initial consonants in English and German words in the 200-item Swadesh list result from

Table 3.3 x^2 values for the results shown in Table 3.1

English	German		
	/ʃ/	/f/	Other phonemes
/s/	15.03 (+7.9)	3.63 (−3.6)	0.71 (−4.24)
/f/	2.25 (−2.25)	72.97 (+12.02)	6.93 (−9.77)
Other phonemes	1.73 (−5.625)	4.30 (−8.39)	5.06 (+14.02)

chance alone, then we can demonstrably reject that hypothesis at the 1% level. It seems justifiable, given the magnitude of these numbers, to conclude that there is some reason beyond chance for those recurrent English–German matches.

However, although χ^2 is a very robust test for such contingency tables, it does have one particular statistical problem for use with language data. As we have seen, in calculating χ^2 the observed deviations from the expected numbers in each cell are scaled by the number expected in that cell. This creates a major problem when the expected number in a cell is 0, because dividing by zero is a mathematical impossibility; and in fact the statistic should not be used where the expected number is less than 1. Unfortunately, for all but the most frequent segment comparisons the expected number of chance matches over short, Swadesh-type meaning lists *will* lie between 0 and 1. To see why, just consider German and English. Comparing the 200-meaning Swadesh list, we find 18 initial segments in German and 21 in English (grouping all vowel phonemes into a single class), giving a table of 378 possible matches. However, since we are comparing only 200 slots, there can only conceivably be 200 matches to populate the table. One way round this difficulty would be to increase the number of items compared: Ross (1950) in fact used over 1,000, but still found far too many zeroes for comfort; and Kessler (2001: 47) suggests that 'with about 10,000 pairs of words, the table would fill out nicely'. Although this is a possible solution in principle, there is an obvious and problematic balance to be struck between statistical probity and practical possibility. Another approach would involve collapsing segments into groups according to shared phonetic features, but this would inevitably lead to a loss of significant information and might mask true relatedness (Kessler 2001: 47–9). Our Tables 3.1–3 in fact operated on just this kind of clustering basis, with individual pairs of segments compared to 'all others', and the consequent χ^2 was 112.6 for Table 3.3. Comparing this to Kessler's (ibid. 49) value of 895 for the same languages, where the higher χ^2 indicates a much more significant deviation from chance, shows just how much information is lost by lumping segments together.

3. 1. 3. 3 The Binomial Approach to Meaning-List Comparisons

Starting from similar contingency tables, and again working with initial sounds, Ringe (1992) developed a slightly different approach to testing the significance of the observed correspondences. Recall that using the χ^2

statistic is problematic when the expected values are between 0 and 1. However, it is really only those cells, like /s/ : /ʃ/ in English and German, where values exceed 1 that can be taken as indicating a real relationship between the languages over and above chance correspondence. Ringe consequently developed a statistical strategy to test each of these frequent matches separately, effectively ignoring the cells with 0 or 1 'hits'. He assumed that the number of matches in any given cell can be treated as a binomial problem, like the 10-coin-tosses example above, such that we can calculate the probability of that number of matches (or more) arising from a series of 100 'tosses' if we set the probability of each toss being successful (p) to the product of the language-specific frequencies of the two initial sounds. So, for example, in a comparison of English and German the probability of success for /s/ : /ʃ/ would be p = 0.165 × 0.125 = 0.0206 and the probability of not matching would be (1−p) = 0.9794. The number of successful outcomes to be tested against the binomial expectation would therefore be r = 12, a result that is well outside the 99th percentile of the binomial distribution.

Of course, the next problem is finding appropriate lists to test this method on. If we pick unrelated languages (which was the approach adopted by Bender (1969), a forerunner of Ringe's work here), then we are begging the question: How do we know they *are* unrelated? Ringe's solution was not to use real-language data at all, but rather a series of randomly generated numerical 'vocabularies'; and his conclusion was that this approach did not generate a worryingly large number of false positive results. On the contrary, it appeared to detect no more than the predicted level of approximately 1 out of 20 phoneme pairs lying outside the calculated 95th-percentile range (that is, the 5% confidence limit). When Ringe then moved back to real-language data, comparing American English and High German, he found 16 correspondences above the 99th percentile, and 7 above the 99th percentile for Latin and English. On the other hand, he encountered 2 above the 99th percentile in a comparison of Turkish and English, which is close to the expected value for chance resemblance alone.

3. 1. 3. 4 The Binomial Approach and Mass Comparison

After trialling his methodology with simulated and real languages in binary comparisons Ringe (1992) next asked what effect altering parameters in the list comparison had on the probability of chance matches; and these results have particular relevance for mass comparison. First, Ringe argues that doubling the number of meanings per list has effectively no impact on his approach: although it increases the number of resemblances necessary for significance, it also increases the number of actual matches, so, assuming both lists are unbiased, the results will be the same. This may not be strictly true, since with a longer list some of the true correspondences between rarer morphemes have a higher probability of being observed at a better-than-chance level, whereas they may be only of borderline significance in a smaller list. Even so, the effect is likely to be marginal, except at greater time depths, where such rare matches may be the only residual indication of true relationship. Next, Ringe asked what would happen if near synonyms were allowed to count as a match—in other words, if he relaxed the requirement for absolute semantic matching. In fact, this greatly increases the number of potential chance matches: for the 100-meaning list Ringe was able to identify a further 50 semantically close pairings such as 'I' with 'we'. He notes that this will not affect the number of true cognates in the list, but does increase by over 50% the number of potential random matches between two unrelated lists that need to be accounted for in a rigorous testing of statistical significance.

Finally, Ringe returned to randomly generated vocabulary lists to see just how many chance phonetic matches occur across semantically aligned words in multiple list comparisons. Table 3.4 shows his calculations for a particular phoneme pair and demonstrates that the number of matches between at least two 'words' of the same 'meaning' (recall that these were in fact lists of random numbers, rather than real language data) rises rapidly with the number of languages included in the comparison. In this example, the sound 't' is assumed to have a word-initial frequency of 0.2 in each list. Obviously, in real-life situations there will be variation in the frequencies of particular phonemes and the phonotactic generalizations governing their distribution, but the general observation that the number of chance resemblances between pairs of lists rises rapidly with the number of lists compared will still hold.

Ringe therefore predicted over 400 chance matches of 't' : 't' among 15 compared synthetic 'languages', and actually observed 431 matches in his comparisons of 100-item synthetic lists, very close to the value predicted by his model. If we repeated this for all the frequent sound comparisons between a group of 15 real languages, it is not too difficult to imagine that a few random associations might begin to look like a constellation of

Table 3.4 Number of expected chance matches in a simulated mass-comparison experiment: calculation of the number of chance matches between simulated vocabulary lists with 100 items for an initial consonant 't' with probability of 0.2 in each list

Number of languages	Pairwise comparisons	Chance frequency of 't' : 't'
2	1	4
3	3	12
4	6	24
5	10	40
6	15	60
7	21	84
8	28	112
9	36	144
10	45	180
11	55	220
12	66	264
13	78	312
14	91	364
15	105	420

similarities between different subgroups of the 15 in a large multilateral comparison. Remember also that in mass comparison the phonetic and semantic criteria for a match are very much relaxed compared even to Ringe's least stringent assumptions; that some of the languages may indeed be truly related, forming real groupings; and that only a limited number of matches between any of the representative languages in any two groups are required to justify higher-order lumping. The strong implication is that relaxing the criteria for matching in either domain will increase the possible space for chance resemblances. Greenberg (1987) sets great store by the sheer number of resemblances he identifies, and in effect argues that the method cannot be wrong, because the volume of evidence is so great. However, Ringe's tests make it clear that simply increasing the number of languages being compared cannot possibly help us guard against chance resemblances, *unless we also insist that the resemblances are found in more of those languages.* If we do not make this additional requirement, then including more languages in the comparison simply increases the likelihood that we will find (and be fooled by) chance resemblances. These problems are discussed at greater length in McMahon and McMahon (1995); but already it must be clear that mass comparison can at best act as a starting point for further linguistic investigation.

3. 1. 3. 5 Problems with the Binomial Approach

(*a*) *Constant Probability of Matches* Ringe's use of the binomial to calculate the expected significance of recorded matches has been criticized (Greenberg 1993; Baxter and Manaster Ramer 1996, 2000; Ringe 1999), most cogently on the grounds that it requires the assumption of a constant probability of matching. This assumption is in fact incorrect, since in a finite list each matching of a pair of phonemes removes those phonemes from the list available for subsequent matches. Thus, the probability of two phonemes matching is different for each meaning in a list, depending on the pairings that have gone before. There is a statistical distribution, the hypergeometric, that allows for this sort of variation in probability, but it is complex to calculate even with modern computers, and statisticians often use the binomial as a good approximation to it. However, with small lists the difference can, under certain circumstances, be extreme. Baxter and Manaster Ramer (1996) have illustrated just how poor the approximation of the binomial to the hypergeometric can be by taking the extreme situation of two lists in which each word starts with a different consonant. In this unlikely situation the resultant 100×100 table would consist of 100 cells with exactly 1 observed matching of one sound in one language with that in the comparable meaning in the other language, and 9,900 cells with 0s. In this case the relative frequency of matches in the table could never provide evidence of a relationship, and yet Ringe's approach, purely because it assumes a constant probability of matching phonemes, would calculate that these results indicated 100 phoneme pairings above the 99th percentile—highly significant proof of an entirely unreliable relationship. Nonetheless, this is a very extreme situation, and in more ordinary conditions the difference between the hypergeometric and the binomial will be much less severe. In any case, no critique of Ringe's exact numbers can affect the central observation that large numbers of chance matches must be expected with multiple-list comparisons.

(*b*) *The Test Is Too Rigorous* The other criticism of Ringe's approach is that his method is too rigorous to confirm close relationships within Indo-European, let alone to test alleged relationships that are less secure: Greenberg contends that Ringe's method 'makes easy cases difficult and difficult cases impossible' (Greenberg 1993: 89). In one respect this criticism is justified, since Ringe has biased his test towards considering only the most extreme results, effectively ignoring any cells in the comparison that are not significant at the 1% level, regardless of whether they might indicate some sort of relationship if combined together. The χ^2 statistic could in principle include such information; but, as we saw above, Ringe's approach was in effect a direct response to the impossibility of applying this test to a table with very low expected numbers in the cells. However, computers open up another way of dealing with this problem using permutation testing.

3. 1. 3. 6 More Sensitive Statistical Tests—Permutation Testing

All the possibilities discussed above are complex, and either rely on potentially problematic background assumptions or have been constructed on artificial data. A simple method based on material from real languages might seem too much to hope for; but in fact there is an excellent (and unjustly ignored) candidate in the form of the shift test, as proposed by Oswalt (1970). This operates with two standard meaning lists from real languages. The items in the list are compared to one another—but not only in the usual way. In a normal list comparison we would compare item 1 in language A with item 1 in language B, and go through comparing the items in the same slot until we reach item 100. The shift test, or permutation test, adds to that initial comparison a set of further permutations of the list, beginning by comparing item 1 in language A with item 2 in language B, item 2 in A with item 3 in B, and so on until the end (which will be item 100 in A, with item 1 in B). Any similarity metric can be applied here: let us assume that we are checking whether initial consonant matches are in fact recurrent correspondences in the two languages. In the shift test the data are real, and any quirks arising from individual language probabilities will be retained, because the lists are absolutely standard. Ideally, every position in list A would be compared with every position in list B, moving on to a comparison of item 1 with item 3, item 2 with item 4, round to item 100 with item 2, and continuing sequentially, shifting one place on every time. The combination of all these displaced list comparisons gives a background score for the degree of chance similarity across the two lists; this can then be compared with the score obtained from our initial, 'normal' comparison of item 1 in language A with item 1 in language B, through to item 100 with item 100.

In languages which are not really related, we would expect the score for the 'real' comparison to be much the same as in the shifted comparisons; if they are related, we will expect to see a significant difference.

The type of permutation testing pioneered for linguistics by Oswalt (1970) has been developed more recently by Lohr (1999), Baxter and Manaster Ramer (2000), and Kessler (2001). One problem with such tests is that although ideally we should perform all possible realignments of the lists, this would be impossible in practice—as Kessler (ibid. 49) observes, '100 words would require 100! (almost 10^{158}) arrangements' (100! is mathematical shorthand for $100 \times 99 \times 98 \ldots \times 2 \times 1$). The shift test does provide a sample of 100 possible results, with the interesting characteristic that each word in each list is paired once with every other word in the other list. However, this procedure might introduce a degree of bias if adjacent meanings in the list are semantically related, and therefore not truly independent. It is likely that this bias will increase the randomized χ^2 values, giving a relatively conservative estimate of significance, although this could be argued to be a good thing anyway.

Any bias in the data could be minimized by resorting to Monte-Carlo sampling to generate the list pairings. In this approach the second list is treated rather as if it were a bag of words from which 100 are chosen in a random order to be matched against the first list, with perhaps 1,000 or 10,000 test lists being prepared and used to construct the chance distribution of χ^2s for comparison. Using this approach, Baxter and Manaster Ramer (2000) have shown that with just the initial consonants of a 33-word test list it is possible to demonstrate a significantly greater than chance relationship between English and Hindi. Kessler (2001) goes even further, demonstrating that this approach using initial consonants alone discriminates powerfully between known relationships and chance. However, he points out that the significant relationship thus detected might not always be due to a shared common ancestor, but could also include other types of shared common history such as borrowing. Significance in such similarity metrics will therefore indicate common history, but further inspection will still be required to exclude contact, either before or after testing.

The use of permutation analysis opens up the possibility of other types of linguistic comparisons, as yet not fully developed. Kessler (ibid.), for example, proposes R^2, one possible recurrence metric which tries to establish the significance of recurrent sound correspondences of the sort central to the comparative method. In his approach each cell of the contingency table is given a value 'R' equal to the number of matches in the cell minus one: so for German : English /f/ : /f/ the value of R would be $14 - 1 = 13$. These values are then squared and summed together to give a metric for the degree of 'recurrence' in the table. This R^2 metric ignores all cells with single sound matches, getting round the problem small numbers cause for χ^2, and increases in value in a non-linear fashion with the number of recurrent matches in a cell, capturing the intuitive aspect of the comparative method which suggests that the more matches there are, the more significant the particular cell should be. Monte-Carlo permutation of the two lists then allows calculation of a distribution for random arrangements of the words and associated R^2s, which can then be used to determine the significance of the R^2 calculated for the lists aligned by meaning. Such resampling strategies can be used to test the significance of any metric, and we shall return to their use in determining the significance of phylogenetic approaches and phonetic comparisons in more detail in later chapters.

These innovative techniques, then, are useful, and offer the potential of separating more and less reliable methods of comparison. However, they again illustrate the point, raised in Chapter 2 for lexicostatistics, that results for comparisons over particular meaning slots do not only involve meaning: what we are in fact evaluating is primarily phonetic matchings, and the likelihood of different phonetic comparisons reflecting regular sound change and common ancestry. In other words, no method of comparison is uniquely concerned with a single area of the grammar, just as was the case for the comparative method, which crucially identifies and evaluates recurrent resemblances in sound *and* meaning. As we have seen, the comparative method is also closely connected with hierarchical, family-tree representations; yet the methods explored in this section do not produce hierarchized classifications. In the next section we turn to a further computational project which includes sound, meaning, and morphosyntax, and which also generates and attempts to test family trees.

3. 2 Computerizing the Comparative Method

3. 2. 1 Introducing Computational Cladistics

At the end of the last chapter we cited with approval the view of Kroeber and Chrétien (1937: 85), who believe that statistical analysis can 'validate and correct insight, or, where insight judgments are in conflict, help to decide between them. In short, it increases objectivity, sharpens findings, and sometimes forces new problems'. This is particularly relevant to the comparative method, since here we have a generally adopted technique, which appears to be validated by external evidence (like the decipherment of Linear B, which followed the reconstruction of the main aspects of the Proto-Indo-European sound system). However, the independent and objective testing of the method and its results does not currently seem feasible. It is not viable simply to repeat the comparative method for the same data, to see if we achieve the same results—partly because it is a gradual, cumulative process. Worse still, Embleton (1986: 22) notes that 'Intentionally or unintentionally, IE historians may discuss only features which tend to reinforce their prior conclusions'. Colleagues applying the method may have worked in good faith, but it is hard to guarantee that individual preferences could not have crept into their analyses. It is therefore impossible to ensure that the results are objective and repeatable, and extendable to other language groups, without some kind of truly independent testing. In the same way, we are unable to demonstrate that the family tree produced for a particular putative group is significant among the mass of possible trees we have not considered. Asking another linguist to repeat the procedure is not an option either, since if one linguist can bring preconceptions and preferences to the task, and have her judgement coloured for the unavoidable reason that she knows more about one branch of a family than another, for example, then so can another.

In the computational-cladistics project, based at the University of Pennsylvania (<http://www.cis.upenn.edu/~histling>, accessed March 2005), Ringe and his collaborators (Warnow, Ringe, and Taylor 1996; Ringe, Warnow, and Taylor 2002) are essentially attempting to computerize aspects of the comparative method. Their methodology is character-based: that is, it involves a fixed set of pre-selected features. A character can be seen as a historical equivalent of the familiar sociolinguistic variable. For example, the modern English variable (r) has a variant [ɹ] in *star* for speakers of rhotic accents, who pronounce [ɹ] whenever there is an <r> in the spelling; but there is an alternative variant, zero, for non-rhotic speakers who will pronounce [ɹ] in *ripe, pry*, but not *star, part*. In the same way, each of Ringe et al.'s characters represents a category, with different values across the range of languages being compared: 'every character is a linguistic property which languages can instantiate in a variety of ways, and languages which instantiate the character in the same way are assigned the same state of that character' (Ringe, Warnow, and Taylor 2002: 71). Languages can be grouped according to whether they share a state for a particular character or not; and the more characters we have, the more data we can use in establishing these groups and subgroups. Example (2) below shows 3 of the 22 phonological characters from Ringe, Warnow, and Taylor (ibid.), along with the different states, or variants, observed in the daughter languages.

(2) Phonological characters and states (Ringe, Warnow and Taylor 2002: 113)
P1 *p . . . k^w > *k^w . . . k^w
1, absent [ancestral]; 2, present; 3, obscured by merger; 4 etc., no evidence
P3 'ruki'-retraction of *s
1, absent [ancestral]; 2, present; 3, 4, obscured by merger or orthography
P7 word-initial *ye- > e-
1, absent [ancestral]; 2, present

In each language under comparison the state for each character will be determined, and entered into a matrix of the kind in (3). Ringe, Warnow, and Taylor work with 24 Indo-European languages, though only 6 are included here.

(3) Matrix for 3 characters in 6 languages (Ringe, Warnow, and Taylor 2002: 115)

	P1	P3	P7
Hittite	4	1	2
Vedic Sanskrit	1	2	1
Old English	1	1	1
Old Irish	2	1	1
Old Persian	1	2	1
Latvian	1	4	1

Ringe et al. provide a much more comprehensive matrix and list of states in an appendix to their paper: examples (2) and (3) are very selective, but can still illustrate the workings of the method. What (2) and (3) tell us is that, for instance, some languages in the sample have a particular sound change assimilating /p/ to a following labiovelar: this is phonological character P1. This change has not happened in Vedic Sanskrit, Old English, Old Persian, or Latvian, which have a 1 in the matrix to show that they retain the ancestral state. The change has taken place in Old Irish. In Hittite there is no relevant evidence to tell us whether the change has happened or not, so we find a special code, 4. Turning to character P3 we find a division between languages coded 1 (like Hittite, Old English, and Old Irish), which have not undergone a change backing Proto-Indo-European *s in the context of a number of sounds including /r u k i/, and another set coded 2 (like Vedic and Old Persian), where the so-called 'ruki rule' has taken place. In Latvian, the 4 indicates that we cannot tell, for reasons to do with the spelling system, whether the change has happened or not. From these matrices, over a large number of characters, we can retrieve information about the likely subgroups into which the languages fall. This example also shows that not all the data are always clear-cut: sometimes we will find unclarity, sometimes alternative possibilities, and sometimes a form which makes no sense at all. The important thing is that we use a special code to show that the form is exceptional, for whatever reason. The more kinds of exceptionality there are for a character, the more codes we need. If we had only the possibility of using two codes, 1 where the change has not happened and 2 where it has, we would risk setting up spurious connections, and missing real ones. If we have the option of any number of codes, to indicate any number of language-specific uncertainties or peculiarities, then we can ensure that languages behaving oddly are set aside for the calculation of that parameter. We have to hope that there are enough other parameters where that language does show affinities with others for it to be placed in its own subgroup accurately.

Of course, all this will work only if we have identified suitable characters in the first place. Ringe, Warnow, and Taylor (ibid.) are mainly concerned with the first-order splitting of Indo-European, and therefore choose characters which identify particular subfamilies, either individually, such as Tocharian, or as groups, like Italo-Celtic. Since Indo-European and its component subgroups have already been very thoroughly investigated, these characters are ones that have emerged from prior philological work. This is why the approach can be seen as a means of computerizing the comparative method; and again Ringe, Warnow, and Taylor (ibid. 66) stress that their subgrouping method 'is *not* intended to replace already existing methods, but to supplement them'.

As (4) shows, these characters are not all phonological; there are also morphological and lexical examples.

(4) Distribution of characters in Ringe, Warnow, and Taylor (2002)
    22 phonological characters
    15 morphological characters
    333 lexical characters

Morphological and lexical characters work in much the same way as the phonological cases above. Morphological characters sometimes have states involving different forms (such as M8, which has 13 possible states depending on whether the most archaic superlative suffix in a language is *-isto-*, *-ismo-*, something else, or nothing at all) or may be more general and systemic (like M1, which has 8 states reflecting the overall organization of the verb system as having one stem per lexeme, as opposed to a present/preterite contrast, or a contrast of present/subjunctive/preterite, for instance). Turning to lexis, 'Every meaning on a basic wordlist is a character, ... [and] languages are assigned the same state if and only if they exhibit true cognates in that meaning' (ibid. 71). As one might expect, there is greater diversity in the number of states per lexical character, and unique states are quite commonly assigned because there is no evidence in the language at issue, or no cognate with the same meaning in the database—or, less commonly, because the item found is a loan. As (4) shows, there are many more lexical characters, simply because they are much easier to find. Phonological and morphological characters are both problematic for different reasons: the former because natural sound changes will tend to be repeated independently in different languages at different times, so that the mere presence of a change need not signal common ancestry, and the latter because it is hard to tell which inflectional states are ancestral and which have been innovated. Of course, lexical characters bring problems of their own, particularly in terms of ruling out loans, as we shall see below.

Once the characters have been selected and scored, the computational part of the process begins. Ringe, Warnow, and Taylor make the assumption that what they call 'backmutation' (the absolute reversal of a change) 'is either impossible or vanishingly rare' (ibid. 70); they also assume that loans and independent, parallel changes can be discovered and discounted. If backmutation, borrowings, and parallel innovations are excluded, 'the true tree defined by the remainder of the data becomes a mathematically interesting object with properties that we can exploit in order to recover it from linguistic information present in its leaves' (ibid. 70). Of course, this method is generating and evaluating trees; and the limitations of the family-tree model are well known: Bloomfield (1933: 317) notes the 'insoluble problem' created for the tree model by conflicting evidence and differential overlap, which led to the development of Schmidt's (1872) wave model. Nonetheless, the family tree is well established as a tool for modelling and visualizing common descent with differentiation in historical linguistics, with the further advantage of being tightly definable in mathematical terms, making it particularly suitable for quantitative methods requiring testability. Many of the deficiencies in the family-tree model are in any case connected with contact and borrowing, and if we accept for the moment that Ringe et al. can identify loans and effectively remove them from the analysis (by assigning the borrowing a unique code for that meaning), there is no reason why a tree model should not be acceptable and accurate.

The next step involves the use of 'perfect-phylogeny' software, which searches for the best tree. The perfect phylogeny itself will be compatible with all the characters considered. Briefly, for a character to be compatible with a particular tree, all the languages sharing a particular state for that character must form a single group or a continuous subgraph. If a single state is shared by languages which must (because of other characters) lie in different, discontinuous regions of the tree, the relevant character is not compatible with that tree. Failing an absolutely perfect phylogeny, the best tree will be the one consistent with *most* data. There is also some limited prioritization among the characters: although lexical characters are more numerous, Ringe et al. contend that non-lexical characters provide far better evidence of relatedness, and their program is constructed to 'fix' the phonological and some of the morphological characters, automatically rejecting any tree which is incompatible with these (Don Ringe, personal communication). Trees can therefore be ranked for consistency, potentially allowing further support for existing, accepted hypotheses, as well as an additional means of evaluating more controversial ones. As it turns out, finding a perfect phylogeny, a tree compatible with all Ringe et al.'s 370 characters and 24 languages, is too much to ask: but one of the best trees is shown in Figure 3.1.

In many respects Figure 3.1 looks like a fairly orthodox hand-drawn Indo-European tree. True, the number of languages included is limited,

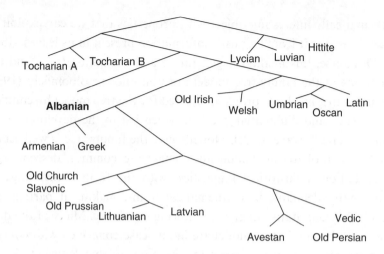

Fig. 3.1 A close-to-perfect phylogeny, redrawn from Ringe, Warnow, and Taylor (2002: fig. 8)

but they seem to fall into the subgroups we would expect: Latin, Oscan, and Umbrian are grouped together, but Oscan and Umbrian form a separate subgroup within this Italic subgroup; likewise, Avestan and Old Persian are grouped together, but Vedic is included at the next highest level. This is all as it should be from the perspective of the comparative method, and it must be stressed that finding computational results which match existing hypotheses is precisely what we hope for at an initial stage of testing any quantitative method. If linguists feel confident about the general outline of Indo-European, then we would hope that a quantitative approach which aims to model aspects of the comparative method will provide the same general outline; and this is the case here. This does not, however, render the quantitative method pointless or supernumerary: if we can show that the two methods provide matching results in the clear cases, we support both, and leave open the possibility of also applying the quantitative method to provide some adjudication on unclear cases.

   Despite more than a century's intensive work on the structure of Indo-European, there remain some subgroupings which are hotly debated. One of these is the so-called Italo-Celtic hypothesis: Is there a split in the tree which includes both Italic and Celtic, which then branch off separately, or should each branch off as a separate daughter group in the first place? The Ringe et al. (2002) tree in Figure 3.1 seems to support Italo-Celtic; and in the same way it suggests that Greek and Armenian form a valid genetic grouping (see also Clackson 1994), and that the first, immediate branching under Proto-Indo-European opposes Hittite (and its relatives Lycian and Luwian) to the rest of the group—this is the Indo-Hittite hypothesis. Having said that, aspects of the computational-cladistics project might possibly bias the trees in these directions. First, the perfect-phylogeny software is set up to require binary branching at each level: if three-way splits were allowed, would Italo-Celtic emerge as a unity, or would the two branches simply emerge separately? In other words, is Italo-Celtic (and perhaps Greek-Armenian) 'real', or is it an artefact of computational restrictions on the tree? Second, the tree is generated on the basis of pre-selected characters, and if we choose characters where Italic and Celtic share states, it is not altogether surprising that the resulting tree generates an Italo-Celtic branch. There may be no alternative: there may be no other generally valid, useful characters for which Italic and Celtic emphatically do not share states, in which case the linguistic data are telling us the only possible story. But we must remember Embleton's note of caution (1986: 22) about the comparative method, which applies also to methods based on that method: 'Intentionally or unintentionally, IE historians may discuss only features which tend to reinforce their prior conclusions'.

All of this relates to the problem of how we know the tree in Figure 3.1 really is the best possible tree. Ringe et al. (2002: 91) note that exhaustive searching of all the options is impossible, given the staggeringly large number of possible trees: 'The number of sets of 318 characters that can be chosen from 322 is 445, 197, 684', and clearly a search of more than 445 million sets is not feasible. Recall that situations where characters are not compatible with a generally acceptable tree are likely to reflect either undiagnosed parallel developments, or loanwords which have been mis-coded as cognates: in both cases, these will work against the real subgroupings, pushing us to set up subgroups which are supported by parallel changes or loans, but which do not really reflect immediate common ancestry. If we are to discover where the problem lies, the first step naturally involves identifying the incompatible characters, and assessing whether these are consistently of a particular type, or concentrated in particular languages. In the case of Figure 3.1, the tree is only incompatible with four characters, and all of these are lexical: recall that Ringe et al. argue for phonological and morphological characters as more reliable indicators of relatedness. All four lexical characters 'beard', 'one', 'tears', and 'nine' may involve contact; and no better tree can be obtained by adjusting the tree so it becomes compatible with any of them. In fact, trying this makes things discernibly worse, since any tree compatible with one of these lexical characters automatically becomes incompatible with more than four others, and at least one of those characters is always non-lexical.

There is, however, another problem with the next-to-best tree in Figure 3.1: it does not include all Ringe et al.'s 24 languages. The omission is not accidental. A tree incompatible with as few as four characters can only be obtained if Germanic, in the shape of Old English, Old High German, Gothic, and Old Norse, is excluded. When Germanic is included, as shown in Figure 3.2, the resulting phylogenies become very much less than perfect.

The Germanic languages share states with a wide variety of other groups (including Italic, Celtic, and Baltic). Indeed, of 18 problematic characters, shared by discontinuous sets of languages, Germanic is involved in 16! In early pilot work Ringe et al. (ibid. 88–9) report that Germanic was therefore very unstable, and that 'its position in the tree shifted from run to run of the software; it was variously grouped together with Balto-Slavic and Indo-Iranian, or with Greek and Armenian, or with Italic and Celtic'. In later trees, generated from a modified data set,

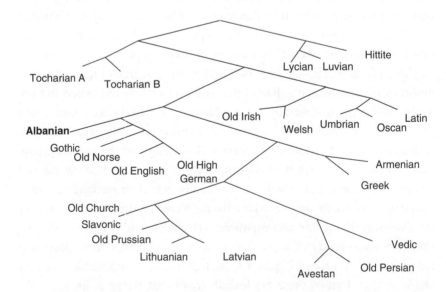

Fig. 3.2 Best tree for all 24 languages, redrawn from Ringe, Warnow and Taylor (2002: fig. 7)

Germanic is more stable, appearing fairly consistently as it does in Figure 3.2; but although consistency may be preferable to inconsistency, the price of consistency here is a bizarre grouping of Germanic and Albanian. The odd distribution of shared states with various subgroups also remains; and there is a price to pay computationally too, since 'Apparently because so many characters are incompatible, running the software on this dataset on a dedicated state-of-the-art machine takes about eight days' (ibid. 86 n. 16). When Germanic is excluded the running time drops to less than 24 hours (ibid. 89 n. 19). As Ringe, Warnow, and Taylor (ibid. 88) argue, 'The obvious inference is that there is not necessarily anything "wrong" with these characters, but there might be something very peculiar about Germanic.' Just as we can celebrate the fact that methods of this kind sometimes echo and therefore support the results of the comparative method, so it is vitally important that we should investigate and explain, rather than simply write off, cases where there is less coherence between the two. Consequently, the next obvious question is what this 'something very peculiar' might be.

3. 2. 2 Computational Cladistics and Contact

As we have already seen, the perfect-phylogeny approach is, by its very name, reliant on the family-tree model; and the tree model, in turn, is only applicable where contact-induced change can be ruled out. Ringe, Warnow, and Taylor (ibid. 65) argue that 'the tree model of linguistic speciation is normally appropriate, if the loss of contact between diverging dialects has been relatively abrupt and no discontinuities of transmission can be demonstrated for any of the languages in question'. It follows that prioritizing a method which is (at least currently) heavily reliant on trees necessarily means downplaying the effects of contact.

The past thirty years in historical linguistics have seen the development of a keen interest in contact-induced change, and in attempts to classify and categorize its effects (for a survey see Thomason 2001). Although any mention of language contact will certainly bring loanwords to mind, it is now abundantly clear that lexical borrowing is not the most extreme manifestation of contact-induced change. This is not to suggest that lexical borrowing is insignificant: it is certainly the most widespread type of change found in contact situations, and is often implicated in more radical types. However, as Thomason (ibid. 11) observes, 'It is not just words that get borrowed: all aspects of language structure are subject to transfer from one language to another, given the right mix of social and linguistic circumstances.'

Thomason (ibid. 10) proposes that 'The various linguistic results of language contact...can be viewed as a hierarchical set of typologies, starting with a three-way division at the top level into contact-induced language change, extreme language mixture (resulting in pidgins, creoles, and bilingual mixed languages), and language death.' We shall exclude any serious consideration of language death from what follows. Borrowing does take place from the dominant into the endangered language in many cases of language shift, but the types of borrowing in such situations do not seem to be radically different from other cases in languages which are not dying, so we assume the difficulties they will raise for classification are broadly the same. Attrition of the endangered language's structure may also remove some evidence for that language's genetic affinities; but, again, such changes also happen in languages which are not dying, and must be confronted in any attempt at classification. At least the social context of language death is relatively clear, so that we might hope to recognize such situations and anticipate the kinds of disparities we might encounter between a dying language and its relatives, though undoubtedly more research is needed on such questions.

Returning to Thomason's remaining typological categories, there is general agreement that in relatively casual contact situations borrowing is likely to be restricted to non-basic vocabulary; but as contact becomes more intense there may be borrowing of basic vocabulary, and also structural borrowing of phonology, morphology, and syntax. Although she stresses that this is intended only as an outline statement of probabilities, Thomason (ibid. 70–1) proposes an approximate division of borrowing situations into four types, some examples of which are given in (5).

(5) Thomason's borrowing scale (after Thomason 2001: 70–4)
   Type 1: casual contact
   Bilingualism not essential. Borrowing of non-basic vocabulary only; typically nouns. No structural consequences.
       Southwestern Pomo (N. California): borrowed words for 'sack', 'wheat', 'milk', 'coffee', 'tea', 'apple', 'socks', etc. from Russian during Russian occupation of local territory 1811–40.

Type 2: slightly more intense contact

Bilinguals more common but still a minority. Borrowing of non-basic vocabulary, function words, plus slight structural borrowing.

Formal **Turkish** loans from Classical Arabic: Arabic loanwords, conjunction *wa* 'and', several Arabic phonemes used in loan-words only.

Type 3: more intense contact

More bilinguals; language attitudes favour borrowing. Borrowing of basic vocabulary; verbs as well as nouns and adjectives; closed class items like pronouns, numerals; derivational affixes. More serious structural consequences, including new phonemes outside loanwords; prosodic phenomena; word order; possibly inflectional affixes.

Ossetic (Iranian) from Georgian (Caucasian): heavy lexical borrowing; extension of glottalic sounds to native vocabulary; new cases; agglutinative expression of case and number; word order shift towards subject-object-verb, with associated structural features including postpositions.

Type 4: intense contact

Extensive bilingualism; social factors strongly in favour of borrowing. Heavy lexical and structural borrowing, which may lead to major typological shifts in the borrowing language.

Asia Minor Greek from Turkish: heavy lexical borrowing, roughly equal numbers of verbs and nouns; borrowing of conjunctions, postpositions; some Greek phonemes replaced by Turkish ones; borrowing of phonological rules (including vowel harmony); shift from inflectional to agglutinative morphology in some dialects; general shift towards Turkish syntax.

All these four types fall into Thomason's category of contact-induced language change, though the divisions between the types are fluid: descriptors like 'slightly more intense contact', 'more intense contact' and 'intense contact' do not lend themselves to strict or absolute interpretation. This is as it should be, since, as Thomason stresses, we are dealing in contact situations with both linguistic markers of contact and social attitudes; and in both cases we are faced with continua. Furthermore, there is some potential leakage between Type 4, intense contact, and

Thomason's second major category of extreme language mixture, to which we turn shortly.

Note, however, that (5) above applies only to situations of contact between two languages, where it is clear which is the source and which the recipient. There are also situations of bilateral or multilateral contact, where more than two languages are involved, and the source may be one language for some features and another for others: indeed, it may not always be clear where a feature has come from. Such situations are known as linguistic areas, and the changes which take place in them fall under the heading of convergence, and typically involve the diffusion of more grammatical than lexical features. Although most issues in contact linguistics are controversial, convergence is particularly so: Thomason (ibid. 99) notes that 'what we understand about linguistic areas is depressingly meager, compared to what we don't understand about them', while Campbell (forthcoming: 2) argues in favour of 'abandoning the search for an adequate definition of "linguistic area" and concentrating instead on individual instances of borrowing'. The nature and status of convergence, in other words, is both fascinating and uncertain (see also Matras, McMahon, and Vincent forthcoming); but it is not directly relevant to our main concerns here. We assume that bidirectional borrowing will cause the same sorts of problems for attempts to recognize and deal with loans as unidirectional borrowing, though the changes may be harder to disentangle if the source of some features is unclear; we therefore set the specific circumstances of convergence aside in what follows.

In some contact situations borrowing is so intense that it creates something entirely new: Thomason (2001: 158) suggests that in these cases we find contact languages. Such systems are not affected but effected by contact-induced change:

a contact language is any new language that arises in a contact situation. Linguistically, a contact language is identifiable by the fact that its lexicon and grammatical structures cannot all be traced back primarily to the same source language; they are therefore mixed languages in the technical historical linguistic sense: they did not arise primarily through descent with modification from a single earlier language.

Thomason argues that contact languages fall into two main sets, the former comprising pidgins and creoles, and the latter what she calls bilingual mixed languages. Pidgins and creoles are discussed extensively in Holm (1988, 1989), McMahon (1994, ch. 10), Arends et al. (1995), Sebba (1997), and Singh (2000), and the summary here is necessarily brief and glosses over a number of central issues and controversies. A pidgin develops in a contact situation involving more than two groups, where there is no common language but communication is essential for some reason, perhaps trade or master–slave interaction. The result is a structurally simple system, which is nobody's first language, and is typically also functionally restricted. If such a language becomes the native language of some part of the speech community, it will necessarily extend its range of domains of use, and concomitantly become more complex lexically and grammatically: such a functionally and structurally expanded language, with a pidgin ancestor, is a creole.

Thomason (2001: ch. 8) argues that bilingual mixed languages form a separate category from pidgins and creoles. Mixed languages typically develop in situations of contact between just two languages, with widespread bilingualism; so a new language is not a necessity for communication between communities to take place. Mixed languages are neither structurally nor functionally restricted, and in Thomason's view they do not arise through imperfect learning. On the other hand, imperfect learning is commonly implicated in the development of pidgins, since often the speakers of the less prestigious substrate languages will lack sufficient access to the more prestigious superstrate language to allow full, normal learning: this may be encouraged by the superstrate speakers, who historically often had a vested interest in keeping the pidgin speakers linguistically and socially separate, and may also have believed that the substrate speakers were intrinsically incapable of learning the more 'sophisticated' superstrate, often a European colonial language.

Bilingual mixed languages have not yet been studied extensively: as Thomason (ibid. 198) suggests, the first studies only appeared in the 1960s, though much more information can now be found in Thomason and Kaufman (1988), Bakker and Mous (1994), Arends et al. (1995), Bakker (1997, 2000), Muysken (1997), Thomason (1997), and Matras (2000). There is no single characterization of a mixed language. For example, Michif, a language spoken in North Dakota, Manitoba, and Saskatchewan by the Metis people and studied mainly by Bakker, is a mixture of French (which supplies the noun phrases) and Cree (the source of verb phrases and most aspects of higher-level syntax). Media Lengua, spoken in central Ecuador, has mainly Spanish vocabulary and Quechua grammar; while Kormakiti Arabic, investigated in Maronite Christian communities in Cyprus in the 1960s, had both Greek and Arabic elements of grammar and vocabulary. Thomason suggests that what is common to these systems is not so much their linguistic shape, which always involves elements from two languages but otherwise can be very different from case to case, but the motivation for their development, which she sees as reflecting deliberate choices on the part of the speakers. Thomason divides the resulting mixed languages into two groups: one type has developed due to 'the gradual loss of a group's language under relentless pressure, over a period of hundreds of years, to assimilate to a surrounding dominant community' (2001: 205); this usage in a persistent ethnic group would characterize Anglo-Romani and Kormakiti Arabic, for example. These, then, are cases of long-term and gradual but extreme borrowing. On the other hand, bilingual mixed languages may develop more abruptly, to act as a linguistic marker of a newly developing ethnic group or community. This would be true of Michif and Media Lengua; but these cases are not, in timescale or result, like 'normal' borrowing.

Clearly, the first of these subtypes shows strong affinities to Thomason's Type 4 borrowing (see (5) above): in both cases there is extensive lexical and structural influence of one language on another. Thomason (ibid. 209) notes this overlap herself:

all the individual types of features of these mixed languages that originated in the dominant groups' languages can be found as interference features in cases of ordinary borrowing.... So the only difference between the interference features in ordinary borrowing and the (suggested) interference features in these bilingual mixed languages would be in the quantity: moderate to extensive in ordinary borrowing, extreme in the mixed languages ... Here, as with so many other things in the field of language contact, the determining factors must be social, not linguistic.

Although the determining factors may be social, the consequences are linguistic, since Thomason does not include this category of bilingual mixed languages as a Type 5 of borrowing (presumably, extreme contact); instead, she groups them with the other, abruptly developing mixed languages and with pidgins and creoles as languages lacking any language family and therefore excluded from family trees. Overlaps and unclarities of this kind are to be expected of contact linguistics, and perhaps especially of mixed languages, which have been studied for such a short time. However, this particular instance of overlap has implications for computational cladistics and, indeed, for any quantitative method, as we shall see below.

Contact languages, then, would not exist without the contact situations that have given rise to them. They have more than one ancestor, and therefore 'are not members of any language family and thus belong in no family tree' (ibid. 158). Other languages may have been in contact, but they still retain at least elements of continuity with a single ancestral system: English has borrowed from French, but it remains a Germanic language, and Asia Minor Greek is still (a variety of) Greek, though it has a fair amount of Turkish in it. Consequently, languages of this second kind do have families, and can be placed in family trees, though the nature and extent of the contact-induced changes they have undergone might make it difficult to locate them accurately and appropriately in the tree where they belong. For most languages our job as comparative historical linguists is to disentangle the influences reflecting common ancestry from those showing contact, and to remove the latter; but for contact languages this is impossible in principle, since in the absence of contact no such language would have developed in the first place.

How, then, is this typology of contact linguistics relevant to Ringe, Warnow, and Taylor's computational-cladistics approach (2002)? Ringe et al. also divide the consequences of contact into two types (as Thomason does, at least if we exclude language death, as we have argued we should, for present purposes). On the one hand, they assume that lexical borrowing will happen, but that 'most words borrowed from foreign languages can be identified as such in a language's basic vocabulary' (ibid. 78). The few that are not will cause peculiarities in the tree, and will tend to stop a perfect phylogeny being generated; but if the number of characters affected is small, the effect should be minor. Secondly, Ringe et al. (ibid.) assume that other consequences of contact-induced change are relatively marginal in historical linguistics, and can be recognized and excluded straightforwardly.

However, the similarities between this two-way division and Thomason's typology are more apparent than real. The closest affinity between the two systems is the opposition of 'normal' borrowing to language mixing. But Thomason (2001) divides her category of 'normal' borrowing into four subtypes to cover a range of social situations and linguistic effects ranging from minor borrowing of non-basic vocabulary to intense lexical and structural borrowing which can alter the typological nature of the recipient language, while Ringe et al. mention only lexical borrowing in this category—it is not clear how they would handle structural borrowing. Indeed, at one point they seem to deny its existence, arguing that 'natively acquired sound systems and inflections are resistant to change later in life; attempts to acquire a non-native phonemic contrast, phonological rule or inflectional category are at best only partially successful' (2002: 61). Ringe, Warnow, and Taylor take languages with 'mixed grammars' to result from discontinuities in transmission; these are either creoles or are 'descended from an imperfectly learned second language which became the community norm' (ibid. 64). The crux of this argument seems to be their assertion that 'mixed grammars are not known to result from native-language acquisition' (ibid. 63), so that discontinuous transmission alone can result in mixing. Furthermore, 'to judge from the aggregate of languages whose histories are actually documented for at least a few centuries, such discontinuities appear to be infrequent' (ibid. 63). In other words, any situation where it would be possible to argue that a language has more than one ancestor, as signalled for instance by the presence of apparent structural borrowings, would automatically be incompatible with a family-tree model, and therefore with any computational approach based on trees.

As might be expected from the discussion of language contact above, things cannot be that simple. Thomason (2001) seems to see structural borrowing of even quite extreme kinds as compatible with a family-tree model; only when there is genuinely a new language can we justify excluding that system from any language family. Ringe, Warnow, and Taylor seem to suggest that inflectional morphology and phonology are virtually unborrowable, and clearly this is reflected in their prioritization of non-lexical characters in subgrouping; but how are we to reconcile this with Thomason's view (ibid. 63)?

What can be adopted by one language from another? The short answer is, anything. Various claims can be found in the literature to the effect that this or that kind of feature is unborrowable, but counterexamples can be found (and have been found) to all of the claims that have been made to date.

Even if we accept the dichotomy between mixed languages (which are excluded from the family-tree model) and 'normal' borrowing (which is compatible with such a model, though problematic), there are clear problems in deciding where the line between them falls. Ringe, Warnow, and Taylor (2002) seem to suggest that any non-lexical borrowing might qualify as mixing, and mixing is intrinsically non-tree-like, while Thomason (2001) includes a range of structural borrowing types in the 'normal' category; she might even be interpreted as allowing one type of bilingual mixed language, the sort used in persistent ethnic groups and reflecting an extended history of borrowing from a dominant language, in this class. There is a particular issue here with imperfect learning, which Thomason (ibid.) invokes in the development of pidgins and creoles but excludes from the histories of bilingual mixed languages, since she assumes widespread bilingualism in the relevant communities. On the other hand, Ringe, Warnow, and Taylor (2002: 64) see imperfect learning as central to 'A surprising number of examples of the supposed borrowing of foreign morphosyntax by native speakers', which they ascribe instead to languages 'descended from an imperfectly learned second language which became the community norm'.

In one respect this seems like splitting hairs: whether the mixing is a result of influence from an L2 on an L1, or from imperfect learning of an L2 with influence from the L1 and hence in the opposite direction, surely does not affect the overall outcome, in the sense of a language with more than one historical contributor. Subsequent generations of speakers will indeed have to learn that mixed system; they may not be doing the mixing online, as it were, and they may not see the system they are learning as anything out of the ordinary, but from the perspective of a historical linguist that system is still undeniably a mixed one, and therefore problematic for the family tree. Whether we suggest that such cases must automatically be excluded from trees and from families will depend in part on our confidence in identifying such cases. Ideally, of course, we would have a series of diagnostic features which would tell us without question when we are dealing with a language with a history of contact-induced changes, or with creole ancestry, or with discontinuities in transmission. We do not currently have such a set of features, as evidenced in part by the lack of a clear division between Thomason's 'normal' borrowing category and one type of bilingual mixed language. Turning to mixed languages, Ringe, Warnow, and Taylor (ibid. 65) note that 'there remains a tiny handful of languages that exhibit unarguably mixed grammars but do not seem to be typical creoles', for which they cannot account. Given the relatively small amount of research to date on mixed languages, it seems unsafe to assume that the category is necessarily insignificant. Thomason (2001: 218), for instance, argues that 'the study of bilingual mixed languages is still in its infancy', and that 'the wide range of variation already evident in the languages currently available for study is likely to be the proverbial tip of an iceberg... anyone who believes that sweeping generalizations or strong predictions about these languages are possible in our current state of knowledge is at best overoptimistic'. At present, then, excluding any such cases a priori would seem premature.

In fact, Ringe et al. themselves invoke contact to deal with the peculiarities caused by Germanic, which, as we have seen, is implicated in 16 out of 18 problematic characters and represents a considerable obstacle to generating anything approaching a perfect phylogeny. This invocation of contact might initially seem surprising; but just because Ringe et al. (2002) see contact as the exception rather than the rule in linguistic history does not disqualify them from using it as an explanation for the odd behaviour of Germanic. Indeed, the procedure followed by Ringe et al. has the advantage of *demonstrating*, rather than simply asserting, that Germanic cannot have developed as the straightforward result of tree-like descent. The argument here is that Germanic shares a number of inflectional morphological character states with Balto-Slavic, Indo-Iranian, and Greek: 'since those are the characters that are the most reliable indicators of genetic descent, it appears that Germanic should be placed in what we are calling the core of the family—the residue after the departure of Anatolian, Tocharian and Italo-Celtic' (ibid. 110). Of the relevant lexical characters, Germanic shares states with either this core group or with Celtic or Italic, suggesting that (ibid. 111):

Germanic was originally a near sister of Balto-Slavic and Indo-Iranian... that at a very early date it lost contact with its more easterly sisters and came into close contact with the languages to the west; and that that contact episode led to extensive vocabulary borrowing at a period before the occurrence in any of the languages of any distinctive sound changes that would have rendered the borrowings detectable... In sum, it is clear that the development of Germanic exhibits some characteristics which cannot realistically be modelled with a 'clean' evolutionary tree, but it is not clear what historical developments have given rise to those anomalies.

As we have seen, the exclusion of Germanic allows a close-to-perfect phylogeny which is only inconsistent with four characters, all lexical.

This is certainly a good result, though it is achieved only on the assumption that non-lexical characters are indeed better indicators of common ancestry than lexical ones; and, as we have seen, Thomason (2001) allows quite extensive structural borrowing without ruling languages out of family trees. Although accepting Ringe et al.'s arguments that structural borrowing is likely to reflect imperfect learning and hence discontinuous transmission might exclude such cases from family trees in principle, it does not remove the risk that these will be problematic for tree construction in practice. If we are unaware that contact of this kind has happened, we might inappropriately try to include languages with this sort of history in trees and generate false representations anyway.

Of course, other questions must be raised in any full evaluation of the computational-cladistics project. For instance, although the use of non-lexical characters is an extremely promising development, the number of phonological and morphological characters which are actually useful and informative turns out to be very low, and the evidence for first-order branching is sparse and mainly lexical: as Ringe, Warnow, and Taylor (2002: 98) argue, 'the higher-order subgrouping of the IE family has remained an unsolved problem for so many generations partly because the evidence is genuinely meagre'. Ringe et al.'s findings are also absolutely reliant on prior philological work, because the characters must be identified and coded before involving the software; this means that while the *method* could be generalized to other language families, there can never be direct comparability, because the diagnostic *characters* will inevitably be different from family to family. Ironically, the only characters we can rely on extending to other groups are again the lexical ones, in the shape of basic vocabulary lists, for instance.

We believe that there are three lessons to be learned from this extremely promising computational work. First, it seems unwise to discontinue work on lexically based methods like lexicostatistics; we might be willing to consider and even to prioritize non-lexical data, but we cannot guarantee that in the actual analysis we will not be reliant on lexical material and calculations, so it pays to make these as watertight as we can. In addition, Ringe et al.'s results are highly dependent on their presumed ability to discount contact-induced changes, either philosophically, by assuming that structural 'mixing' is marginal and rare, or analytically, in the case of lexical borrowing. If we are to accept that borrowing does not present a significant problem, we must be able to show that loans, either in the lexicon or in other areas of the grammar, can indeed be excluded reliably; and even Ringe, Warnow, and Taylor (ibid. 78) have their doubts here:

> though most words borrowed from foreign languages can be identified as such in a language's basic vocabulary, there is always the possibility that a few will fail to exhibit the usual diagnostics of loanwords by sheer chance, especially if they were borrowed from closely related languages. That has been known for some time, though there has never been an effective way of dealing with the problem.

Finally, we understand the motivation for excluding many contact-induced changes from trees; but, stepping outside genetic classification for a moment, we might not wish to lose the data they provide. It is a matter of considerable interest to prehistorians, for example, to be able to assess which populations might have been in contact with one another in the past; and linguistic borrowings might give us a way of establishing this. In addition, setting aside evidence which is not compatible with a family tree only answers half the question: Can methods be developed to prove that contact is the source of these problematic innovations, and perhaps to trace the source reliably in cases where we have too little written history to be sure? Finding that the histories of some languages, or some aspects of the histories of others, are not compatible with a family-tree model does not mean that those languages or developments are intrinsically uninteresting. If we wish to understand and use those non-tree-like histories then we need alternative models; and here Ringe, Warnow, and Taylor (ibid. 110) again indicate one way forward in suggesting that 'the diversification of the IE family must be modelled at least in part as a network rather than a tree'. We return to the development of network models in Chapter 6; but first we must pursue the question of whether even lexical loans can be diagnosed accurately. If so, we shall ask whether excluding these loans is our best option; or whether retaining and using them in our analyses can tell us more about linguistic and human history and prehistory.

4

Tree-based Quantitative Approaches: Sublists

4. 1 Excluding Lexical Borrowing

In the last chapter we considered Thomason's typology of contact linguistics (2001). There is a paradox inherent in typologies of this kind, since the most extreme types of contact are not necessarily the most problematic for language classification. Although it might initially appear that contact-induced changes which affect all areas of the grammar, sometimes radically, might have most impact on our attempts to group languages into families, in fact many contact situations of this kind are particularly obvious, and therefore less likely to mislead us into proposing a relationship where there is none, or a closer relationship than was historically the case. On the other hand, contact involving only lexical borrowing, especially when that borrowing has been gradual but continual over a lengthy period of time, can be particularly difficult to trace, and to distinguish from the effects of equally gradual, differentiating change on a common ancestral system.

Take, for example, English *street* and German *Strasse*, which show the same regular sound correspondences as many pairs of cognates, like *foot/Fuss, eat/essen*, and so on, all with English final /t/ corresponding to German /s/. The meanings of these forms are the same, and there is nothing irregular about the apparent correspondences between them. Yet what we see here is the result of borrowing from Latin into Germanic, with subsequent differentiation into the daughters, though the item borrowed is the second rather than the first element of *via strata* 'a paved road', again making the loan particularly hard to spot. Likewise, all Romance languages have a word for 'coffee', and for the most part these also seem related by the expected sound correspondences; but this is a relatively late loan which has spread through the family, not a common ancestral form inherited from Latin. It follows that low-level lexical borrowing within a family or subfamily can be the greatest challenge for language classification, especially where there has been enough time for subsequent sound changes to obscure the nature of the loans, and even more particularly when the classification is based predominantly or uniquely on lexical lists.

Historical linguists have tended to react to these difficulties by assuming that lexical loans can be identified and excluded. In nineteenth-century historical linguistics two completely separate systems of representation were developed, the family tree for common ancestry (Schleicher 1863), and the wave model for contact-induced changes and feature spread (Schmidt 1872). Although neither can tell the whole story for most languages, and although contact can be difficult to trace, this differentiation has led to a policy of exclusion. In language classification today it is still very commonly assumed that language contact can be excluded philosophically, since it is so marginal and insignificant that it can comfortably be ignored; or excluded analytically, by selecting the data appropriately, or 'cleaning up' the data retrospectively. As we have already seen, it cannot be assumed that even the most basic of meaning lists will be immune to borrowing; in this chapter we shall show that we cannot guarantee removing loans from lexical lists after the fact either.

In any case, it does not seem to us that exclusion is the right policy. Borrowing is a fact of linguistic life; languages may fit into more or less tree-like patterns, but their histories are just as interesting and legitimate either way. It also seems unfortunate that historical linguists working on language change from past to present should currently be so strongly focused on contact, while historical linguists trying to reverse change up the tree and classify languages are effectively trying to pretend contact does not happen, or at best attempting to discard its effects. We shall argue that there are positive benefits in recognizing and using loans, though accessing those benefits requires new quantitative, computational techniques.

First, however, we should demonstrate that it is *not* possible to remove borrowings. We take it for granted that a 100- or 200-item Swadesh list will contain meanings which are more universal and less susceptible to borrowing than a randomly selected list of the same length; but, equally, there are going to be exceptions. It is well known that basic vocabulary can be borrowed, as English *they*, *them*, *their*, *sky*, *skin* were from Norse, for instance. Thomason's work (2001) reported in the last chapter also indicates that contact situations are common, so that marginalizing and ignoring contact-induced change is not a possibility either. Instead, Embleton (1986) accepted that borrowing will inevitably take place, but proposed an algorithmic correction for its effects.

Embleton points out, quite rightly, that the typical reaction on identifying borrowing affecting a meaning in a basic vocabulary list is to exclude that meaning; the problem is that if you keep excluding all the meanings where borrowing ever happens, the list will get smaller and smaller, and the results will be less and less robust. Instead, Embleton tries to build borrowing parameters into list calculations, by making an adjustment of b/k_x for the borrowing b into language X from each of its k_x neighbours. Although 'ideally of course b is supposed to be zero for the Swadesh-lists' (ibid. 79), we know there are cases of loans in the basic vocabulary; the question is how Embleton calculates b.

The answer is straightforward, but sadly ungeneralizable. Embleton begins with Germanic, and initially lists all the identifiable borrowings. Those are added up to give a value of b for each language pair, and then that value is fed back into the calculations, effectively correcting for those identified loans. The problem is that Embleton's calculations are specific to each pair of languages; worse, when she turns to Romance she finds that the borrowing rates she calculates do not give the right dates, so she has to build in what she accepts is a fudge factor, 'with the borrowing rates all arbitrarily increased by half' (ibid. 141). Finally, because this method relies absolutely on finding the loans first, it cannot help in cases where we are unsure whether borrowing has taken place or not; and yet these are the very cases where we most urgently need methodological help in identifying loans. Embleton (ibid.) herself finds a whole range of inter-borrowings within Indo-European, for the Swadesh 200-meaning list, including 12 loans from French into English, 16 from North Germanic into English, 11 from Danish into Norwegian, 15 from Dutch into Frisian, 19 from Danish into Faroese, and, moving outside Indo-European, 6 from Hebrew into Yiddish, and 5 from Tolai into Tok Pisin. However, we must ask whether we can realistically expect to have caught all the loans that exist using conventional techniques—or could there also be undiagnosed loans lurking in our lists? And if there are, what effect could that be having on our analyses?

The opposite approach is illustrated by Kessler (2001), who uses the term 'historical connection', defining as historically connected any two languages which are similar to one another, whether those similarities come from common ancestry or from borrowing. His aim is to distinguish historically connected languages from unconnected ones, not to distinguish common ancestry from borrowing—and he quite often uses the term 'cognate' to mean 'similarity reflecting historical connectedness', so his figures may include measures of traditional cognates and loans summed to give a composite similarity score: this issue is discussed at length in Kessler's chapter 8. However, we believe that Kessler is combining two different contributions to history which we might want to keep separate: it should be possible to agree that borrowing and common ancestry are both important, without having to go to the extreme lengths of collapsing the distinction.

4. 2 Identifying and Using Lexical Borrowings

Our view is that we can learn to identify and use lexical borrowings by applying quantitative and computational methods, and that we can derive these methods, at least in part, from work already done in biology. We return in the next chapter to correlations between the results of genetic and linguistic investigations; here, we simply note that it is not necessary for historical linguists to reinvent the wheel, when methods are already available, tried and tested, in the closely related discipline of population genetics.

Adapting methods from population genetics is particularly appropriate because, as Cann (2000: 1008) notes:

There is a close connection between comparative linguistics and evolutionary biology. Both seek to account for the overall resemblance between entities that are now distinct; in both there are confounding cases of horizontal transfer of information; and both are bedevilled by spurious similarities that arise from convergence, parallelism or reversals in character states.

In other words, both population genetics and historical linguistics are working with systems which persist and change over time, and which are susceptible to influence from outside, by admixture from other populations, or other languages. There are even family trees in both disciplines.

However, the difference between the methods used to reach conclusions about relatedness could not be more marked. Geneticists incline towards sophisticated computer technology, objective quantitative methodologies, and statistical testing; comparative linguists, on the other hand, have tended to prioritize depth of knowledge of one particular language group on the part of the individual scholar, rather than generalizable techniques which allow the processing of large quantities of data, regardless of region or family. In our own project, 'Quantitative Methods for Language Classification', we have therefore been investigating the borrowing of biological computer programs into linguistics. In this respect our work parallels that of Ringe's group, who also base their research on algorithms developed elsewhere, this time in computational mathematics.

One point of agreement with Ringe et al. involves the absolute requirement for historical linguists to show why a particular proposed family-tree configuration is the right one, or at least the best available. As we saw in Chapter 3, Ringe et al. assess their trees according to fit with a pre-selected set of characters; our approach is not character-based, but distance-based (though we return to character-based methods in Chapter 6). All distance-based methods start by calculating degrees of similarity (or of difference, if you prefer); the resulting matrix of distances between systems is then input to computer programs. On the positive side, distance-based methods allow generalization across groups, because there is no need to pre-select salient features or work with known shibboleths; on the other hand, not all aspects of language are suitable for measuring distances and deriving matrices. The method we outline here uses standard Swadesh-type meaning lists; we hope to show that additional information can be derived from already available data by using quantitative approaches. Nonetheless, we accept that methods based only on a single area of the grammar are inevitably limited, and will turn in Chapter 8 to the possible development of additional quantitative approaches to phonetics and phonology.

There are undoubtedly difficulties with the use of meaning lists: as we saw in Chapter 3, lexical data are generally regarded as inferior to phonological or morphological data in demonstrating relatedness, and are arguably most susceptible to contact-induced change. On the other hand, as Ringe et al.'s work also demonstrates, lexical data may be the only evidence supporting particular subgroupings, even in well-attested families. Despite problems of translatability across languages, and of potential subjectivity in choosing the 'unmarked' translation, meaning lists do have the very considerable advantage of being collectable even when available data is sparse; we should therefore at least consider testing the approach.

4. 3 An Initial Test: Optimal List Length

Thus far we have talked generally about Swadesh-type basic meaning lists, without committing ourselves to exactly which list we might wish to use: as we saw in Chapter 2, there are many variants, but perhaps the most important decision in quantitative terms is the choice between 100 and 200 meanings. This therefore seems a useful first test of our quantitative approaches.

There is a very common assumption that the 100-meaning Swadesh list is more universal, more basic, and more resistant to borrowing than the 200-meaning list: certainly, as Kessler (2001: 67) observes, 'the Swadesh 100 (a subset of Swadesh 200) is meant to be even more universal than the fuller list', while Hymes (1960: 7) notes that, for English at least, there is a higher proportion of more frequent words in the 100-item list. However, although there is a clear implication that list length, universality, or frequency should correlate with propensity to borrowing, this does not appear to have been validated directly. We have therefore tested the two standard lists to see whether they contain the same proportions of loans.

This test is extremely simple, and involves extensive use of data from Kessler (2001), who marks loans very carefully in his data, supported by an extensive etymological appendix. We selected 5 of Kessler's languages, all with fairly high levels of borrowing—these are Albanian, English, French, German, and Turkish. For each language we calculated the proportions of loans for both the 100- and 200-meaning lists. The overall borrowing rate across these 5 languages is 12.3% (which in itself is quite high for lists which, remember, are meant to be maximally resistant to borrowing); but these borrowings are not evenly distributed. In short, there is a lower proportion of borrowings in the 100-meaning list, with 8.6%, as compared with the meanings present in the 200-item list but removed to form the shorter list, where the rate is 15.7%. This difference is highly significant ($\chi^2 = 10.7$, p < 0.001).

This test has obvious implications for the optimal length of list, and perhaps the most obvious reaction would be to assume the 100-meaning list is inherently preferable, and prioritize this list in the rest of the book. However, as with all test results, we must be careful to consider all the implications. It is certainly true that if we were interested above all in 'purifying' the data we would be well advised to use the 100-meaning list. But even the shorter list still contains a fair proportion of loans; we do not face a straightforward choice between many borrowings on the one hand and virtually none on the other. In addition, there is a further and opposing argument that more data points are better: as Kessler (ibid. 67) puts it, 'sample size does matter. All things being equal, it pays to have more words in the sample.' Swadesh himself notes that his preference would have been to extend rather than to reduce the list from 200 items: 'An obvious way to improve the testlist, if possible is to make it longer' (1952: 457). However, Swadesh reports that he was not able to find enough suitable items: 'The first list, in its earlier and modified form, contained about 200 items, and the author hoped at one time to enlarge it in order to gain increased statistical accuracy, however only a handful of really sound new items were found' (1955: 124). Embleton (1986: 92–3) carried out a range of simulations on lists of various lengths, and concluded that 'comparison of results for N = 200 with those for N = 100 shows that accuracy . . . is considerably decreased by using a 100-word list. Hence the conscientious researcher must prefer a 200-word list over a 100-word list'; though she also notes that simply continuing to increase list length does not pay the same kind of dividend, since the benefits of a 500-word list are not sufficient to outweigh the practical problems of list collection.

In what follows, then, we shall use a standard Swadesh 200-meaning list, even with its greater propensity to loans, for two reasons. First, sheer weight of numbers: as Matisoff (2000: 336) observes, 'Surely the more words we have to go on the better.' However, we also opt for the extended list because it can be subdivided in helpful ways, reflecting the fact that 'it is not to be imagined . . . that its component items are of uniform stability' (Swadesh 1955: 128). In other words, within the 200-item list we will predict finding a greater range of retention rates. Clearly, if we had to assume a constant retention rate, most probably because of an application to dating the splits in family trees (a practice central to glottochronology, and one against which we will argue in Chapter 7), this would constitute an insuperable problem. However, Lohr (1999: 210) notes that, if we leave aside issues of dating, a variety of retention rates can actually be a major advantage:

If we wish to use the method to examine very ancient relationships, we need meanings which are as stable over time as possible; if, however, our concern is with more recent splits, we would prefer meanings with lower retentiveness to provide a more detailed sub-classification (e.g. if numerals up to ten were used as our test-list, we could say virtually nothing about the sub-classification of the Indo-European languages, since cognate roots are used in almost every case).

As we shall show below, we can use this spread of retention rates to our advantage: subdividing the longer Swadesh list allows us to diagnose even unsuspected loans.

4. 4 Subdividing Meaning Lists

4. 4. 1 The Dyen, Kruskal, and Black (1992) Database

Having decided to use 200-meaning lists in our tests, we now need to find as many examples of such lists as possible. There are, as we saw in Chapter 2, inevitable problems with list collection, whether they involve choosing the right translation equivalent, or dealing with cases where there is no single candidate form; and yet the quality of the data included in these lists will be absolutely vital for the quantitative methods we apply. It might be argued, then, that we should have gone out into the field in every case and collected all the relevant data ourselves, first-hand, noting each problem as it arose; and, indeed, this was the process we followed when dealing with the Andean data, collected by Paul Heggarty, discussed in Chapter 6. However, we chose for the first stage of our analysis to use an off-the-peg database for Indo-European instead.

There are several reasons for this decision. First, a great deal of relevant groundwork in this area has already been carried out by Dyen, Kruskal, and Black (1992), whose database we selected. If respected historical linguists, using a range of carefully vetted sources for languages with a long history of intensive and detailed study, have already constructed a database going well beyond our own level of expertise in many of the languages and varieties included, it goes against our guiding principle of not reinventing wheels unless absolutely necessary to rush out and do it all again. In addition, however, one might expect that any large and complex database, gathered over a lengthy period of time and using a wide range of sources, might well include some errors and miscodings; and in fact we were rather hopeful that this might be the case. This is not a misplaced case of academic *Schadenfreude*: we are delighted to put on record here our debt to Dyen, Kruskal, and Black, and it is worth saying in advance that the errors we detected in the end were very few, given the size of the initial undertaking. However, it does allow us a possible further test of our tree-drawing and tree-selection methods, in assessing whether they might allow us to identify errors in the data which had not been identified by prior linguistic analysis. If it turned out that such miscodings could be tracked down by our computational methods, this would both provide further validation of the methods for Indo-European and give us greater confidence in applying them to other language families. We therefore used the Dyen, Kruskal, and Black database completely without prior investigation or checking.

What, then, is the Dyen, Kruskal, and Black (henceforth DKB) database? In short, it is based on Swadesh 200-meaning lists for 95 Indo-European languages and dialects; and the database itself falls into three parts. First are the list items themselves for each language. Second, and forming the database proper, are judgements of whether any two items are cognate for each language pair; although this is considerably simplified for present purposes (and a fuller discussion appears in Chapter 6 below), there is a score of 0 for non-cognate items, 1 for cognates, and a further, unique code is assigned in cases where there has been borrowing. This unique code effectively removes the item in question from further computation, flagging up the fact that there is something peculiar going on. Finally, from each pairwise language comparison of these codes a single index of the degree of similarity is derived, and this in turn is used to construct a distance matrix. What this means is that the DKB database relies absolutely on prior, comparative-method work, which enables us to assess where we have cognates. It is important, especially for non-linguists, to appreciate this fact, since in many disciplines the data in comparisons are considerably more direct, with numbers derived directly from measured similarities between the items. In historical linguistics, and therefore in the DKB database, the data are actually judgements made on the basis of those similarities in the light of historical knowledge and investigation: but they are crucially judgements, rather than algorithmically derived measures of similarity. Quantification is therefore strictly two steps away from the original linguistic material, being a numerical transformation of linguistic cognacy scores.

This may raise questions over the reliability of the database itself, which is clearly potentially open to 'contamination' from subjectivity; there are three points to be made in response. First, a case has already been made, in Chapter 1, for the comparative method as vitally important in historical-linguistic research, and our quantitative methods do not seek to set this approach aside but to provide support and validation for it, and to allow us to extend our practice into language groups where we cannot apply the comparative method, for whatever reason. Second, it follows that quantitative and computational approaches are not intended to replace linguists and their accumulated knowledge: it is not a question of elbowing aside highly trained and experienced professionals, but of providing them with new tools. Finally, however, we share the discomfort of any scientist faced with an assertion that the data are potentially compromised, and we are actively seeking other, independent and more direct measures of linguistic similarity to supplement lexical list-based approaches; we turn to phonetic methods in Chapter 8.

4. 4. 2 Tree-drawing and Tree-selection Programs: Verifying What We Know...

Although Dyen, Kruskal, and Black produced a set of box diagrams from their distance matrix, they did not convert their data into language family trees. Recall that one advantage of quantitative approaches is the possibility they offer for testing familiar modes of representation like tree diagrams, to assess whether a particular tree is consistent with the data, and indeed is the most strongly supported by the data. We used three different programs from Felsenstein's PHYLIP package (2001), a suite of programs developed to draw and select biological trees. These programs, of course, are simply working with numerical data, and neither know nor care whether these data are derived from allele frequencies in biology or percentage cognacy scores in linguistics, so we simply treated our data as if they were analogous to genetic information. The great advantage of this approach is that the PHYLIP programs are not simply *drawing* trees: they are not the computational equivalent of one linguist and a pencil. These programs generate all or many of the possible trees, and then select from this set the tree most consistent with the distances in the data matrix. The selection criteria are objective; the entire process is automatized; and the result can be evaluated statistically.

Of course, no method of this kind can absolutely guarantee to find THE best tree, given the volume of candidates to be considered. Ringe, Warnow, and Taylor (2002: 86) are quite right in noting that the best tree cannot plausibly be identified by exhaustive searching, since the number of possible trees for their 370 characters, or our 200 meanings, will run into many millions. For example, on excluding Germanic from their analyses, Ringe et al. are searching for the best tree consistent with 318 of 322 characters, and calculate the relevant number of sets as 445, 197, 684. Similarly, the number of possible trees for our 95 languages and 200 meanings is approximately 6×10^{161} (which, if you are not used to very big numbers, is 6 followed by 161 zeros; for comparison, Page and Holmes (1998: 18) discuss the number of possible trees for a slightly larger data set of 135 human genetic sequences, as opposed to our 95 languages, and calculate that this number, 2.113×10^{267}, comfortably exceeds the number of particles in the known universe). However, biologists are quite satisfied with the heuristics included in programs of the PHYLIP type, which exclude at the outset large areas of the tree population which simply cannot be strong contenders; and, in any case, one can do further statistical-evaluation work in assessing how well a particular tree fits the data, as we shall see below.

Although we used three PHYLIP programs (namely Neighbour, Fitch, and Kitch), we shall focus here only on the first of these, since its neighbour-joining approach most accurately reflects the route which would be taken by a linguist drawing a single tree. Each step involves clustering the closest two languages (in terms of percentage similarity), then adding the next closest, and so on. This is a fairly crude but computationally simple procedure which takes less than 10 minutes to run for the DKB data on a 700 MHz PC (for comparison, recall that the Ringe et al. program took approximately 8 days with Germanic, and 24 hours after Germanic was excluded). On the other hand, the maximum-likelihood approach of the Fitch and Kitch programs attempts to minimize the differences between the branch lengths in the tree and the distances in the matrix; it also allows the entire tree to be globally rearranged after each addition, rather than regarding the previously drawn branchings as sacrosanct, as neighbour joining does. This means the population of possible trees considered is substantially larger under the maximum-likelihood approach, so the results may theoretically be better (because in considering a larger population of trees it is less likely to miss the true tree), but the cost is greater complexity in computing, with a run taking between 3 and 6 hours. For completeness, note that within the maximum-likelihood approach Kitch differs from Fitch in assuming a constant rate of change throughout the tree, while Fitch allows for different rates down each individual branch, meaning that the relative lengths of branches in Fitch trees show cases where languages have changed more or less since the common ancestor. At present any benefits from using the maximum-likelihood rather than the neighbour-joining approach seem marginal, since all programs generate several hundred thousand trees, and thus far produce strikingly similar results: for comparison, neighbour-joining and Fitch trees for the DKB data are presented in McMahon and McMahon (2003), and the outputs are virtually indistinguishable.

A neighbour-joining tree, drawn using the Neighbour program (Felsenstein 2001) is shown in Figure 4.1. Neither neighbour-joining nor maximum-likelihood trees resemble conventional language family trees, because they are unrooted: instead, the diagrams look like stars, with the members of each subgroup branching off together from the centre. Labels have been added to the arcs in Figure 4.1 to make this clearer.

It is, however, possible to convert these star diagrams straightforwardly into representations which do resemble classical linguistic trees, by rooting the tree artificially. Imagine the tree in Figure 4.1 as a mobile lying spread out on the floor—the kind found in children's rooms, for instance, with moons and stars or dinosaurs round the edge. Any part of that mobile can be picked up and hung from the ceiling, and all the rest will hang down, in a tree configuration. In exactly the same way we can select any of the languages or groups in Figure 4.1 as the root, and 'suspend' the other subgroups from that. Figure 4.2 shows the result when Figure 4.1 is rooted using Albanian, and redrawn using the program TreeView (Page 1996), which assists display on a personal computer. By choosing Albanian we make no assumption that it is older, or more archaic, or privileged in any way whatsoever. We chose Albanian solely for convenience, since it is not typically included in any larger subgroup, and there will consequently be no disruption of other languages in the tree. But any language could, quite arbitrarily, have served equally well as the root.

It is quite clear that these trees 'find' the usual suspects, in the shape of the generally recognized Indo-European subfamilies. Recall, though, that this could be a lucky fluke: the program is choosing from a population of

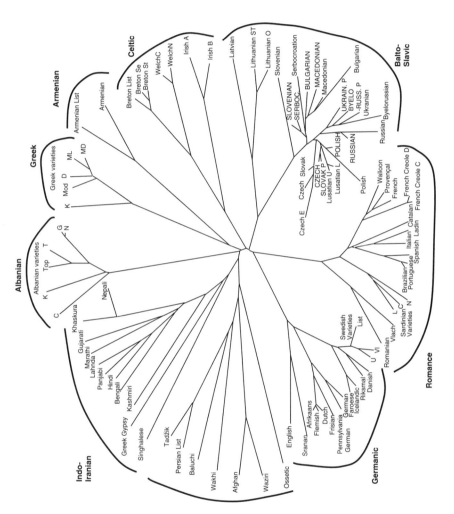

Fig. 4.1 Neighbour unrooted tree for DKB data

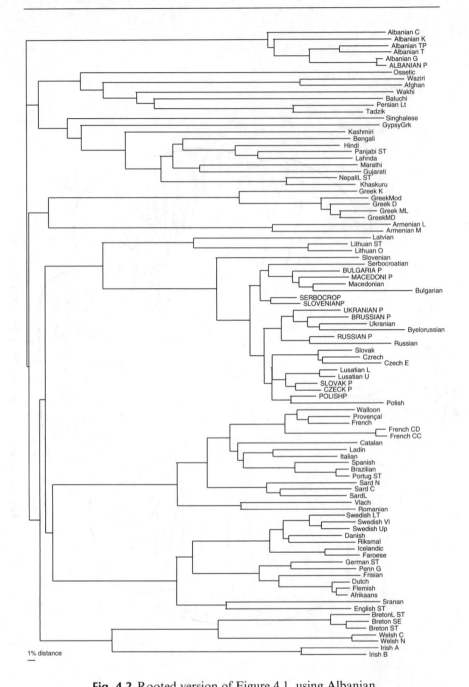

Fig. 4.2 Rooted version of Figure 4.1, using Albanian

several hundred thousand trees at the very least, and it might have stum-
bled over a decent-looking tree by accident; or there might be an even
better tree in the input set, which the program has unreasonably rejected.
It follows that we must also check how good these trees actually are, by
testing statistically how much confidence we can have in any particular
branching, and therefore cumulatively in the tree as a whole. The main
statistical method here is bootstrapping, which essentially means resampling the data sequentially to test the robustness of any given part of the
tree. Of the data, 5% are excluded at random (for our 200-meaning list, this
means removing ten meanings), then those empty spaces are refilled, again
by randomly choosing ten meanings from the same data set; and the whole
procedure is run again. For the most part, ten meanings will therefore be
removed and another ten will be doubled up on each run. In theory, it is
possible that the ten substitute meanings will all in fact be the same (it is
highly unlikely that, say, meaning 77 will be selected randomly ten times in
a row, but it is not strictly speaking impossible), or that the same ten
meanings that were randomly excluded on a particular bootstrap iteration
will, by a fantastic accumulation of chances, be randomly selected straight
back in again; it follows that the more bootstrap runs we can perform, the
better. This is, however, a time-consuming process, since the exclusions
and resamplings have to be done by hand—it is a type of permutation
testing of the kind discussed in Chapter 3 (Sect. 3. 1. 3. 6) above. Figure 4.3
is a bootstrap tree, showing the percentage support for each branch, for
neighbour-joining iterations only. The results show that the subfamily
branches are extremely robust, recurring in all runs. Again, the use of
bootstrapping helps address the criticism that the whole space of possible
trees cannot be searched exhaustively to identify the best tree.

4. 4. 3 … and Finding Something New

This use of biological tree-selection programs, along with bootstrapping,
demonstrates the robustness of the Indo-European subfamilies (Romance, Germanic, Celtic, Slavic and so on). This is a good result, since
it allows us to verify something historical linguists feel they have already
established, providing us with an independent check on results arrived at
partly by intuitive means. However, the devil's-advocate argument at this
point would suggest that Indo-Iranian, Celtic, Germanic, and so on were
always bound to emerge from these analyses, since they are built on a

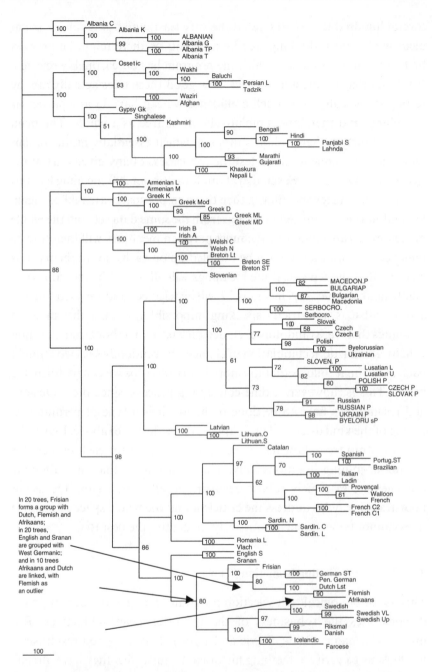

In 20 trees, Frisian
forms a group with
Dutch, Flemish and
Afrikaans;
in 20 trees,
English and Sranan
are grouped with
West Germanic;
and in 10 trees
Afrikaans and Dutch
are linked, with
Flemish as
an outlier

Fig. 4.3 Strict consensus neighbour-joining phylogeny for 100 × 5% boot-strapped iterations. Numbers to the right of a branch point indicate the percentage of resampled trees including that branching structure. Three examples of alternative branching patterns are shown for the Germanic subfamily for illustration.

distance matrix derived from cognacy scores: and if we have told the programs that there are more cognates within Germanic than between Germanic and Celtic, say, it is scarcely surprising that those same programs then obediently generate Germanic and Celtic as separate groups, rather than opting for Celto-Germanic. Reinforcing agreed results in the field, then, is an important aspect of this kind of work. But to become really convincing, and to justify extension of the methods to new areas and new questions, we have to demonstrate that we can also find out things we did not already know.

Let us turn, then, to two underlying assumptions about meaning lists. It is commonly assumed that borrowing should not be a major issue for basic vocabulary: we have, following Embleton (1986) and Kessler (2001), modified this assumption slightly, noting that such lists can contain loans, but that they should nonetheless be at a lower frequency than in other, nonbasic areas of the vocabulary. In the DKB database in particular the use of unique codings to mark loans should mean borrowings have been identified and filtered out, so that the cognacy scores submitted for computation really should approximate the ideal of loan-free basic vocabulary. There is a further but generally unstated assumption that individual items in meaning lists should be contributing equally to the analysis by changing at the same rate. Evidence from our initial bootstrap tests argues against both assumptions. It is true that subfamily groups do emerge routinely, but the numbers in Figure 4.3 show that some lower-level branchings are less well supported. This is because certain languages shift within their subgroups: not all reruns are giving exactly the same result, and yet the variation is not entirely random either, because the same languages seem consistently to be involved in the shifting. The question is how we can identify the meanings responsible for these shifts, and what is causing them.

There have already been suggestions that not all basic vocabulary changes at the same rate, and that some 'basic' items are more likely to be culture-specifically altered. Swadesh himself (1955: 122) observed that differential rates of change opened up new possibilities for lexicostatistics:

Since lexicostatistical work thus far has been keyed to the estimation of time-depths and has purposely sought to use those lexical elements which are least subject to cultural influences, it follows that only a fraction of the total phenomena have been studied. Eventually it will be desirable to study rates of change in the various types and levels of less stable vocabulary and to develop a complete theory of the factors affecting the rate of vocabulary change.

We argue that the best place to start on this enterprise is by maximizing the information provided by variation within the list itself. The issue of different rates of substitution has already been illustrated in a preliminary way by, for instance, Kruskal, Dyen, and Black (1971) and Pagel (2000); but what has not been demonstrated so far, though it has surely been suspected (see e.g. Clackson 1994: 26 ff.), is that these differential rates of change might have an impact on the shape of the resulting trees, perhaps explaining the kinds of shifts we observed in our different PHYLIP runs.

So, if all basic vocabulary is universal, but some meanings are more universal than others, how are we to identify the most and least conservative types? Both Lohr (1999) and Starostin (2000; and see Baxter and Manaster Ramer 2000) have been concerned with defining the 'best' meaning lists in an objective way, attempting to isolate shorter lists which are maximally stable and maximally resistant to borrowing.

Lohr (1999) approached this question by developing two scales, of relative reconstructability and retentiveness, on which meanings can vary. She considered reconstructions of four proto-languages for different families: Proto-Indo-European (Buck 1949), Proto-Afroasiatic (Ehret 1995), Proto-Austronesian (Zorc 1995), and Proto-Sino-Tibetan (Luce 1981). She then collected lists of meanings which could be reconstructed for 2 or more of these proto-languages; the argument is that 'such meanings are likely to be relatively basic, universal, and stable, since they reflect cultures of several millennia ago, cross at least two cultures, and were able to be reconstructed from descendant languages' (Lohr 1999: 54). Lohr found 61 meanings which were reconstructible for all 4 proto-languages, 196 meanings shared by 3 proto-languages, and 281 meanings shared by 2 proto-languages.

Lohr then went on to estimate the retentiveness, or the likely relative rate of change, of a set of these meanings, for Indo-European only. She traced the histories of a range of meanings in Buck's dictionary, with the addition of some particles, numerals, and pronouns, for the language groupings in (1): in each case the figure in brackets is the time period in millennia from the first-mentioned language state to the second.

(1) Lohr (1999): time periods for calculating rates of replacement
    Proto-Indo-European to Classical Greek, Sanskrit, and Latin
        (approximately 2.5 millennia in each case);
    Proto-Indo-European to Proto-Germanic (2.7);

Proto-Indo-European to Old Church Slavonic (3.7);
Classical Greek to Modern Greek (2.5);
Proto-Germanic to Proto-West-Germanic (0.7);
Vulgar Latin to French, Italian, and Romanian (1.8 in each case);
Proto-Germanic to Danish (2.3);
Proto-West-Germanic to English and German (1.6 in each case);
Old Church Slavonic to Serbo-Croat and Russian (1.3 in each case).

Lohr calculated how often a different form is documented with each meaning (or, put slightly differently, the number of replacements for that meaning) in this range of periods and languages within Indo-European. The number of replacement events per meaning was calculated for each time period in (1), and then summed for the combined time period of 31 millennia. Consequently, the replacement rate, as shown in (2), is expressed as the average number of millennia one might expect to wait for a replacement event for that meaning.

(2) Lohr (1999): average Indo-European replacement rates per meaning

Visible replacements over time period	Replacement rate in millennia	Number of meanings
0	Infinite retentiveness	17
1	31.3	40
2	15.7	20
3	10.4	25
4	7.8	37
5	6.3	44
6	5.2	53
7	4.5	56
8 or more	3.9 or lower	138

In many ways Lohr's work is preliminary. Her database is relatively small (though still larger than anything else available), with only 4 proto-languages considered for the calculation of relative universality, and only a single source for each of these. In terms of the retentiveness calculation, some of the time periods are known and secure, since we can date texts for Latin or Old Church Slavonic, for example; but others are much less clear, since we do not know with any certainty (see also Ch. 7) when Proto-Indo-European was spoken. One might therefore argue over the time periods Lohr allocates to the PIE–Latin, Greek, and Sanskrit intervals.

Nonetheless, Lohr's calculations seem a convincing starting point. For one thing, shortening or extending the specific periods between PIE and its immediate daughters would not greatly affect the relative results. Since PIE is unattested, and we therefore have no records of diachronic variation until the first daughter-language texts, we cannot in any case project many replacements for these periods; and consequently, although changing the projected date for PIE would alter the overall number of millennia in the calculations, it would not affect the number of replacements or the relative ranking of rates for different meanings.

It is also possible to provide some external, independent evidence for Lohr's set of maximally retentive, maximally reconstructible meanings, on the basis of Starostin's 35-word list of highly persistent meanings from the Swadesh 100- and 200-word lists, collected independently and from a different set of languages. We constructed a list of 30 meanings from the DKB database which scored as highly as possible on Lohr's indices of reconstructability and retentiveness, all being reconstructable for at least 3 proto-languages, and with no more than 3 replacements. This list and Starostin's 35-item list (presented in Baxter and Manaster Ramer 2000) are shown in Table 4.1.

These two lists overlap in 13 meanings. If we were to randomly select 30 items from DKB, the probability of picking 10 or more items overlapping with the Starostin list is less than 0.1%. Given the significance of this result, it appears much more likely that both Lohr and Starostin have independently identified some of the factors which do indeed mark out these sublists as highly universal and resistant to borrowing.

Both Lohr and Starostin established their clines of reconstructability and retentiveness in order to identify the maximally conservative items, which they then prioritize in their further analyses. The same is true of earlier work by Dolgopolsky and Dryer, who again attempted to isolate

Table 4.1 Comparison of 30-item list from Lohr/DKB with 35-item Starostin list

Starostin	Overlap	Lohr/DKB
blood, bone, die, dog, egg, eye, fire, fish, hand, know, louse, nose, stone, tail, this, water, what, who, year	ear, give, I, name, new, one, salt, sun, thou, tongue, tooth, two, wind	come, day, eat, five, foot, four, long, mother, night, not, other, sleep, spit, stand, star, thin, three

*full, *horn, *moon, *Not in DKB

the most retentive meanings, proposing lists of 15 and 20 items respectively: both are arguing for a limitation on the volume of data we require 'by in effect using only the items that carry the most information (in the technical sense) about genetic relationship' (Embleton 2000: 152–3). In all these cases the strategy is to identify the most extremely retentive meanings, and reject the rest.

Our approach is different: rather than dispensing with all the less conservative items, we drew up a contrasting sublist which scored conspicuously low on Lohr's indices of retentiveness and reconstructability. This sublist consists of 23 DKB meanings which were reconstructable for only two proto-languages, and which had 8 or more visible replacements in the 31.3-millennium total sample: we opted for meanings reconstructable for two proto-languages rather than only one because a collection of complete cultural one-offs, which really would be at the extreme low end of the reconstructability spectrum, would offer far less potential for cross-cultural generalizability of our results. We call the two contrasting sublists, which are given in Table 4.2, the 'hihi' list (for high in reconstructability, or universality, and high in retentiveness, or resistance to change), and the 'lolo' list (low in reconstructability and low in retentiveness; in other words, less universal, and more changeable). The numbers in the two classes do not match because 6 meanings in the more stable, hihi class were cognate across the whole of Indo-European, and thus totally uninformative. In a few cases one of these six meanings is absent from an individual language in the DKB material because of some

Table 4.2 Hihi and lolo sublists; criteria for list assignment after Lohr (1999)

Sublist	
Hihi	Lolo
30 meanings, from DKB Reconstructable for at least 3 proto-languages; no more than 3 replacements	23 meanings, from DKB Reconstructable for only 2 proto-languages; at least 8 replacements
four, name, three, two, foot, give, long, salt, sun, other, sleep, to come, day, to eat, not, thin, five, mother, ear, I, new, night, one, to spit, star, to stand, thou, tongue, tooth, wind	grass, mouth, stone, heavy, year, bird, near, smooth, wing, man, neck, tail, to walk, back, to flow, left (hand), to pull, to push, river, rope, straight, to think, to throw

language-specific change; but none of these changes is shared by a whole subfamily, and there is therefore no salient information for tree-drawing purposes, since a unique innovation (or loss, for that matter) affecting only a single language is consistent with any possible tree.

Rerunning different bootstrap iterations on the full 200-meaning list led to certain inconsistencies in the positions of particular languages. Our hypothesis was that isolating the top and bottom ends of the full list, in terms of most and least conservative meanings, might bring differences between resulting trees into sharper focus, and perhaps isolate the meanings responsible for the shifts we observed. Let us consider just two differences involving the hihi and lolo sublists, both within Germanic.

When only the lolo meanings are used (Fig. 4.4) Frisian appears as a sister of a group containing Afrikaans, Flemish, and Dutch, as is also the case with the full 200-meaning list.

However, with the hihi sublist (Fig. 4.5) Frisian is related to these languages only at a deeper level, and the tree indicates an earlier split of Frisian as against the rest of the West Germanic group.

In the second case, English, which in the full 200-word-list tree and the tree for lolo meanings (Fig. 4.4) appears (along with the creole Sranan) as a relatively deep, distant sister of the whole Germanic group, 'migrates' into the West Germanic group in Figure 4.5, based on the hihi meanings. McMahon and McMahon (2003) also give trees for Romance, which show a similar effect for Romanian: although we do not repeat these trees here, in the lolo tree Romanian is marginal to Romance, while in the hihi tree it is much more integrated, forming a subgroup with Ladin and Sardinian.

Our hypothesis is that these shifts of individual languages arise from borrowing; a similar suggestion is made by Ogura and Wang (1998),

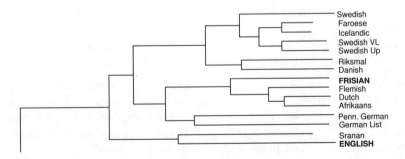

Fig. 4.4 Lolo meanings, Germanic

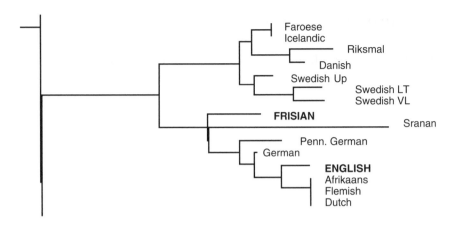

Fig. 4.5 Hihi sublist, Germanic

which was sent to us after we had completed our own investigations. Ogura and Wang (ibid.) also used the DKB database and PHYLIP, but only for Germanic; they found that the most unstable languages are typically those noted by Embleton (1986) as having most borrowing, but do not pursue this correlation further. However, the hypothesis of borrowing seems to be supported by the languages that are moving, and the direction in which they move. Within Romance, Romanian has borrowed extensively from Slavic. In the case of Frisian there is heavy borrowing from Dutch, towards which Frisian gravitates in the lolo tree. For English there is considerable early borrowing from North Germanic. (Embleton (ibid. 100–1) finds 15 Dutch to Frisian loans in the Swadesh 200-word list, and 16 from North Germanic to English.) English does not move into the North Germanic group altogether; but this is quite possibly because of additional, extensive borrowing from Romance, which is effectively pulling English towards the margins of the Germanic subfamily. (Again, Embleton (ibid. 100) reports 12 borrowings from French into English in the 200-word list.)

4. 4. 4 Testing the Hypothesis of Borrowing

4. 4. 4. 1 Computer Simulations

So far all the signs are positive for our hypothesis that the differences between the positions of certain languages in the PHYLIP trees drawn from the hihi and lolo sublists reflect the effects of borrowing in the latter.

Lohr's criteria (1999) have allowed us to define contrasting sublists, and items in the lolo list ought by those criteria to be more susceptible to borrowing; it is also true that the languages which shift around from run to run are those we know independently to have a substantial amount of borrowing in their histories; and, finally, the direction in which those languages move in the lolo trees is uniformly towards other languages we know to be sources of at least some of those loans. Nonetheless, all this evidence, though cumulative, remains circumstantial. How can we demonstrate conclusively that borrowing is the cause of these shifts in our trees?

The problem is, in fact, a more general one. In the case of Indo-European we are already in possession of a considerable amount of evidence about which items have been borrowed, and the direction in which they have travelled. It is therefore possible, as we shall see below, to reverse-engineer our trees, focusing on individual meanings to assess whether these are responsible for a particular shift. However, this is not directly generalizable to cases where the history is poorly understood and it might be unclear whether borrowing has in fact happened or which languages are particularly affected. We have therefore carried out some computer simulations. If borrowing of particular types and intensities creates a typical signal for our tree-drawing and -selection programs, we can look for just that signal, or variants of it, in trees we generate subsequently from real data.

Our simulation technique is based on an Excel spreadsheet, generated from a single ancestral 'language' consisting of a 200-item list. This provides the best match with the Swadesh 200-meaning list in the DKB database, though the simulated items are only lists of numbers, not linguistic material. In each generation there is a fixed probability of any item in the list changing. We modelled the emergence of 12 daughter languages, labelled A to L, over 220 generations, with each bifurcation taking place at a specific, set time point. Each time the program is run there is the same history of bifurcations, but which of the 200 items mutates, and when, is stochastic. That gives a 'real' history for the family, which is represented in Figure 4.6: each number is the date of the relevant split, expressed in generations.

The next step was to carry out different runs, with the equivalent of a very conservative, simulated hihi list, set to the equivalent of one mutation per item per run, and a more changeable lolo list, set at double that mutation rate. At the end of each run we calculated the cognate frequencies, created a distance matrix, and put the data through the PHYLIP

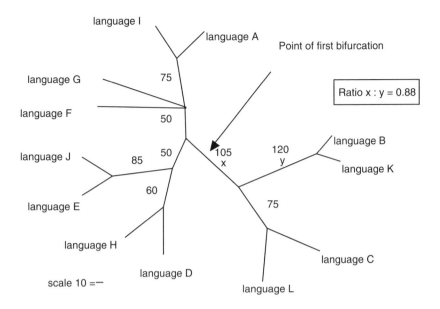

Fig. 4.6 Actual history of simulated language family in generations

tree-drawing programs. The resulting tree for the hihi list, in Figure 4.7, is very close indeed to the real history, except that the branch length at the root is shorter: this can be seen by comparing lines x and y in Figures 4.6 and 4.7. This reflects the fact that certain early changes will have been obscured by later changes to the same items, hence becoming unrecoverable; this gives the impression, in Figure 4.7, of slightly less change having happened than was really the case.

The recovered history from the lolo list, shown in Figure 4.8, is almost identical again, with the same shortening of the root.

It may initially seem surprising that the simulated hihi and lolo lists give such similar results; but this simply reflects the fact that for these initial simulations we set the history so no borrowing is allowed at all. This enables us to model the case where only the rate of change is different between sublists (where, as Figs 4.7 and 4.8 show, the simulated lists produce strongly similar trees) against the case where both the mutation rate and the possibility of borrowing are higher. The next stage therefore permitted recent borrowing, within the last 20 generations; and in the relevant trees we have included a completely unrelated language M, which indicates the position of the root. We have also allowed borrowing at different rates from the list for language B into the list for language A.

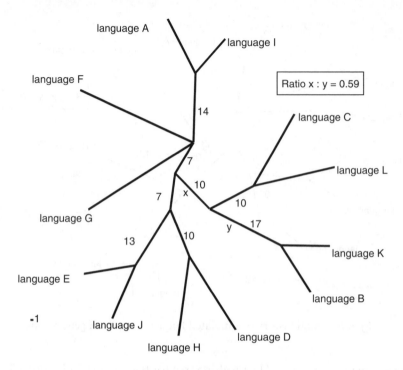

Fig. 4.7 First 'recovered' history from low-mutation-rate simulation (hihi list)

First, borrowing is permitted at a minimal 1% rate, and the result is essentially identical to the earlier trees, as shown in Figure 4.9, except for the trace of a reduction in the lengths of the branches containing A and B, suggesting a reduction in the distance between them.

With 5% borrowing, the branch containing A, and its sister language I, is noticeably shifting away from its sister group containing F and G, and towards the root, as shown in Figure 4.10, though we only observed this effect in approximately 15% of runs.

The trend is the same, but much clearer at the 10% borrowing level modelled in Figure 4.11, where the dotted line shows the group of A and I splitting from the root earlier than the group with F and G: in the real history, shown in Figure 4.6, this was not the case, but reflects the contact between B and A. We saw this pattern in more than 80% of our runs.

Finally, we modelled 20% borrowing, shown in the two rooted trees in Figure 4.12. On the right, the real history with no borrowing from B into A, these two languages appear in totally different lineages, and are only quite distantly related. On the left, with 20% borrowing from B to A, A

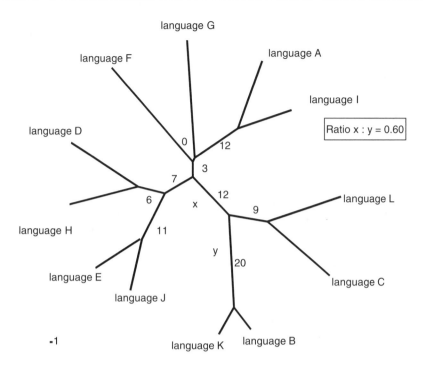

Fig. 4.8 First 'recovered' history from high-mutation-rate simulation (lolo list)

(along with its subgroup of I, F, and G) shifts into a cluster with B—which, as we know from a comparison with the known, real history, never existed at all.

The effect shown in Figure 4.12 is close to the pattern we found with some Indo-European languages, which changed position within trees in the lolo runs. This does not, however, mean we must assume the borrowing in the real data took place over a relatively short time period: although our simulations above allowed borrowing over only the previous 20 generations, we found that 5% borrowing over 20 generations is identical in its simulated structural consequences to 1% borrowing over a much longer period of 100 generations. This is potentially important because more gradual borrowing over a longer period might be harder for linguists to identify, as older loans will have had longer to come into conformity with the phonotactic requirements of the borrowing language; but the program will give the same picture in both cases. This may therefore help us identify just those problem cases of early and long-standing borrowing where the linguistic evidence on its own is insufficient.

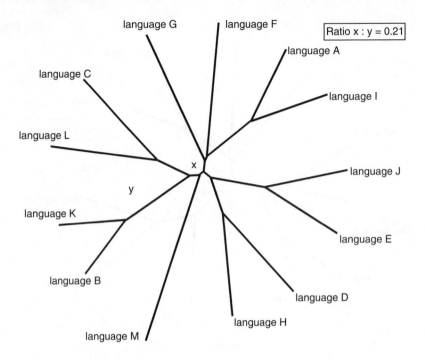

Fig. 4.9 Simulation with high mutation rate and 1% borrowing from B to A

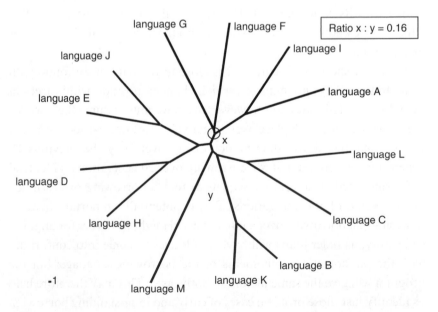

Fig. 4.10 Simulation with high mutation rate and 5% borrowing from B to A

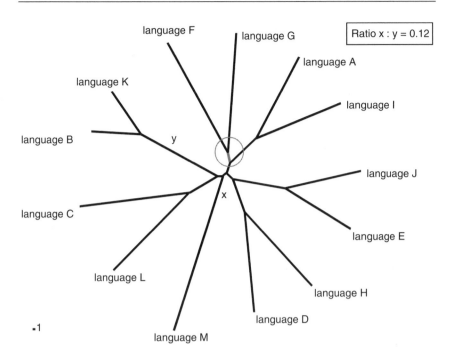

Fig. 4.11 Simulation with high mutation rate and 10% borrowing from B to A

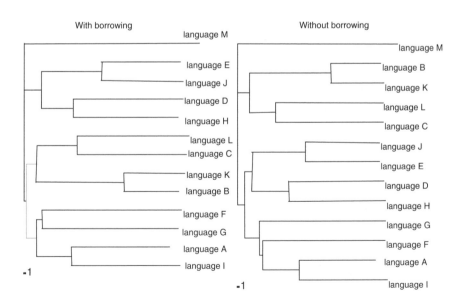

Fig. 4.12 Comparison of rooted tree with 20% borrowing from B to A, and without

4. 4. 4. 2 Erroneous Codings in the Database

The use of these computer simulations contributes a further piece of evidence that the patterns we have observed in our hihi versus lolo Indo-European trees reflect the greater propensity of our lolo data to borrowing. However, this is still not decisive. First, the evidence remains circumstantial, though powerful: it is possible, though unlikely, that other factors could have affected the real data, creating patterns coincidentally resembling those arising from borrowing in our simulated data. And there is a more serious problem: since DKB provide unique codings for loans, and do not mark them as cognates, surely there really ought not to be any effect of borrowing in our lolo data, as any loans should already have been factored out?

We tested this possibility by checking whether any of our hihi or lolo items appeared on the lists of borrowings within Germanic produced by Embleton (1986). At least 6 borrowed items ('wing', 'left (hand)', 'to pull', 'to push', 'river', and 'to throw') are in our lolo list, but none at all is in the hihi list, supporting the argument that the lolo items have a greater propensity to borrowing. We then selected a sample of lolo items, and returned to the original DKB codings, to check whether these had all been entered correctly. In fact, there are some miscodings in just these cases—a small number, given the volume of data involved, but tellingly affecting the overall distance matrix and consequent trees, by allowing loans in certain cases to count as cognates. For instance, four loans from Frisian into Dutch are miscoded as cognates by DKB, and these include both 'left (hand)' and 'river' from the lolo list; and nine loans from North Germanic into English are erroneously coded as cognates, including 'wing' from the lolo list.

This is, then, conclusive proof that the different configurations we have found for trees generated from more conservative and less conservative sublists in fact reflect, at least in some cases, the effects of loans. In Chapter 6 we shall see that using other programs, such as Network and NeighbourNet, allows further testing: Network, for instance, is much more sensitive to the effect of even a single miscoded item. We shall also extend this approach to detecting loans to languages outside the Indo-European family. Network programs, like the PHYLIP programs, were originally developed for use with biological data; and before introducing network-based analyses for language we turn to the possibility of much closer and more direct connections between biology and linguistics.

5

Correlations Between Genetic and Linguistic Data

5. 1 The 'New Synthesis'

An approach which can diagnose and use even unknown loans turns out to be of considerable relevance when we turn to another area of controversy, this time moving beyond linguistics per se to a set of observed though contentious interdisciplinary correlations. It is easy to see language families as abstractions, and perhaps our conventional representation of each language, reconstructed or attested, as a single node encourages that kind of thinking. But reconstructed languages in the past, like languages today, must have had speakers; so it follows that human histories, rather than simply linguistic histories, are necessarily involved.

However, it is impossible to find out about those human histories through linguistic work alone: we have to take an interdisciplinary approach. One possibility, which is much in the scientific news at the moment, is the 'new synthesis'; and its proponents argue that we can bring together evidence from linguistics, genetics, and archaeology, assess whether meaningful correlations exist between these disciplines, then use this cumulative evidence to provide clues to the histories of human populations. Moreover, work of this kind might help us understand the features of populations today, by revealing prehistoric affiliations and contacts.

The idea of constructing trees for linguistic and genetic groupings and measuring the degree of similarity between them is, of course, not a new one: we might trace the start of work on mappings between linguistics and genetics to the publication of the well-known Cavalli-Sforza et al. (1988) parallel linguistic—genetic tree, which is shown in Figure 5.1.

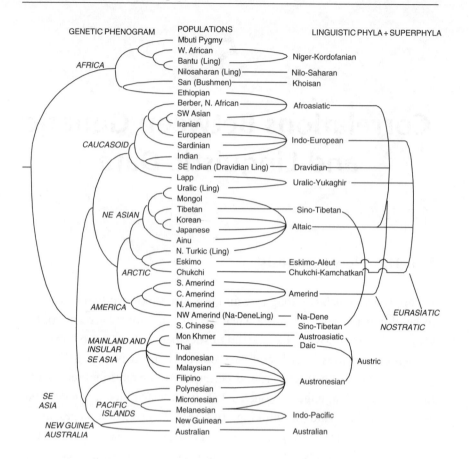

Fig. 5.1 Cavalli-Sforza et al. (1988) tree, redrawn

As is well known, there has been a good deal of criticism of this tree
(Bateman et al. 1990; McMahon and McMahon 1995; Sims-Williams
1998), both because of lack of independence of the populations sampled
(some genetic populations, like Na-Dene, are defined on the basis of the
language spoken in the community, which rather begs the question) and
because it includes very long-range comparisons—many historical linguists would consider constructs like Amerind, Nostratic, and Eurasiatic
essentially unfounded (Campbell 1988; McMahon and McMahon 1995).
However, it would naturally be unreasonable to reject any prospect of
meaningful matches because of problems in a single early application. We
can, however, learn two lessons from the Cavalli-Sforza tree and its
critics. First, any reasonable attempt to establish correlations must be

based on good genetics, and good linguistics: if the methodology or results on either side are suspect, the best we can hope for is Matisoff's vision (1990) of two drunks supporting each other. Good science cannot come to good conclusions on the basis of bad data. It follows that our discussion below will rule out from the start any correlations based on Greenberg's mass comparison (see Ch. 1 above), or involving long-range language megafamilies—which we see as currently unsupported. Second, we cannot expect any successful and enlightening attempt to identify correlations between genetics and linguistics to involve straightforward, one-to-one matches: both genetic and linguistic histories are too complex for that. Indeed, it is precisely the common, but independent, characteristics of the two systems, since both involve gradual divergence along with contact phenomena, that make parallels between the two, methodologically and in terms of results, so attractive. But dealing with that complexity will involve the interpretation of equally complex patterns, not writing equations of the $x = y$ type.

Even accepting these concerns, hopes for the so-called 'new synthesis' of disciplines are high: Cavalli-Sforza (2000: vii), for instance, introduces his recent book as follows:

This book surveys the research on human evolution from the many different fields of study that contribute to our knowledge. It is a history of the last hundred thousand years, relying on archaeology, genetics, and linguistics. Happily, these three disciplines are now generating many new data and insights. All of them can be expected to converge toward a common story, and behind them must lie a single history. Singly, each approach has many lacunae, but hopefully their synthesis can help to fill the gaps.

However, the promise of the new synthesis has not yet been achieved, and Renfrew (1999: 1–2) is rather more cautious in his assessment, noting that 'We may be on the brink of seeing some convergence in our understanding of issues of genetic diversity, cultural diversity, and linguistic diversity. It may be possible, then, to work toward a unified reconstruction of the history of human populations. It is much needed, because certainly we do not have such a unified history at the moment.' Sims-Williams (1998) also provides a careful, critical overview of the whole area and its prospects. Before proceeding to consider some suggested correlations, then, it is important to review some possible misunderstandings and problems.

5. 2 Correlations Between Genetics and Linguistics: Cautions and Caveats

We should begin by defining, at least in a very general way, just what we mean by correlations between genetics and linguistics. Most importantly, of course, there is no claim of determinism between genetics and linguistics (which at its most problematic and simplistic would mean that the genes an individual carries determine the language she speaks). This is a notoriously difficult area, since we do not wish to reject the hypothesis that there is a genetic component underlying language either: it is entirely possible for the human species to be predisposed to language learning and use without any of that genetic hard-wiring corresponding to characteristics of English, as opposed to Estonian or Quechua. Exploring these issues further is beyond the scope of this book; but it is worth simply reiterating that establishing population-level correlations between linguistic and genetic features does not imply any causal connection between the two systems.

It is also worth stressing the necessity of working at the population level when exploring these correlations. Calculations will ideally be based on many individuals, involving averages and probabilities across groups, not absolute values for individuals. Although molecular genetics has had a higher public profile recently, because of the advances in the Human Genome Project, for instance, it is not the best genetic correlate for linguistic variation. One of the immediate concerns about cross-disciplinary comparisons of the kind we are proposing involves the apparently discrete and absolute nature of genetic haplotypes at the DNA level, where we either have a sequence of GTA, or ATG, and not something in between; quite reasonably, linguists see this as contrasting absolutely with the naturally variable and choice-ridden data of language. However, the right comparison, we believe, is with population genetics, or evolutionary biology, rather than molecular genetics. When we scale up the molecular material for a whole population we do see variation and 'choice', so that at the same locus we might find 10% of one population with GTA and 90% with ATG, and the opposite ratio in a second population, while yet a third has 10% GTA and 90% ATA. This looks much more like the shifting, variable patterns linguists know and love.

It is also worth reminding ourselves that populations are abstractions, like speech communities. It would clearly be unrealistic to expect, in a sociolinguistic survey, that each member of a speech community would use a particular variant 33% of the time, or that all middle-class women would use that same variant in precisely 95% of their formal speech (even assuming that we are confident we can define relativistic constructs like 'middle-class' or 'formal' in such a definite and non-overlapping way). As linguists, however, we can transcend the individual level, and interpret data of this kind in terms of its reality for the speech community. Individual speakers are not robbed of their identity or their uniqueness by being grouped together into broader categories; and for different purposes we can study the individual or the group.

Exactly the same is true of genetic studies of populations. Individuals are important; but there are some studies for which we need to take a broader view, and categorize people into groups according to the average of their genetic characteristics. It may seem unlikely, looking at cosmopolitan, modern, urban European populations, for instance, that we can ever reach any meaningful conclusion on their genetic characteristics, since each individual will have his or her own highly specific history. But averaging over a sufficiently large number of individuals can indeed reveal particular frequent, key attributes for the group, alongside the individual markers which signal a history outside that population as unusual and marginal. Put in linguistic terms, we might doubt, listening to several speakers from the same area, that we can subsume their distinct and individual accents under a single system; but grouping together a whole range of such speakers may well reveal shared characteristics. We both have noticeably Scots accents; closer inspection reveals that one author has acquired a marginal contrast of /æ/ versus /ɑ/ over 15 years of living in England, though typically Scots lack this distinction and have a single, undifferentiated low mid /a/ vowel (the other author is holding out and has no such contrast). This does not remove the general impression of Scottishness when either of us speaks; and it does not contradict the observation that most Scots lack the *Sam–psalm* opposition. Both observations are valid, and relevant for different purposes. It is also important to note that contemporary urban populations, with their history of input from widely divergent genetic (and linguistic) sources, are by no means the norm either diachronically or diatopically: smaller, closer-knit communities with greater continuity represent a more usual basis for human histories.

This has three implications for work of the sort discussed below. First, it is important that we should collect both linguistic and genetic data from 'older', more isolated populations before admixture levels out many of the signals in which we are interested. Second, those of us who are urban speakers and rejoice in our mixed and exotic heritage have to accept that we are relatively unusual in global terms, and therefore that our own experiences and expectations do not amount to a necessary rejection of these methods and results. Equally, however, we cannot simply ignore all those mixed populations that do exist, and of course admixture at some level occurs even in the smallest and most traditional of groups (see McMahon 2004): hence, we must as a matter of urgency investigate means of recognizing and, where necessary, factoring out admixture. This will be a recurring theme in the discussion below, and, as we shall see, differences in practice here between geneticists and historical linguists represent a significant threat to progress in the 'new synthesis'.

These preliminaries are important in breaking down possible misperceptions of the meaning of genetic/linguistic correlations. Turning to a broad definition of those correlations, we mean simply that, all else being equal, when the languages spoken by two populations are closely related we might expect genes present in the two populations to be similar; and, conversely, when the languages are only distantly related (or unrelated) the genetic profiles of the two populations should also show considerable differentiation. We can then hope to use these affinities between linguistics and genetics to help us cast light on the histories of particular populations. Since populations, after all, consist of people who both carry genes and use languages, it might be more surprising if there were no correlations between genetic and linguistic configurations. The general observation goes back to Darwin (1996 [1859]: 342), who suggested that 'If we possessed a perfect pedigree of mankind, a genealogical arrangement of the races of man would afford the best classification of the various languages now spoken throughout the world.' This might now seem somewhat overstated: clearly, 'The correlation between genes and languages cannot be perfect', because both languages and genes can be replaced independently; but the relationship 'Nevertheless...remains positive and statistically significant' (Cavalli-Sforza 2000: 167).

This correlation is supported by a range of recent studies, and we explore several of these in detail in the following section. To take just one example, Barbujani (1997: 1011) reports that 'In Europe, for example,...several inheritable diseases differ, in their incidence, between geographically close but linguistically distant populations'. In this case and others we find a general and telling statistical correlation between genetic and linguistic features, which reflects interesting and investigable parallelism rather than determinism. Where we observe genetic and linguistic parallels today, we therefore hypothesize earlier ancestral identity: as Barbujani (ibid. 1014) observes:

Population admixture and linguistic assimilation should have weakened the correspondence between patterns of genetic and linguistic diversity. The fact that such patterns are, on the contrary, well correlated at the allele-frequency level... suggests that parallel linguistic and allele-frequency change were not the exception, but the rule.

The 'new synthesis' may look promising, but at present it is limited, since most recent work has involved correlations between archaeology and genetics: Renfrew and Boyle (2000) coin the term 'archaeogenetics' for exactly this bilateral disciplinary match. There remain some doubts over the feasibility of including linguistic evidence, in large part because of the generally non-quantitative approaches favoured by historical and comparative linguists, and the consequent difficulties of establishing repeatable, demonstrably correct results, let alone parallels with other disciplines. Archaeology and, to an even greater extent, genetics are quantitative in their approaches and methods, and in their evaluations of results; and if their practitioners are to understand and use historical-linguistic data, linguists must therefore deal in probabilities and degrees of relatedness. Here we have a further motivation for the development of quantitative methods in historical linguistics: if we are genuinely interested in interdisciplinary research, and do not supply numbers of our choosing, we cannot be surprised if archaeologists and geneticists attempt to provide their own. To give just one example, Poloni et al. (1997: 1017–18) adopt the following methodology:

Linguistic distances between pairs of populations were defined as simple dissimilarity indexes... two populations within the same language family are set to a distance of 3 if they belong to different subfamilies; their distance is decreased by 1 for each shared level of classification—up to three shared levels, where their distance is set to 0... a dissimilarity index of 8 was arbitrarily assigned to any pair of populations belonging to different language families.

What this means is that Poloni and her colleagues, urgently requiring some numbers to feed into their computations, have almost arbitrarily assigned grades of relatedness of 0, 1, 2, and 3 to pairs of languages, with a score of 8 for pairs generally thought to be unrelated. If we as linguists feel that these are crude overgeneralizations, then the onus is very much on us to provide better-reasoned alternatives. Not all colleagues may agree that linguists should feel under any obligation to change the way we do linguistics, just because other disciplines are interested in our results; Smith (1989: 185) takes the more insular view that 'linguistic theory is not affected by the fact that its subject matter can also be of interest to others: the hydrologist's theories are not affected by spitting'. As the last four chapters suggest, we take a very different view, and see the development of quantitative and computational methods as crucial to progress within historical and comparative linguistics, for discipline-internal as well as interdisciplinary reasons. Clearly, we are not alone, either: after a gap following Embleton (1986), there is now something of a resurgence in interest in quantitative methods among historical linguists and colleagues in other disciplines (Kessler 2001; Ringe, Warnow and Taylor 2002; McMahon and McMahon 2003, 2004; Heggarty et al. forthcoming; Forster, Toth, and Bandelt 1998; Forster and Toth 2003; Gray and Atkinson 2003; Renfrew, McMahon, and Trask 2000). As quantitative methods develop further, one of the main barriers to integrating linguistics into the 'new synthesis' seems set to disappear. It is therefore timely to consider some general issues relating to correlations specifically between linguistics and genetics.

5. 3 Evidence for Correlations

5. 3. 1 Genetic Evidence and Sampling

A range of recent studies in the genetics literature discuss evidence for correlations between genetics and linguistics at the population level. Looking ahead, we shall see that there are interesting parallelisms, but that correlations seem less significant in some cases than others. As we shall show, a very influential factor here, which has not so far been taken into account, is the different attitudes of linguists and geneticists to admixture between systems.

Considerations of space mean it is possible to discuss only four studies; Sokal (1988), Poloni et al. (1997), Gray and Jordan (2000), and Rosser et al. (2000). An overview of current literature on genetics—linguistics correlations at the population level is provided by McMahon (2004), who also focuses on two general issues, namely the type of genetic evidence used and the techniques and rationale involved in sampling.

First, no single type of genetic feature is consistently included in these comparisons: we cannot simply say that all relevant studies compare 'genes'. Three main types of genetic evidence have been included in studies of correlations with language, and these are the so-called 'classical set' of genetic polymorphisms, such as the ABO blood groups (see Cavalli-Sforza et al. 1994); mitochondrial DNA; and Y-chromosome material. There are other genetic systems which promise to be even more informative, notably involving microsatellite DNA and repeat sequences which are unique events and therefore provide excellent markers for group membership, but these have not yet been applied in interdisciplinary research. Not all these genetic markers seem to correlate equally well with linguistics: Poloni et al. (1997) argue that the clearest results typically come from comparisons with Y-chromosome DNA, which contains the gene determining maleness and is therefore passed on only from fathers to sons; and McMahon (2004) surveys a range of studies of Europe which indicate that prioritizing classical set, Y-chromosome, or mitochondrial DNA evidence (the last being passed on only through the female line) can give different results. This might seem to constitute an open and shut case for rejecting such correlations altogether; but it is much more likely to indicate that men and women in populations may sometimes have different histories, providing both a more complex and a more interesting picture. In turn, this may reflect the higher variability in male reproductive success, as well as indicating cases of partial migration or organized intermarriage systems between groups.

Even more important and potentially problematic is the issue of population sampling (Cavalli-Sforza et al. 1994; Moore 1994). Most genetic variants predate the geographical break-up of the human species and therefore differ between human groups only in relative frequency; it follows that investigators cannot validly define populations after the fact on the basis of the variants they do or do not have, but must crucially define the boundaries of the population in advance in order to be explanatory. Random sampling on a physical-grid approach might be ideal, but is both socio-politically and scientifically challenging; and so far sampling has often been on the basis of named, culturally significant groups, such as villages or ethnic groupings. These are commonly defined by language affiliation, with unfortunate consequences for the independence of linguistic and genetic data. In addition, the result of such non-random sampling is that small, disappearing tribal groups character-ized on the basis of their language are often treated as equivalent to similar-sized samples drawn from large, modern nation states. As MacEachern (2000: 361) points out 'the Hadza of Tanzania, with a total population of about 1,000, occupy the same analytical status in Cavalli-Sforza *et al.*'s regional genetic reconstructions [1994] as do the South Chinese (approximate population 500,000,000) and the French (approxi-mate population 60,000,000), yet these three ethnonyms define entirely different types of human population unit'. McMahon (2004: 4) notes that

This approach has provided perfectly acceptable samples for addressing large-scale questions of human origins, such as the Out of Africa vs Multi-Regional Hypotheses...where only a few representative populations are required from each continent. However, when we are asking questions about the relationships between human groups and their languages, to base the sampling criteria in one domain on data from the other automatically weakens the importance of any relationships detected.

It could be argued that sampling strategies based on language groupings might be appropriate for groupings with pre-agricultural social organiza-tion; but powerful evidence against this simplistic assumption is provided by the extended studies of the Yanomani tribal groups living in the Amazon basin of South America summarized in Merriweather et al. (2000). Fission and fusion, intermarriage and warfare amongst the roughly 150 villages that make up this linguistic group have led to a situation where several villages are genetically closer to geographically close but linguistically and culturally distinct groups than they are to other Yanomani villages. These hunter-gatherer villages have at least as much evidence of complex interactions as anywhere else, so that a choice of members from a single village to represent the Yanomani could be as misleading as choosing a group of Londoners to represent Western Europeans. We shall touch on issues of evidence and sampling in con-nection with the four studies to be discussed below.

5. 3. 2 Four Specific Studies

Our first case study is Gray and Jordan (2000), which reports on the use of unpublished data from Blust's *Comparative Austronesian Dictionary* to construct a phylogeny of the Austronesian languages. The main idea behind this paper was to test two competing hypotheses on the origin and spread of Austronesian languages and speakers: these are the 'express-train-to-Polynesia' and 'tangled-bank' models. Gray and Jordan's phylogeny was strongly congruent with the 'express-train' model, which is well supported by archaeology and all three types of molecular genetic evidence, and assumes a rapid population expansion from an original source population in Taiwan, with a unidirectional series of population movements covering the 10,000 km to Polynesia in approximately two millennia. Any possible contribution of contact is also minimized, since the archaeological culture of these early Austronesians exploited island coastlines, meaning that where they did arrive on already populated islands they were unlikely to interact much with the inland-dwelling prior inhabitants; many other islands would have been unpopulated. We might anticipate that this sort of history, involving continual change with clear punctuations as populations split and move on, and rather little contact, might produce patterns in keeping with relatively simple models of divergence, like the family tree. Gray and Jordan's paper is a paradigm case of the approach advocated in earlier chapters, where quantitative work can validate existing proposals; here they provide evidence for a particular tree of the Austronesian languages which was originally put forward by comparative linguists, but can be shown to be supported by data from other disciplines.

Our second case study, Poloni et al. (1997), used genetic data mainly from a single region of the Y-chromosome, in 45 published populations, and 13 collected by their own group. The total sample included 3,767 individuals, with a worldwide distribution, but some bias in favour of African and European populations. Poloni et al. demonstrate a strong correlation between linguistic and genetic distance among their 58 populations; in particular, they identify four essentially non-overlapping clusters on the basis of members' genetic characteristics and whether they spoke an Indo-European, Khoisan, Niger-Congo, or Afro-Asiatic language.

Our third case, Sokal (1988), again seems to support the existence and exploitability of correlations between linguistics and genetics; this time the genetic data studied were 'classical-set' autosomal genetic polymorphisms. Sokal demonstrates significant correlations between languages and genes across Eurasia using a simple model of linguistic distance, with languages within a subfamily (such as Romance) being set at 0 distance, while languages in different subfamilies within a family (such as a

Romance and a Germanic language within Indo-European) were set to 1, and those from different families (such as Turkish, from the putative Altaic family, and Hungarian from Finno-Ugric) were set at 2. Sokal carried out Mantel correlation analyses of the genetic-distance matrices, using several different estimators for genetic distance, against the resulting linguistic-distance matrix; these were significant for over half of the genetic loci studied.

Although these initial investigations of correlations between linguistic and genetic evidence look positive, clouds start to gather on the horizon when we look at a fourth recent paper. Rosser et al. (2000) used by far the most extensive molecular data set to date, but, perhaps paradoxically, genetics–linguistics correlations here become rather more elusive. Rosser et al. studied 11 separate Y-chromosome polymorphisms on 3,616 chromosomes drawn from 47 European populations, and their main suggestion is that the primary determinant of both the linguistic and the genetic variation seems to be geography. In other words, variation in both linguistic and genetic terms relies on the degree of physical distance between populations. Where the populations compared are on different continents, so that there is considerable physical distance between them, we would expect, and indeed find, a good deal of linguistic and genetic distance too. Exceptional cases of large linguistic and genetic differences between geographically close populations are often associated with clearly identifiable local barriers, such as mountain ranges or stretches of water: for instance, as Rosser et al. (ibid.) note, the Georgian and Ossetic populations are geographically close, but are genetically and linguistically distinct, and separated by the Caucasus mountains.

There are consequently two alternative accounts for our linguistics–genetics correlations. We may have found the real explanatory factor, in the shape of geography; the apparent correlation between languages and genes is then revealed as secondary. On the other hand, it might be that the indubitable effect of geography is not the main, or the only, factor but is masking a true correlation between genetics and linguistics which reflects shared population history. One way to reduce the confounding effect of a third common variable is to use a statistical technique known as autocorrelation analysis to 'remove' the effect of the third variable, leaving a partial correlation of the other two variables of interest. For a partial correlation of genes and language with geography held constant, this amounts to asking what the correlation for language and genes would be for all those populations with the same geographic distance from each other. This then isolates the relevant component of total variation, revealing the extent to which a knowledge of the genetic relationships between populations can be used to infer the relationship between their languages and vice versa.

From this point of view the main difference between the studies we have discussed is that Poloni et al. (1997) did not test for the contribution of geography: they did refer to distance, but of course distance is only one aspect of geography, since, as we have seen already, populations separated by the same distance may be more or less close in languages and genes depending on whether that distance includes a major barrier like a mountain or sea. On the other hand, Poloni et al. (ibid.) were working across continents, and most of their largest-distance figures in language and genes correspond to populations on either side of these geographical barriers. Sokal (1988) removed the effect of geographic distance and found a reduced but still significant correlation between language and genes. Gray and Jordan (2000) are not dealing with populations on different continents in a political sense, but certainly these populations are divided by isolating stretches of water. Similarly, in the Cavalli-Sforza et al. (1988) tree those correlations that seem most convincing and robust are again those that operate across continents. Rosser et al. (2000) were most careful in their treatment of geography, since they considered both local barriers and distance; their conclusion was that, within continents, geography is by far the greatest explanatory force for genetic distances, eclipsing the contribution of language as an independent barrier to gene flow. However, even in their work significant correlations between linguistic and genetic characteristics of populations were found where samples include populations on different continents or otherwise separated by major physical barriers: although Rosser et al. included only European populations in their main analysis, they did also consider two African populations, and in comparisons involving these groups the linguistic–genetic correlations did become significant.

5. 3. 3 The Contribution of Contact

It is self-evident that the likelihood of contact and interbreeding is much lower for populations on different land masses or separated by a major physical boundary than for adjacent or physically close populations.

Indeed, before the development of relatively recent technological innovations, simple distance even within continents would have correlated very strongly indeed with the likelihood of contact between members of different populations. Sewell Wright, whose work in the 1930s led him to be acknowledged as the father of modern population genetics, is said to have held that the single most important factor in reducing the level of inbreeding in human populations was the invention of the bicycle, since before this the norm was for marriage within five miles of one's birthplace, whereas afterwards population admixture quickly became the rule. Genes in populations do naturally change and diverge; this is the basis of the fundamental speciation model of isolation by distance. However, the further apart two populations are geographically, the greater the divergence is likely to be, because in geographically close populations interbreeding and consequent admixture will cause genetic convergence, running counter to the effects of normal divergence. In the most distant cases we would not find even the very limited amount of admixture required (in the order of 1 or 2 individuals per generation (Nei 1987)) to prevent those populations from diverging. It follows that we should expect to find considerably less genetic distance between geographically close populations which are not separated by any significant physical barrier—and if there is anything in the claims of correlation between genetics and linguistics, we should expect that relatively small genetic distance to be paralleled by less linguistic distance. Of course, these distinctions are all more difficult to observe in studies sampling only modern, mobile groups, since technological innovation has led to a greater likelihood of interbreeding between even the most distant populations.

These expectations are supported by our knowledge that contact between two populations does not only have the genetic effect caused by interbreeding. Contact is also possible at a linguistic level, and has its own consequences there (see Thomason 2001; Ch. 3 above). Depending on the intensity of contact, and on other imponderables like language attitudes, prestige, and so on, these effects may range from the occasional, nativized lexical item to wholesale structural borrowing, convergence, pidginization and creolization, language mixing, and the like. And just as interbreeding was less likely, at least until relatively recently, for geographically distant populations, so language contact might be expected to be less intense the further apart two speech communities are.

If neither genetic nor linguistic mixing takes place to any great extent between populations on different continents, or with a major physical boundary separating them, then one can well understand why the correlation between the two types of evidence seems relatively strong for populations under these circumstances: greatest genetic distance equals greatest linguistic distance. However, where populations are geographically close, with no intervening physical barrier, one would equally expect increased similarity at the genetic level to be mirrored in increased linguistic similarity; and here we have a paradox, because within a continental mass Rosser et al. (2000) suggest that the correlations are less significant. In other words, where populations are geographically adjacent one would expect recent history, and its consequences in terms of admixture, to blur to an equivalent degree any more distant historical relationships in both genetics and linguistics. What seems to happen, however, is that some of these geographically close populations remain more distant linguistically than would be anticipated given the probability of recent contact: here, the expected correlation with genetics is disturbed. For example, in northern populations of Europe a particular Y-chromosomal haplotype has been associated with the expansion of the Ugric-speaking peoples along an eastern to western axis (Zerjal et al. 1997). Rosser et al. (2000) identify this particular haplotype (HG16) in all the Finno-Ugric speaking populations, but also in the adjacent Indo-European-speaking Lithuanian and Latvian populations. However, although the historical spread and current distribution of this haplotype is an excellent example of genetic contact and diffusion, it is happening across the most significant language-family boundary in the region, between Indo-European and Finno-Ugric.

There are two approaches to interpreting this apparent paradox. Either contact between populations does not have any linguistic consequences— or only very minor ones. Or contact-induced change is going on all right in both linguistics and genetics, but linguists and geneticists handle admixture in very different ways. It does not even seem worth testing the hypothesis that language contact does not happen—putting it at its most cartoonishly simple, there are simply many more opportunities for conversation than for interbreeding, especially where the latter must end up in the production of viable offspring if the genetic profile of a population is to be affected by admixture. But there has certainly been a long-standing tendency in comparative linguistics to marginalize or exclude contact-induced changes, as we have seen in earlier chapters. Contact-induced changes are problematic:

they can lead to erroneous hypotheses in terms of family-tree construction, and to false steps in reconstruction. And if our priority is the construction of linguistic family trees, it is only natural that we should attempt to remove the effects of changes which are out of keeping with the tree model, whether by pre-selecting basic vocabulary lists, which should be relatively resistant to contact, or by excluding languages with non-tree-like histories, which Thomason and Kaufman (1988) describe as 'non-genetic'. In fact, the kind of discrepancy that arises can be illustrated quite straightforwardly by considering the case of French. In all our PHYLIP trees discussed in Chapter 4, French falls squarely and consistently inside Romance. However, we can also construct a genetic tree for the French population—admittedly a highly idealized concept, taking into account the concerns about sampling expressed in 3.1 above. Our tree, which covers a range of European populations, is based on average genetic distance for 88 'classical-set' genetic polymorphisms from Cavalli-Sforza et al. (1994), and appears as Figure 5.2. It also shows that French falls clearly inside Germanic, producing a complete lack of parity, in this case, between linguistic and genetic trees.

This disparity arises, then, because if historical linguists can exclude borrowings they will—and they will certainly prioritize data which seem less amenable to external influence. This, however, is exactly what geneticists do not do. The tendency in population genetics has been to recognize and accept migration, and its genetic consequences, and there is a significant history of attempts to provide measures of interpopulation exchange, and indeed models of how this might happen, and the extent of its effects, under particular circumstances. This is all part of quantitative work in genetics which aims to calculate equilibrium gene frequencies and levels of variability, and to assess the contribution of the different forces affecting populations, namely mutation, migration, drift, and selection.

Given this discrepancy in practice between linguistics and genetics, our hypothesis is that the actions of linguists in denying, downplaying, or attempting to screen out the effects of borrowing may have created the appearance of non-significance in the correlation between linguistic and genetic variation for certain populations within continental land masses. The exclusion of borrowings will automatically prioritize and emphasize data indicating common ancestry and earlier history for the linguistic systems concerned, while the genetic systems for the same populations will also include any more recent innovations due to contact and admix-

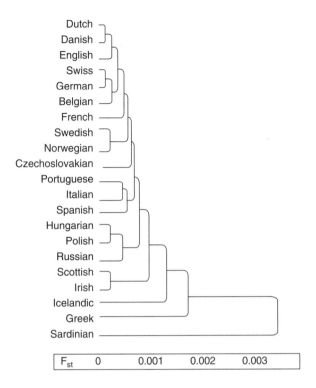

Fig. 5.2 Genetic tree of European populations from genetic distances (= F_{st}) between populations, based on 88 genetic polymorphisms from data in Cavalli-Sforza et al. (1994)

ture. This would create an obvious mismatch between those systems, which would then appear less comparable in geographically adjacent populations, disrupting the overall correlation between linguistics and genetics. But this discrepancy has not arisen because the histories are different—it has arisen because the histories are the same, but half the linguistic history is being analysed out! That is, our linguistic methodologies attempt to exclude contact-induced changes, and this conspires against the recognition of parallels between linguistics and genetics.

Matters get even worse, though, when we consider that last sentence in more detail—our linguistic methodologies attempt to exclude contact-induced changes, yes; but we know that they do not always succeed. Basic meaning lists, as we showed in Chapter 4, have on average 12.3% loans (at least for the five languages we sampled); and even where we are dealing with well-attested and intensively studied languages, as in the DKB database for

Indo-European, and agreed mechanisms for marking and filtering out loans, we have seen that errors can inevitably be identified at some level. This presents even more of a problem, because it means we cannot even rely on the disparity between linguistic and genetic trees being a consistent one: the degree of mismatch we find will depend on how many loans linguists have missed (for instance, because of gaps in their knowledge of certain systems), and that is hardly a factor amenable to statistical modelling.

What our methods offer is a way of avoiding the problems arising from these inconsistencies of practice. We can retain all the data, loans and all, for 'new-synthesis' type work where we are undertaking cross-disciplinary comparison and thinking about population histories; but we can then identify the borrowings and exclude them later for purely linguistic work. In Kessler's terms, we can retain a database reflecting 'historical connectedness' for comparison with genetics or archaeology, but prioritize true cognates when we are drawing our family trees. If our methods can reliably exclude loans, we may not even in principle be restricted to Swadesh-type lists in future, since we will be able to assess the different contributions of different meanings by rerunning our programs and isolating which meanings are contributing to shifts of languages between runs.

5. 4 Looking Forward

We ended the last section with a bright prospect; but there are two outstanding issues to be considered before we leave the topic of linguistic–genetic correlations. First, identifying some apparent disparities between linguistic and genetic trees does not remove the possibility that there may also be real ones: we noted at the outset that comparing these two independent systems would always be a complex undertaking, not a simple one-to-one match, and population movements might have highly significant, but variable, effects on correlations between genes and language. Large-scale directed migration might result in the total replacement of the resident population and their language; or the 'newcomers' may join with the local population, forming a composite group speaking the new language. If the number of incomers is small, they may be amalgamated into the resident population and learn to speak the original language of the area, leaving only a genetic signal in the resulting population. Alternatively, an invading elite may generate an effective cultural change, including resultant replacement of the local language, without significant genetic influence.

In other words, there is no intrinsic reason why genes and culture should show identical lines of descent. Indeed, in areas of Australia native languages appear to be attached more to a particular geographic locality than to any particular resident group of humans: individual Aboriginal tribes in the area are multilingual and speak the language appropriate to their physical position in the landscape (David Nash, personal communication). Thus, as McMahon (2004: 4) notes, 'one extreme possibility for language replacement would be for a language to no longer be spoken as a first language by any single group, but rather be used by two genetically distinct tribes whose ranges overlap where that language was originally spoken by a now extinct third tribe which shared little genetically with either group of current speakers'. Our methods offer the prospect of unearthing real correlations between linguistic and genetic features in cases where earlier differences in disciplinary practice have obscured them: but they can do nothing to resolve those cases where the correlations really do break down, and we must accept that these exist too.

Finally, there is a further question of representation. Our work in Chapter 4 and the investigations reported here have been based on family-tree models; and yet those are by no means universally accepted for language. Dixon (1997) argues that there are areas of the world, notably Australia, and perhaps periods of equilibrium for other language groups, where convergence will be more important than divergence, and the tree offers an inappropriate model. Thomason and Kaufman (1988) see pidgins, creoles, and mixed languages as non-genetic, and therefore as intrinsically incompatible with the family tree. If we are serious about rehabilitating contact-induced change, and want to be able to account for both aspects of Kessler's 'historical connectedness' (2001), then our concentration on trees is problematic.

On the one hand, there will be situations and language groups for which the tree is a wholly appropriate model: it certainly has the advantage of familiarity, clarity of representation, and a built-in diachronic aspect through its vertical dimension. If we have methods which can isolate features arising from contact and exclude those, then arguably for many languages we have a better case than ever for using trees. On the other hand, how are we to represent relationships between languages at the stage before we exclude contact; or in cases where we specifically want to focus on the contribution of contact; or in situations where we are carrying out analyses to assess what the contribution of contact might be? There is something inherently unsettling about using tree-drawing and tree-selection programs specifically to isolate features and changes incompatible with trees, as with the shifts of English, Frisian, and Romanian in the hihi versus lolo trees in Chapter 4. However, if we have learned one thing so far, it is that biology, and specifically population genetics, has many of the same potential problems as comparative linguistics; and, moreover, that many of these problems have already been successfully confronted. It is therefore unsurprising to find alternative programs, beginning with Network (Bandelt et al. 1995; Bandelt, Forster, and Röhl 1999), which allow the representation of features arising through both common ancestry and contact; and in the next chapter we turn to an investigation of network representations for language.

6

Climbing Down from the Trees: Network Models

6. 1 Network Representations in Biology

6. 1. 1 Problems with Trees

The fundamental problems with family trees are the degree of idealization they necessitate and their essential incompatibility with the forces of contact-induced change which, as we have been arguing throughout this book, are as important for at least some languages as descent with differentiation from a common ancestor. Some languages will have an essentially tree-like history, while others are primarily contact languages. Historical linguists, with their propensity for designing opposing methods, might suggest the tree model for one extreme and the wave model for the other: but this does not get around the problem that most languages will occupy some position on the cline between these two end points. We can foresee long and unproductive struggles over deciding when each model is to be used, missing crucial bits of data for each system in the process, whereas in a perfect world what we need is a single model which could sort out for us how much of a language is tree-like and how much non-tree-like, and display the two driving forces, and resulting language features, differently.

Fortunately, we do not need to wait for a perfect world to find such a model: it is already under development in biology. As Pagel (2000: 190–1) notes:

linguists should bear in mind that the glaring, even embarrassing, exceptions are not confined to linguistic evolution. Thus, biological evolution witnesses horizontal transmission of genetic information just as words are borrowed horizontally between languages... Evolutionary biology's response to these phenomena has been to develop, among many other methods, more sophisticated techniques for detecting gene transfer, identifying convergence, and measuring rates of evolution.

We shall return to the vexed question of rates of change in the next chapter, but detecting and displaying gene transfer and convergence are directly relevant to the analysis of contact-induced change in linguistics, and both are tackled in computer programs based on networks.

Network models, at first glance, seem just too good to be true. Bryant, Filimon, and Gray (in preparation: 2) suggest that what we need in dealing with population histories is:

an analytic approach that enables us to assess where on the continuum between a pure tree and a totally tangled network any particular case may lie. More specifically, this approach should be able both to identify the particular populations where admixture has occurred and detail the exact characters that were borrowed.

Network representations can indeed achieve these goals; but to understand how, we must return to their origin, in dealing with molecular genetic data at the level of the individual.

6. 1. 2 Networks in Genetics

The original Network program (Bandelt et al. 1995; Bandelt, Forster, and Röhl 1999; Forster et al. 2001; <http://www.fluxus-engineering.com>, accessed March 2005) was initially developed to deal with cases where a particular genetic sequence has more than one possible history. If there is more than one possible history, then there is more than one possible tree. Network both analyses and represents this ambiguity by collapsing the alternative possible trees into a single network graph. For parts of the sequence where there is only one possible history the diagram will look tree-like; but where there are multiple possible histories the program draws a reticulation, or a box shape, to indicate that the data are compatible with more than one tree structure. An example is given in Figure 6.1, and discussed immediately below.

Figure 6.1 has two parts. The first is a sequence of 12 bases (each base being an A, C, G, or T) of mitochondrial DNA for six molecules *A–F*. *A* represents the common ancestral state, and the differences between this

	1	2	3	4	5	6	7	8	9	10	11	12
A	A	C	T	G	A	C	A	C	G	T	G	C
B	A	**G**	T	**C**	A	C	**T**	C	G	T	G	**A**
C	A	**G**	**A**	G	A	C	A	C	G	T	G	C
D	A	**G**	T	G	**C**	**T**	A	C	G	T	G	C
E	A	**G**	T	G	A	**T**	A	C	**T**	T	G	C
F	A	**G**	T	G	**C**	**T**	A	C	**T**	T	G	C

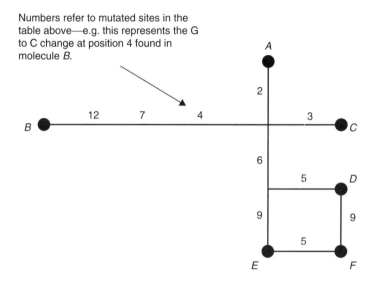

Numbers refer to mutated sites in the table above—e.g. this represents the G to C change at position 4 found in molecule *B*.

Fig. 6.1 Example network for 6 mitochondrial DNA molecules *A–F*, with associated sequence of DNA at 12 positions in each molecule. Nucleotides
in bold represent informative state changes used in constructing the
network.

and the other five molecules are shown in bold: these are state changes, or
mutations. Network is essentially a cladistic analysis (Ridley 1986; Page
and Holmes 1998; Skelton and Smith 2002; McMahon and McMahon
forthcoming *b*), which means that only the mutations are relevant in
constructing the tree: unchanging characters are ignored, as they are
uninformative.

   The graph derived from this set of sequences is the other half of
Figure 6.1. It shows the six molecules *A–F*, and is predominantly tree-
like, with the exception of the reticulation joining molecules *D*, *E*, and *F*.
This reticulation reflects the fact that *F* shares a mutation at base 5 with

D, and a mutation at base 9 with *E*. But because these molecules are mitochondrial DNA, which can be inherited only through the female line and therefore from an individual's mother, *F* cannot be the direct descendent of both *D* and *E*. The problem, in other words, is that these facts are compatible with two possible trees: either the mutation at base 5 happened in *D* and was inherited into *F*, giving the tree in Figure 6.2*a*, or base 9 changed in *E* and was inherited into *F*, giving the tree in Figure 6.2*b*.

In either case one mutation happened once and is then inherited; and the other base has been affected by two independent mutations (the second in each case marked with an asterisk). If Figure 6.2(*a*) is right, both *E* and *F* have independently experienced mutations in base 9, and if Figure 6.2(*b*) is right, then both *D* and *F* have independent mutations in base 5. It is not possible in principle to sort out the actual order of branching from the data we have, so Network simply records the ambiguity in the reticulation it draws. The method respects the assumption, common also in linguistic family trees, that there can be only one direct ancestor in each case, but also signals the fact that we can interpret the available data as pointing to two possible-candidate common ancestors, and invoke an alternative process, here independent mutation, for the remainder of the data.

In the case of these molecular data we are always dealing with a choice for each state change between ancestral mutation and inheritance, or independent, spontaneous mutation. A reticulation means we can't decide which happened: either is possible. What *cannot* be going on at this individual level is any kind of borrowing from an unrelated individual: remember that the mitochondrial DNA can only be inherited from the

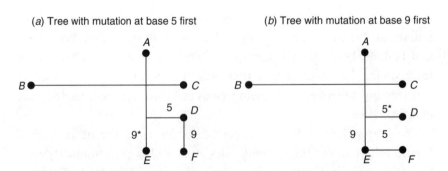

(*a*) Tree with mutation at base 5 first   (*b*) Tree with mutation at base 9 first

Fig. 6.2 Alternative trees contained in the network shown in Figure 6.1

mother, or mutate *in situ*. However, when we are dealing with autosomal DNA (not mitochondrial or Y-chromosome material, but the majority of genes, which are inherited in two copies, one from each parent) common states can again arise from common ancestry or from independent, multiple mutation, but also from recombination. In this case, we need to envisage the three-generation series of events shown in Figure 6.3.

In the first generation the mother and father each have two copies of a particular gene sequence, which they have in turn inherited from their parents. At generation 2 they each bequeath one copy of their own gene sequence to their child, who receives two 'pure' versions of that chromosome, one from each parent. However, in this second-generation individual a process of recombination occurs, such that the 'pure' genetic

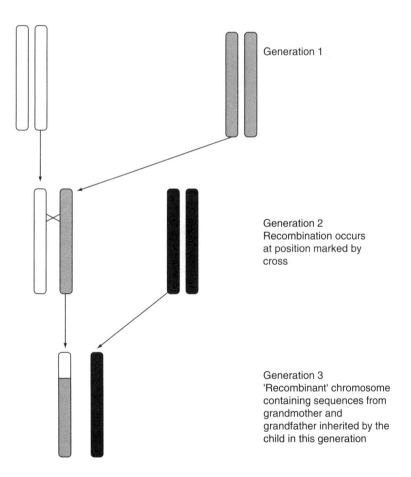

Generation 1

Generation 2
Recombination occurs
at position marked by
cross

Generation 3
'Recombinant' chromosome
containing sequences from
grandmother and
grandfather inherited by the
child in this generation

Fig. 6.3 Three-generation 'borrowing' inheritance

sequences inherited from his/her father and mother are reshuffled together, giving two mixed molecules. One of these mixed chromosomes is
then, at generation 3, passed on to our individual's child, who will
therefore carry as one of his/her copies of that chromosome a mixed
sequence, containing bases from the grandmother, mixed with other
bases 'borrowed' from the grandfather.

In this case too Network would draw a reticulation. This time the
reticulation does not mean the chromosome in question has two *possible*
histories, one involving inheritance and the other independent mutation,
and that we cannot choose between them. Instead, this reticulation shows
that the inherited 'mixed' chromosome has two *actual* histories *at the
same time*: parts of it come from two different ancestors. In both these
examples note that we do not spend time fretting about whether we should
employ a tree-drawing or a network-drawing program: although Network, naturally enough, draws networks where they are appropriate,
cases where there has been neither 'borrowing' (recombination) nor parallel development (the same mutation independently twice or more, also
known as homoplasy) will automatically be represented with the most
likely tree. That is, the program involved draws a tree when the relationships are clear and tree-like, and a more complex network when the
connections are more complex or ambiguous and show more interaction.

6. 1. 3 Split Decomposition

The option of a program which generates trees or networks depending on
the data, or, more accurately, which generates trees interrupted where
appropriate by reticulations, is clearly of interest for linguistic data too;
but before we turn to these applications we should first say a little more
about exactly how the data are analysed by Network. The central process
here is split decomposition (Bandelt and Dress 1992), a technique for
dividing data into natural groups.

Split decomposition for this kind of Network analysis, based on different states, involves three steps (adapted from the excellent account in
Bryant, Filimon, and Gray, in preparation).

First, we need to identify something to count, and then count it. In the
case of our sequences in Figure 6.1 we are counting the number of
molecules with each state: so, we count 6 with the value, or state, A at
position 1; 5 with state G at position 2 and 1 with state C at position 2; 1

with state A and 5 with state T at position 3; 1 with state C and 5 with state G at position 4; 4 with state A and 2 with state C at position 5; and so on.

Second, we then work out the splits generated by this collection of values. This is achieved by figuring out the minimum number of changes of state between each pair of sequences. So, again for the data in Figure 6.1, position 1 tells us nothing at all: there are no changes of state, since all 6 molecules share the same state, and we cannot therefore use this site to split the data. Our first split emerges at position 2, where sequence *A* is the only one with state C, splitting it effectively from the other sequences, which all share state G. At position 3 we have a further split of *C* from all the other sequences; and at position 5, *D* and *F* are separated from all the rest.

The third and final stage involves plotting the resulting splits; this is the role of the Network program. Network will draw branch lengths depending on the number of state changes separating particular nodes, and will, as we have seen, incorporate reticulations where there is more than one possible source for a derived state, giving the diagram in Figure 6.1. So, for instance, at position 5 Network will make a split between *D* and *F* on the one hand, and all the other sequences on the other; but at position 9 it encounters data which seem to force a split of *E* and *F* as against the rest. Clearly, these two splits are incompatible: they cannot be displayed on the same tree, unless we avail ourselves of the possibility of using reticulations to collapse the two possible trees into the same superordinate graph.

6. 2 Applying Network to Linguistic Data

6. 2. 1 Comparing Linguistic and Biological Data

In extending Network to language data it is first important to show how those data can be seen as comparable to the biological sequence data we have been considering so far. A meaning list (our 200-item Swadesh list; or our reduced more conservative, (hihi) or more changeable, (lolo) sub-lists) can be regarded as essentially equivalent to a chromosomal sequence of bases. As noted in Chapter 4, the real data we are interested in for quantitative lexical-list comparisons are not the individual lexical items themselves, with their individual and highly language-specific shapes. What we need is to convert those items into states, comparable with our

A, C, G, and T base labels. The Dyen, Kruskal, and Black (1992) database we have been using incorporates this step, since for each meaning a list of states is provided, with each numerical code signalling lexical items that are cognate, or borrowed, or missing, or unique (see Table 6.1).

In Table 6.1, 0 is used to indicate missing data, and codes between 030 and 050 mark unique states and borrowed items. Other numbers group lexical items deemed to have arisen from the same item in the common ancestor: 003, or 401, or 200, in other words, mark cognate sets. Finally, in the case of borrowed items, the bracketed code following indicates the class the item would belong to if it were mistakenly classed as a cognate rather than as a loan. This additional bracketed code therefore also indicates the likely source of the borrowed item.

As Table 6.1 shows, the equivalent of each sequence in our genetic data is the coded list for a particular language or variety. If for a particular position (or, in linguistic terms, meaning slot) we have a consistent value through all the languages of say 200, then we have an uninformative site, where every list retains a cognate, as in Meaning 109 in Table 6.1. If we have more than one cognate class, then Network will insert a split at the appropriate point, as between 003 and 004 for meaning 001. If there is a borrowing, as with 031 for meaning 003, then this is the equivalent of one of our recombined elements from Figure 6.3, where the common ancestral signal for the language list as a whole includes elements introduced from elsewhere by 'mixing'. In such cases, employing a special code from the range 030–050 instructs the program to ignore the item in question. On the other hand, if we mistakenly coded *animal* in English as 401,

Table 6.1 Examples of cognacy coding for 3 selected meanings in 7 Indo-European languages adapted from the DKB database

	Meaning **001**		Meaning **003**		Meaning **109**	
Language	Word	Code	Word	Code	Word	Code
Sardinian N	tottu	003	animale	401	unu	200
Vlach	tuti	003	—	0	une	200
French	tout	003	animal	401	un	200
Spanish	todu	003	animal	401	un	200
Ossetic	iuyl	030	caeraegoj	030	iu	200
English	all	004	animal	031 (401)	one	200
Danish	al	004	dyr	005	en	200

cognate with the forms in the Romance languages, we would expect a split between English and Danish, and therefore a reticulation, since this character will be incompatible with the tree predicted by the overall pattern of cognacy for these lists.

6. 2. 2 Network and Borrowing: Simulated Data

Borrowing, of course, must be the prime candidate for the type of effect we would hope to detect using programs like Network, so it seems appropriate to begin with an application to a situation of this kind. In Chapter 4 we considered simulated data for the 'real' history of a family, with higher and lower degrees of mutation (corresponding to our lolo and hihi data for Indo-European), and with different degrees of borrowing. At each stage of the simulation trees were plotted using PHYLIP (Felsenstein 2001). Let us see what happens when we apply Network to these simulated data instead.

   The idea of using simulated data, as for the tree analyses in Chapter 4, is that if borrowing of particular types and intensities creates a typical signal in Network, we can look for just that signal, or variants of it, when we apply Network in real cases. Figure 6.4 shows a network for our simulated hihi list. We selected the characters to include here by starting from a full 200-item simulated list with a variable mutation rate, then

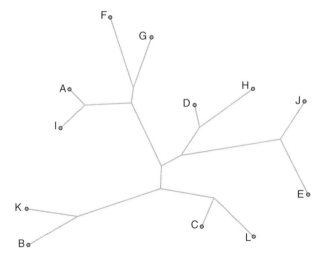

Fig. 6.4 Network for simulated hihi (most conservative) data; no borrowing
      from B to A

choosing the 25 items which were changing most slowly. These least changeable, most conservative characters are clearly the closest analogue to our real hihi sublist. For the full list we set borrowing from language B to language A at 10%, but the fact that we derive such a straightforward tree in Figure 6.4 suggests that in this sublist there has probably been no borrowing at all from B to A.

For comparison, Figure 6.5 shows our simulated version of the lolo list, which is set to change twice as fast. Here, it is evident that Network has had insuperable problems in constructing a single tree, since there are reticulations towards the root of the tree, and these are clearly linking languages A and B, which fall on opposite sides of the group of reticulations.

These differently shaped graphs may look convincing: we certainly get a different signal for cases where the rate of borrowing is likely to be higher as opposed to cases where we would expect less borrowing, since the mutation rate underlying Figure 6.4 is lower than that for Figure 6.5. However, so far this is essentially circumstantial: we have a plausible

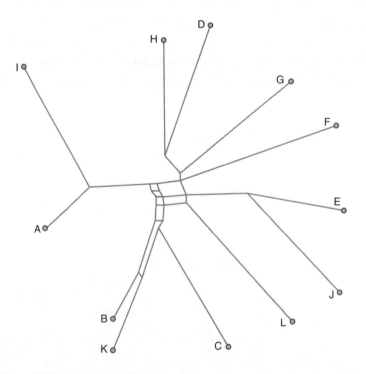

Fig. 6.5 Network for simulated lolo (most changeable) data; borrowing from B to A evident in reticulations

account of the differences, but no real evidence that it is the right one. After all, we have seen that for biological data the same patterns of reticulation can reflect independent mutation as well as recombination. We could opt to rerun Network multiple times, bootstrapping the graphs by assessing how often we get the same picture from the same data, or the same data minus individual items on each run; this is a good way of testing which items are actually causing any discrepancies between the two figures. However, bootstrapping is a particularly time-consuming process, and a further useful property of Network provides us with a convenient short cut. Not only does Network variably construct trees or more complex graphs depending on the complexity of the relationships in the data, it also accompanies each graph with a list of the data points which are most difficult to reconcile with the tree—in other words, those which are behaving in the most non-tree-like way.

When we unpack the Network program and access these lists of non-tree-like characters we find that there are a few inconsistent items for Figure 6.4. However, none of these is a borrowing from language B to A. On the other hand, of the 25 items in the simulated lolo list, where we would anticipate that borrowing should be more common, we find four cases of loans from B into A. Four loans out of 25 items does represent more than 10% borrowing; but our 10% setting was for the list as a whole, and if these 25 items are the ones changing most rapidly we would expect (as for the real lolo data) that borrowing would be particularly concentrated in this sublist. Three of these borrowings are included in the reticulations towards the root of the tree, and the complex pattern of reticulations here indicates that some of these items are also shared by the sisters of A or B, leading to multiplex links between languages. The fourth item has a shared state, by sheer accident, with one language outside the branches for A and B, and therefore does not give a signal leading to an A–B reticulation, though it does appear in the list of problematic items.

6. 2. 3 Network and Borrowing: Real Data

Turning to an equivalent case for real rather than simulated data, Figure 6.6 shows the output of Network for the hihi, most conservative sublist for Romance and Germanic. Since the mutation rate is known to be relatively low for these items, and we have already established that within Germanic at least none of the known borrowings appears in this

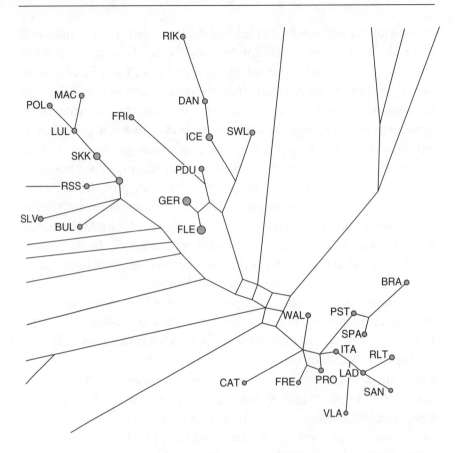

Fig. 6.6 Network for Germanic and Romance, hihi (most conservative) sublist.
Larger nodes contain 2 or 3 languages with identical patterns of cognate
scores (e.g. English and German within the GER node)

sublist (Embleton 1986; Ch. 4 above), it is perhaps unsurprising but
helpfully affirming that Figure 6.6 is highly tree-like. There is a single
reticulation within Romance, reflecting the amount of interborrowing we
know has taken place historically across the Romance group, and some
reticulations towards the root, but these reflect uncertainties in the bigger
Indo-European picture, not relationships specifically between Romance
and Germanic.

   Figure 6.7 shows the graph for Romance and Germanic with the least
conservative, lolo sublist, and has considerably more reticulations, especially at the root of the tree and within Romance.

   However, we might also expect Figure 6.7 to incorporate reticulations
for Germanic, since we know for a fact that there are interborrowings

within Germanic in this lolo sublist: recall from Chapter 4 that Embleton (ibid.) lists 'wing', 'left (hand)', 'to pull', 'to push', 'river', and 'to throw' as falling into this category, and all are included in our least conservative meanings. Yet there are no reticulations in either Figure 6.6 or Figure 6.7 for Germanic.

There are two responses we can make to this. First, the extent to which Network will display reticulations depends crucially on the setting of an internal parameter, ε (Bandelt, Forster, and Röhl 1999). The value for this epsilon parameter determines the sensitivity of Network to conflicting signals in the data, and therefore sets the number of reticulations which will be visualized. Where epsilon is low, Network will tend not to display groupings with low support (in other words, links that involve a small number of characters) as reticulations, but will show new mutations on the relevant branches of the tree instead. Where epsilon is high, Network will attempt to show *any* connection as a reticulation, though this can lead to particularly complex, multidimensional graphs, in which the signal is arguably impossible to disentangle from the noise. We can see this effect by comparing Figure 6.7, where epsilon is set low, with Figure 6.8, where it is considerably higher (< 1 versus 2 respectively).

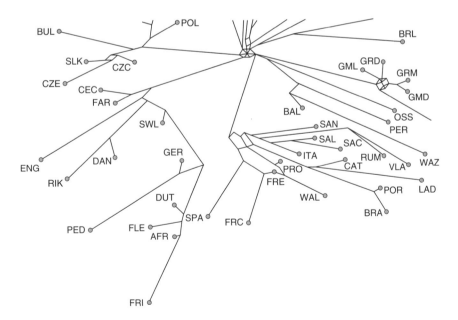

Fig. 6.7 Network for Germanic and Romance, lolo (most changeable) sublist

Figure 6.8(*a*) shows reticulations for Germanic in abundance. But the problem is that there are so many of them, both between and within groups, that the Network is almost impossible to interpret. We have a choice, then, between two types of output from Network. In Figure 6.7 we do not see the reticulations that signal contact in every case, but can check that Network has in fact experienced difficulty in reconciling data

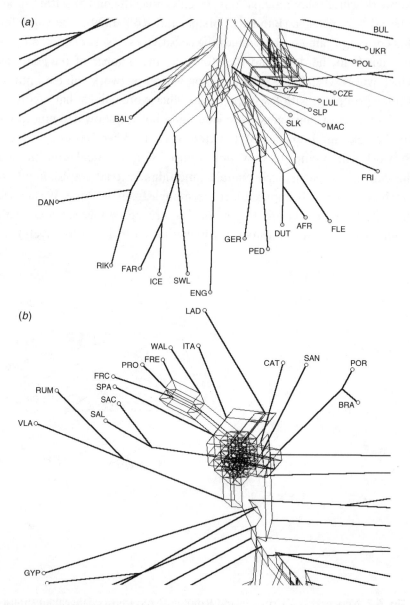

Fig. 6.8 Networks for Germanic (*a*) and Romance (*b*) lolo lists; epsilon = 2

with the displayed tree, and that these data are in fact known borrowings, by accessing the list of problem characters which Network generates automatically. For Figure 6.7 the problem items do include all those items which are (i) borrowed from one Germanic language to another, and (ii) miscoded in the Dyen, Kruskal, and Black database as cognates (see Ch. 4 above). Alternatively, we can visualize an increased number of reticulations as in Figure 6.8, but will still have to sift through the list of problem cases to access the linguistic reasons for each link in the graph.

However, it is also worth noting that Network, even with epsilon set low, shows a particularly clear and sensitive reaction to our undiagnosed loans within Germanic. Specifically, in the most conservative graph in Figure 6.6 English is contained in a cluster with German, and is squarely within West Germanic, while in the least conservative graph in Figure 6.7 English has shifted altogether into North Germanic. Likewise, Frisian, in the same least conservative tree, is clustered with Dutch/Flemish/Afrikaans. Although we are not seeing reticulations in these cases, we do find that subgroups shift within the trees depending on the presence of loans in the data. By way of illustration, Figure 6.9 shows the output of Network with two different codings for the single item 'wing', which is erroneously coded in the Dyen, Kruskal, and Black database as cognate between North Germanic and English, although we know in fact that this is a loan into English.

In Figure 6.9(a), English appears quite clearly as a North Germanic language. In Figure 6.9(b), however, the recoding of that single item as a

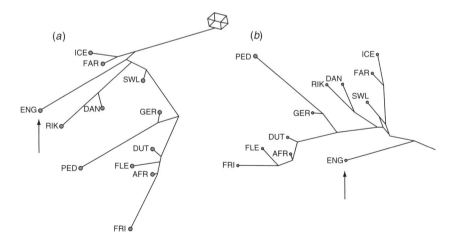

Fig. 6.9 (a) = 'wing' coded as cognate; (b) = 'wing' coded as loan

loan means English appears outside the North Germanic branch. Indeed, in Figure 6.9(*b*) English falls outside Germanic altogether, due to the influence of borrowings from Romance. These have been entirely appropriately coded as borrowings, or unique items, in the database, but the cumulative effect of all these unique states is to distance English from the other Germanic languages which do not share them. It is notable that the coding of even a single item can have such a powerful effect on the structure of the graph.

Clearly, further consideration has to be given to the interpretation of different network patterns, and to the most appropriate settings for epsilon. In any case, we cannot see these programs (just as we argued for the tree generation and selection metrics in Chapter 4) as standing alone: the programs can help us visualize the issues in the data, and focus on the problematic data points, but we still need linguists with detailed knowledge of the languages in question to sort out the real significance of each point. This will also help with a final problematic aspect of Network which we have already encountered for biological data. In biology the presence of a reticulation need not always mean recombination, the closest analogue for individual DNA data of linguistic borrowing. Reticulations can also signal convergent evolution (homoplasy), where the same pattern has arisen more than once by chance; or shared retentions from the common ancestral form which are maintained in certain cases but lost in others. Of course, parallel changes and shared retentions are not unknown in historical linguistics either, so that expert linguistic knowledge is invaluable in sorting out which of the problem cases can be ascribed to either of these less common causes, and which are more likely to reflect contact. In our simulation work we have undertaken a rather partial, indirect test of the effect of shared retentions. As noted in Chapter 4, we found that trees drawn on the basis of simulated data began to be disrupted only at a rate of 5% borrowing, and then only on 15% of runs; more commonly, disruption of tree structure was observed at 10% borrowing. It seems unlikely that we should find as many as 5% shared retentions, let alone 10%; this will depend on the histories of the languages concerned, but in our simulations we found a maximum of 2% shared retentions, with an average of around 0.9%. Nonetheless, this is a further indication that linguists will still have to consider the problem data points generated by Network carefully to ensure that we are not over-interpreting the existence of borrowing where other factors may be responsible.

6. 3 Distance-based Network Methods

6. 3. 1 Distance-based Versus Character-based Approaches

Network clearly offers an interesting range of possibilities for representing and interpreting conflicting signals, which may for linguistic data indicate borrowing, in data sets. We have shown that tests of the method on Indo-European data provide support for Network, which generates meaningfully different graphs for sublists including more and fewer signals of contact, and effectively isolates the items responsible in the form of reticulations, lists of problem characters, or both. It would seem appropriate to assess whether we can now apply Network to cases where we are not so sure about the linguistic history, to see whether we can reach some clarity on the basis of patterns we have observed for known histories. However, before going on to this next step we should report some recent advances in network methodology.

All the illustrations we have provided so far have involved the application of Network, and of the underlying technique of split decomposition, to character data. But this brings inevitable limitations. In biological applications, character-based approaches are applicable only at the level of the individual, in comparing particular molecules, although there exists a much clearer analogue for contact-induced change in linguistics at the level of biological populations. If we were to apply Network to the relationship and histories of populations, we would first have to determine the network for each molecule in the sample, then as a second-order problem assess the distribution of those molecular patterns in populations by plotting each molecule on a map, for instance, to show where its carriers are most typically located. What we cannot do if we are dealing only with character data is to achieve an easily read composite network graph for all the molecules we wish to consider and their relative frequencies in different populations. However, we could do this if we were dealing with composite distances between populations based on a summation of all those individual molecules. Recent network-based approaches have therefore shifted from a character-based to a distance-based method, as in Splitstree (Huson 1998) and NeighbourNet (Bryant and Moulton 2004), though these are still very much models under development.

The development of distance-based metrics also brings considerable advantages for linguistic applications, though these are really still in their infancy (Bryant 2004; Holden and Gray 2004; Bryant, Filimon, and Gray in preparation). In particular, as we saw in Chapter 3 above, there is an inherent difficulty in using character-based approaches for language data: the characters chosen for one language group (say, Ringe, Warnow, and Taylor's phonological and morphological characters for Indo-European (2002)) will be highly unlikely to generalize to other language groups, since they have been selected particularly as specific innovations which are salient in subgrouping for that family. It is true that this is not such a major problem for lexical data, since with our Swadesh lists we are by convention dealing with a set list containing set slots. However, there are still difficulties here. How are we to compare, for instance, a conventional Swadesh list with the adjusted variety developed for Australian languages by Alpher and Nash (1999)? Alternatively, even where we might keep a particular slot there can be serious difficulties in determining which item should fill it for a given language or group: for instance, in Quechua there are two words for 'brother', depending on whether we are discussing a man's brother or a woman's brother, and up to five words for 'wash', depending on whether we are washing hands or clothes, for instance.

This Quechua problem is the direct motivation for Heggarty's proposal (forthcoming) to extend lexicostatistical comparison to provide a more nuanced means of comparing lexical semantics. As we have seen, modified Swadesh lists already exist in the literature, and on the model of Matisoff's CALMSEA list, (1978, 2000), containing meanings Culturally and Linguistically Meaningful for South-east Asia, Heggarty proposes a parallel 150-meaning CALMA list, incorporating meanings Culturally and Linguistically Meaningful for the Andes (for a full list see Heggarty forthcoming and McMahon, Heggarty, McMahon, and Slaska forthcoming). The CALMA list is altered in several ways, discussed in detail in Section 6.3.4 below; but for the moment the most relevant modification is that a single list-meaning may be split into several discrete subsenses where the data warrant such treatment. For instance, the Andean languages commonly distinguish two senses for the Swadesh meaning 'sun', namely 'celestial object' on the one hand and 'sunlight/heat' on the other. Some Andean varieties will have one form for each of these two senses, as for instance Atalla Quechua has *inti* for the 'celestial object' sense, and *rupa-y* for 'sunlight/heat'. Laraos Quechua has both forms too, but it uses *inti* for both these subsenses, and *rupa-y* only in the verb root 'be hot (sunny), burn'. Puki Aymara, however, has only *inti*, and *rupa-y* is entirely unknown. Comparing these varieties reveals a complex set of patterns of overlap, which can be expressed as weighted calculations of degree of similarity; but this immediately means we will require more sophisticated calculations than the usual 0 or 1. Weighted values of this kind, as we shall see, are quite typically incorporated in distance-based calculations, though they disrupt the assumptions of character-based approaches.

6. 3. 2 Split Decomposition and Distance Data

How, then, does the split-decomposition approach work for distance data? Rather than dealing with the approach in biology first and extending this to language data, we shall turn immediately to linguistic applications. In outline, this approach overlaps significantly with the earlier description of character-based split decomposition, though there are some additional steps (see again Bryant, Filimon, and Gray in preparation).

For Splitstree (Huson 1998) the first stage is to derive a distance matrix from the data we are using. In many cases this will involve simply adding up the 1 and 0 values for whether items are cognate or not across the whole list, though as noted above innovations whereby a wider range of intermediate values is included can in principle be accommodated (Heggarty forthcoming). The second step is to generate splits on the basis of the data. For character-based approaches this is a straightforward process, since it involves essentially spotting differences and generating splits accordingly; but for distance-based approaches there is added complexity. For a maximum of four languages or groups, split decomposition calculates the maximum distance **between** each pair, along with the distance separating the two languages **within** each pair. If the distance between pairs is greater than the distance within a pair, then Splitstree generates a split with a branch length equal to that positive value. Cumulatively, these calculations of distance generate a tree, and where we find conflict between the splits, then reticulations will be introduced.

The problem with Splitstree is that it experiences difficulty in dealing with large numbers of languages or particularly complex and messy signals. As Bryant, Filimon, and Gray (in preparation) note, introducing more languages and splits leads inevitably to a reduction in the values for branch lengths, so that it is harder to generate cases of conflict. This means that graphs based on bigger and more complex data sets tend to become more tree-like by default, because the amount of data predisposes to small or negative values for differences between groups, and reticulations therefore rarely arise. Clearly, this makes Splitstree problematic for large data sets, as we shall see below. This problem is being addressed in the development of NeighbourNet, which uses an algorithm similar to the neighbour-joining approach for trees (Saitou and Nei 1987). The details are too complex for full discussion here (though see Bryant and Moulton 2004; Bryant, Filimon and Gray in preparation), but the consequence is that NeighbourNet can deal with much larger data sets and will be able to generate splits and reticulations in even relatively messy cases. The potential drawback, on the other hand, is that NeighbourNet may be such a robust heuristic that it will generate splits and identify conflicts even where the data do not really support them. Furthermore, NeighbourNet is essentially a phenetic method: that is, it works on the basis of observed similarities and distances between languages at a particular time, and does not explicitly seek to reconstruct a history for the group. Outputs from NeighbourNet are strictly phenograms, which give an indication of relative distance, rather than phylograms, which attempt to reconstruct the historical pattern and order of branching.

It follows that an urgent priority for linguists is to assess the operation of these different clustering programs on known data, to allow us to identify the patterns we observe as characteristic of particular types of history. If we do not find consistent representations for consistent types of input, we have a problem with the programs. If we do, then we can start to generalize these approaches to less securely understood cases. We therefore make no apology for returning to our simulations and Indo-European data again.

6. 3. 3 Distance-based Methods and Linguistic Data

It is straightforward to show that NeighbourNet is indeed more sensitive to the presence of contact in the linguistic data than Splitstree. Figure 6.10 shows the output of NeighbourNet on the left and Splitstree on the right for our simulated least conservative data, with 10% borrowing, calculated and printed using the Splitstree 4 beta test version (1 June 2004 release; <http://www-ab.informatik.uni-tuebingen.de/software/jsplits.welcome_ en.html>, accessed March 2005). Clearly, both programs construct reticulations, though they are markedly more extensive for Neighbour-Net. Note that borrowing here is from language A into the unrelated language M (rather than between two of the related languages, such as A and B, as was the case in previous simulations). M has no similarity, prior to borrowing, to any of the other simulated languages; we have selected this option here to minimize any potential interference from shared retentions (see below).

Although we have not shown them here, parallel graphs for our simulated most conservative data set show a more striking difference, since Splitstree here gives a completely tree-like representation, while Neighbour-Net includes a small number of minor reticulations. As we have noted above, these most conservative data do not include any borrowings, so contact cannot be the explanation for these reticulations. In fact, NeighbourNet is here picking up the extremely small percentage of shared retentions, where states from the common ancestor are by chance retained in languages from different branches of the tree, though their immediate sisters have lost those characters. What is more difficult is checking the cause of such reticulations for Splitstree and NeighbourNet: because these programs are operating on distance data, they are applied to a matrix of numbers rather than to the lexical material itself, and they

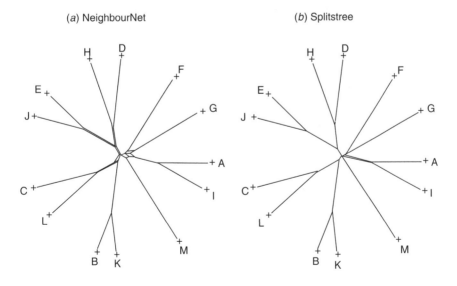

Fig. 6.10 NeighbourNet versus Splitstree, simulated lolo data, with borrowing 10% from language A into language M

do not therefore generate the convenient list of problem items we found so helpful when assessing Network. It is therefore necessary to dig back into the unprocessed data in order to explain the patterns seen in the NeighbourNet and Splitstree graphs.

Next, let us consider some real data from Indo-European. The pattern in Figure 6.11, comparing Splitstree and NeighbourNet again, is markedly similar.

Figure 6.11, based on the least conservative, lolo lexical data for Germanic and Romance, shows a substantially greater number of reticulations using NeighbourNet. These reticulations, if we unpack them, signal known affinities which indicate the utility of the method. For instance, there are clear reticulations linking Sranan, a creole which generally clusters with English, with Dutch, from which it has also adopted a number of lexical items. There is also a great deal of connectivity between the three Swedish varieties, showing the possibility of employing these computational methods also at the level of dialect contact (see Ch. 8 below). Finally, Vlach, although closely connected with Romanian, is here being isolated from Romance by a split which particularly involves Greek, though Greek does not appear on this part of the full Indo-European graph.

The Splitstree diagram, drawn from precisely the same data, fails to illustrate the complexity in the data because it is unable to deal with the large number of incompatible splits. As discussed above, Splitstree therefore has a problematic tendency to generate progressively more tree-like graphs, like the one in Figure 6.11, when confronted with large and complex data sets. If our only goal were to maximize the signals of treeness for a particular data set, then Splitstree might seem more appropriate: on the other hand, as we shall see in the next section, the presence of a large number of incompatibilities in the data set arising from borrowing, for instance, can completely mask these phylogenetic signals. In such cases Splitstree neither diagnoses the underlying tree nor illustrates the more complex interrelationships following from contact.

6. 3. 4 Applying NeighbourNet Beyond Indo-European

All these methods require further comparison and testing, and all remain under active development (see Forster, Polzin, and Röhl 2005 for Network), but for the moment it seems particularly worth continuing with

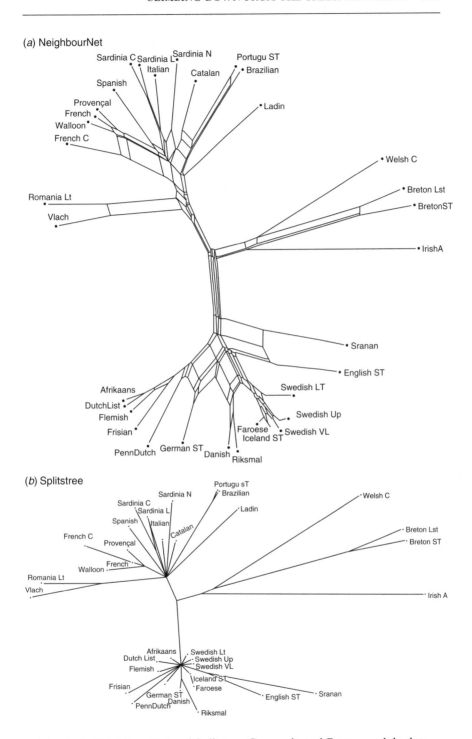

Fig. 6.11 NeighbourNet and Splitstree Germanic and Romance, Iolo data

NeighbourNet, since the algorithm here is apparently set to a good level for detecting relevant signals in linguistic data, without being overburdened by too much noise. It has the further advantage of operating extremely quickly, with runs for our entire Dyen, Kruskal, and Black database taking 40–50 seconds on a 700 MHz PC.

In Chapter 2 we discussed Embleton's stepwise approach to the development of new methods, which is repeated for convenience in (1) below:

(1) Embleton (1986: 3)—steps in quantitative analysis
    (i) to devise a procedure, based on theoretical grounds, on a particular model, or on past experience . . .
    (ii) to verify the procedure by applying it to some data where there already exists a large body of linguistic opinion for comparison, often Indo-European data . . . this may lead to revision of the procedure of stage (i), or at the extreme to its total abandonment;
    (iii) to apply the procedure to data where linguistic opinions have not yet been produced, have not yet been firmly established, or perhaps are even in conflict. In practice, this usually means application to non-Indo-European data. . . .

For NeighbourNet and analogous methods we have now passed Stages 1 and 2, and must devise some appropriate Stage 3 tests. Though there are in principle many situations to which we could apply such methods, and indeed many where linguists would be particularly keen to have a diagnostic for working out the most likely history, we shall content ourselves for the moment with two small demonstrations of the method. Both are designed to assess how NeighbourNet performs when faced with particularly strong and pervasive evidence of contact; the second applies the method to a single situation in South America where the evidence is equivocal as between a hypothesis of common ancestry or a long period of contact and convergence.

First, if we are to pursue our goal of not ignoring or excluding borrowing but learning how to diagnose and use it, we must consider cases of contact-induced change more radical than the few undiagnosed loans our tree- and network-drawing methods have unearthed in a single Indo-European database, extensive though this is. If there is one geographical area where linguists agree that the effects of contact have been particularly widespread, it is Australia. True, the Australian linguistic situation is anything but settled: some linguists argue for at least one substantial, old language family, Pama-Nyungan, with other groupings and isolates (Koch 1997; Bowern and Koch 2004; Evans 2004), while others contend that Pama-Nyungan is not demonstrable, and that the Australian languages are connected primarily by long-standing contact relationships (Dixon 1980, 2001, 2002). This, then, seems an area ripe for methodological innovation.

Our own test here is a very small-scale one, using a severely limited corpus of data from 26 languages of south-eastern Western Australia analysed and published by David Nash (2002). The interrelationships of these languages are poorly understood, and the available data frequently consist of an incomplete meaning list (based on the Alpher and Nash (1999) modified Swadesh list), collected in most cases from a single speaker. These data possibly represent a worst-case test for phylogenetic methods: we cannot select our data, since the sources are intrinsically limited, and we have no comparative-method work to fall back on, so that judgements of likely cognacy are necessarily based simply on recurrent similarity.

For comparison, a NeighbourNet graph for the whole Dyen, Kruskal, and Black database (hence, 200 items for 95 languages and varieties) is shown in Figure 6.12. This clearly produces a tree, though there are obvious reticulations too, particularly in the Balto-Slavic group (note that Splitstree provides essentially the same outline topology, but with considerably fewer reticulations, as we would expect from the comparisons made earlier).

However, Figure 6.13, drawn again using both Splitstree and NeighbourNet for comparison shows that the phylogenetic signal is very considerably weaker in the Australian data. In Figure 6.13(a), the Splitstree graph collapses 20 of the 26 languages as a single node: any phylogenetic structure there may be has been concealed completely by the effects of contact. As discussed above, Splitstree therefore has the dual disadvantage, at least in current versions, of maximizing tree-like structure and failing to illustrate signals of contact, but equally failing to discern tree-ness when the data set is very complex. The NeighbourNet graph in Figure 6.13(b) constitutes a step forward, with some vestiges of a tree-like signal emerging, though the volume of reticulations is still considerable. Note that in both these graphs the alphabetical language codes are those used by Nash (2002).

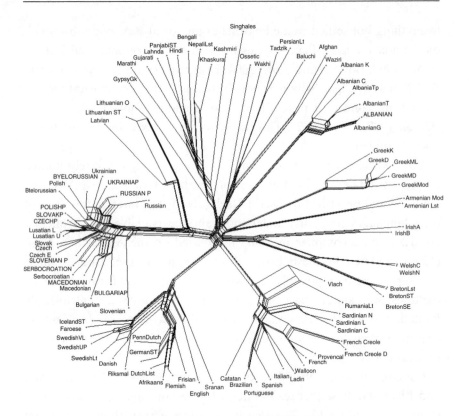

Fig. 6.12 NeighbourNet, full DKB data set

The next step would be to ask linguists with a particular interest in these languages to assess whether the groups which are emerging in the NeighbourNet graph are likely to be linked primarily by the apparently underlying phylogenetic structure rather than by reticulations; this is not something we can pursue further here. Finally, however, note that putting even this highly convergent data through a tree-drawing program like PHYLIP (Felsenstein 2001) Neighbour, which operates on a neighbour-joining algorithm, will inevitably produce a tree. Figure 6.14 shows a tree of this kind, drawn for Nash's Australian data using the neighbour-joining algorithm also available in Splitstree. Programs which cannot analyse out conflicts in the data cannot diagnose the effects of contact; and the fact that they draw trees cannot be taken as evidence that we have languages with a fundamentally tree-like history, since trees, by defini-

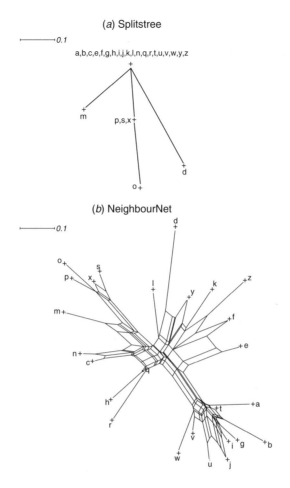

Fig. 6.13 Graphs for 26 Australian languages: (*a*) using Splitstree, (*b*) using NeighbourNet

tion, are all they can conceivably draw. Bootstrapping would, it is true, be highly likely to show very poor support for any particular tree configuration with data of this type; but the fact remains that such doubts could only emerge from further processing and testing of the tree, whereas network-based approaches offer us the possibility of establishing how tree-like our data are from the outset.

These Australian data, however, are unlikely to be accepted as anything approaching a cast-iron test of any method or model, partly because the Australian situation is recognized as such a recalcitrant one, and partly because the data analysed here are so fragmentary. In addition,

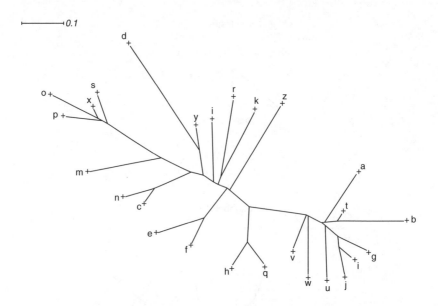

Fig. 6.14 Neighbour-joining tree of Australian data, drawn using Splitstree

though we turn in detail to issues of dating and time depth in the next chapter, Australia is generally agreed to have a long settlement history, dating back to at least 40,000 years BP (before the present): this leaves a great deal of time available for linguistic splits and differentiation to accumulate, and for contact relationships to develop and change, meaning that the chances of successfully recovering a single, accurate history for these languages are inevitably small using any method. If the social and historical forces obtaining since settlement have predisposed to contact and convergence, these effects will be correspondingly greater. Our second test, therefore, involves a range of Andean languages. Here, the issues are at least clearer, and we have access to a considerable database of material collected first-hand by Paul Heggarty, mainly between 2001 and 2004.

The material we have used here from Heggarty's database (see also Heggarty forthcoming) involves 150 lexical items from each of 14 varieties of Quechua; 3 varieties of Aymara; and Kawki and Jaqaru, which are typically classified as independent Aymaran languages. The central question here is whether Quechua and Aymaran are related, or whether the undoubted affinities between them rather reflect extensive contact— the Quechumaran question. Terminology in this area is rather fluid, with various proposals for the name of the cluster containing Aymara, Jaqaru, and Kawki: this has variously been called Aru, Jaqi, and Aymaran. Here, we shall use *Aymara* when referring to the single language, three varieties of which are included in Heggarty's database, and *Aymaran* for the family containing Aymara plus the subgroup composed of Jaqaru and Kawki.

As discussed briefly in Section 6.3.1 above, Heggarty's 150-item CALMA meaning list overlaps significantly with the Swadesh list used elsewhere in this book. However, the CALMA list is modified in four ways. First, not all 200 meanings from the Swadesh list were collected, either because they refer to concepts not native to or otherwise unknown in the Andes, or more commonly because two Swadesh meanings share the same root in Andean languages: this is the case for 'one' and 'other', for example, or 'woman' and 'wife'. The shared roots mean these pairs of items are not independent, so they have been collapsed into a single slot in the CALMA list. Second, a few pan-Andean items which provide good indicators of local relatedness through particular correspondences were included: these are similar to, though not identical with, items in the Swadesh list. For instance, CALMA includes 'fox', 'be ill', and 'finger-nail' in place of 'wolf', 'sick', and 'claw' respectively. Third, where all the languages and varieties Heggarty is comparing differentiate between meanings in a similar way (as, for example, with the case of 'man's brother' versus 'woman's brother', a distinction consistently expressed by two discrete forms in Quechua) Heggarty splits this single meaning from the Swadesh list into two separate list meanings. This means that 'brother', and similarly 'sister', 'old', and 'young' each occupy two slots in the CALMA list. Finally, cases where Andean languages may have different forms for two or more subsenses, as in the case of 'sun', with the subsenses 'celestial object' and 'sunlight/heat', are assigned a single slot in the CALMA list. However, the score when two languages or varieties are compared will be intermediate between 1 and 0, depending on the overlap of subsenses between the varieties.

This brings us to a further innovation inherent in Heggarty's revised lexicostatistical model. Not only does comparison between languages and varieties involve weighting and intermediate values (and recall that this will require analysis using a distance-based rather than a character-based Network approach), but we also have to revise our initial stage of data processing. Up to now we have worked with the Dyen, Kruskal, and Black database, which incorporates judgements of whether items are cognate or not; these are reflected in the codings (recall Table 6.1

above) of 401 for all the Romance 'animal' forms, but the unique state 031 assigned to English *animal*, to mark it as a likely borrowing. However, assigning values based on cognacy judgements in the Andean situation simply begs the Quechumaran question. How can we reach an objective evaluation of whether the undoubted similarities we find here are due to common ancestry or contact if we use terminology and codings which presuppose that items are cognate?

The answer here involves a revision of our terminology which is not purely cosmetic, but underlines a difference in approach. Where we have considerable knowledge of the histories of languages, and of their likely relationships (and this is likely to involve prior application of the comparative method), we can use traditional lexicostatistics, mark up our lists according to plausible cognacy, and talk about cognates as we have done for Indo-European and for our simulated data (where we know the history because we created it) in the examples above. However, when we turn to less securely charted linguistic waters we need to be more circumspect about what we are and are not claiming, and must make our comparisons on a more neutral basis. Heggarty (forthcoming) therefore suggests that in such cases we refer not to cognates but to **correlates** between languages.

What this means is that in situations where we indubitably find significant numbers of matches between languages but it would appear that any signal in the data lies beyond the reach of the comparative method, we should deliberately not beg the question of whether such matches are cognates or loanwords, but should use a term neutral between the two possible interpretations. Correlates, then, are striking form-to-meaning correspondences which are highly unlikely to be due to chance, but might well reflect either common ancestry or contact. Heggarty (forthcoming) suggests that potential correlates should be rated on a 0–7 scale expressing levels of 'plausibility'. These different scores express how far the degree of phonetic similarity observed between correlate sets appears to constitute a correlation significantly greater than chance. To give some outline examples, a case for the 'sun' slot where two varieties both have *inti*, and therefore identical forms, would score 7; *inti–rupa-y* would score 0, at the other extreme, since there is really no basis for assuming correlateness in this case; *p'iqi–piqa* is rated at 5, but **quʎu – *urqu* (= 3) and **huma – *qam* (= 2) are seen as less convincing and more speculative. These assessments are based on a number of principles, discussed in

Heggarty (forthcoming), and are predicated on known sound changes typical within the Andean languages. They also draw on Cerrón-Palomino's (2000: 311) categories of obvious loanwords, very probable cognates, probable cognates, and obviously unrelated forms. Beyond that, there is some subjectivity in these characterizations; but the nature of the scales involved will mean the impact of such subjectivity on the figures is kept to a minimum, causing generally at worst a shift of the order of 0.1 to 0.2. A misidentification in traditional lexicostatistics, of course, would mean a shift of 0 to 1 or vice versa.

Heggarty's approach is also gradient in another way, since he allows intermediate values between 1 and 0 in comparisons, based on the degree of intelligibility between languages (or indeed varieties, making this approach helpfully applicable to dialect as well as language relationships). Often, of course, we will still be dealing with values of 1 or 0. For instance, where there is full, total intelligibility between two varieties, a coding of 1 will be entered: this is the case for Laraos Quechua and Puki Aymara, both of which use the single, identical form *inti* for the list-meaning 'sun', making no particular distinction of separate subsenses. At the other extreme, Chetilla Quechua uses only *rupa-y*, while Puki Aymara uses only *inti*, and the two words clearly do not resemble one another formally; the obvious similarity coding is 0. There are, however, a range of intermediate values, which are shown in (2); we cannot go into details here on the precise method of calculation used, but see Heggarty (forthcoming) and McMahon, Heggarty, McMahon and Slaska (forthcoming) for further information.

(2) Correlate scoring on a descending scale of mutual intelligibility

    (i) Laraos – Puki   Full correlates *inti* in all senses of 'sun'. Score 1

    (ii) Laraos – Atalla   Full correlates *inti* for the 'celestial-object' subsense.

                                For 'sunlight', Laraos speaker uses *rupa-y* only for 'burn', otherwise *inti*; Atalla speaker uses *rupa-y* for 'heat of the sun', otherwise *inti*. Score 0.83

    (iii) Puki – Atalla   Full correlates *inti* for the 'celestial-object' subsense.

                                For 'sunlight', Atalla speaker uses *rupa-y* for 'heat of the sun', otherwise *inti*; Puki speaker has only *inti*. Score 0.78

(iv) Chetilla – Atalla   For the main 'celestial-object' subsense, Chetilla speaker has only *rupa-y*; Atalla speaker has *inti*, but will understand *rupa-y* as 'heat of the sun'.
For 'sunlight', full correlates *rupa-y*. Score 0.56

(v) Chetilla – Laraos   Chetilla speaker uses only *rupa-y*; Laraos speaker uses *inti*, and will understand *rupa-y* only as 'be hot (sunny), burn'. Score 0.17

(vi) Chetilla – Puki   No correlates in either sense; Chetilla speaker uses only *rupa-y* for both senses, Puki speaker uses only *inti*. Lexemes are not correlate. Score 0

These measures of intelligibility and overlap between subsenses provide a graded rating of similarity, but that is all—any network plotted from these results would be purely a phenogram, giving information on distance, and not a phylogram, which tells us about the history of the different groups. And yet, especially if we include Aymaran as well as Quechua data, it is precisely insight into the more likely history that we need. How, then, are we to reconcile our intentionally neutral, correlate-based approach with our search for a resolution to the Quechumaran problem?

The answer, again, lies in our use of sublists, which allow us to place a historical interpretation on our phenetic results. In keeping with our methodology for Indo-European, we have excerpted from Heggarty's database two groups of 30 items corresponding to our earlier hihi and lolo sublists—those which are most retentive on the one hand, and those most prone to change and borrowing on the other. These sublists are shown in (3), and though membership is not identical with the hihi and lolo lists for Indo-European, the overlap has been maximized as much as possible given the different compositions of the Swadesh and CALMA lists (overlapping items are shown in bold). As (3) shows, 25 items from the Andean hihi list are also included in the Indo-European one; the overlap for the lolo list looks poorer, at 18, but recall that our Indo-European lolo list included only 23 items: we increased the hihi list to 30 to compensate for the presence of 6 totally uninformative meanings, which were cognate across the entire group.

(3a) Andean hihi list, 30 items

one	two	three	four	five
one	**two**	**three**	**four**	**five**
I	**thou** (you sing.)	**not**	**ear**	**tongue**
tooth	**foot**	**fingernail (claw)**	heart	**name**
day	**night**	**sun**	**star**	shadow
wind	**salt**	green	**new**	**come**
eat	**sleep**	live (be alive)	**give**	sew

(3b) Andean lolo list, 30 items

year	left (-hand side)	face	mouth	lip
year	**left** (-hand side)	face	**mouth**	lip
neck	(upper) **back**, shoulder	skin (human)	breast	**bird**
tail	**wing**	**man (male adult)**	**river**	**stone**
bread	branch	**grass**	**rope**	red
straight	sick (be ill)	empty	**heavy**	far (away)
hot	**walk**	swim	**think**	**push**

Although these sublists are not identical to those considered earlier for Indo-European, they can be shown to be differentially affected by borrowing in the same way. Spanish borrowings can be identified relatively readily in all the Andean languages and varieties, and we find an average of 2.7% Spanish loans in the hihi sublist, but 6.7% in the lolo sublist, nearly three times as high. This difference is significant at the $p < 0.001$ level (paired t-test; $t = -4.1$, $df = 18$).

This operational difference between the more and less conservative sublists is encouraging, but it remains to be seen whether these can also be used as a basis for deciding between the alternative histories of Quechua and Aymaran. Recall that our use of graded similarity scores in some comparisons, following Heggarty's introduction of subsenses, means distance-based rather than character-based programs are clearly more appropriate. The graphs in Figure 6.15 were therefore generated using NeighbourNet.

For the networks in Figure 6.15, Spanish loans have been excluded by marking them, as usual, as unique states. It is very clear in both these graphs that the 14 Quechua dialects cluster together; so do the three Aymara varieties, plus Jaqaru and Kawki, which however constitute a separate branch within Aymaran. The most interesting aspect of these

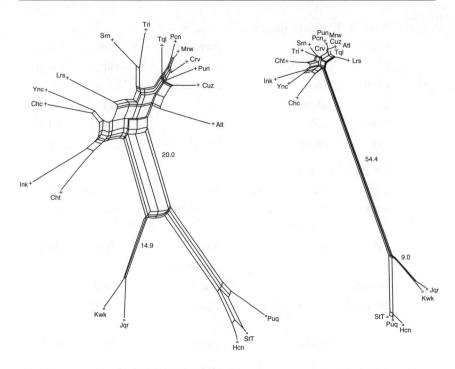

Fig. 6.15 Comparison of the Andean languages for the 30 low-retentive (left) and 30 high-retentive (right) meanings; values are 'lexical-distance' measures (percentage correlate similarities), 10% approximates to 3 lexical items' distance. Calculated using NeighbourNet with power set at 0 (i.e. using crude distances)

graphs, however, is the calculation of distance between the root nodes for those two Quechua and Aymaran groups, which in the lolo network is just over 20%, while for the hihi one it is 54.4%, nearly three times as high. Lexical distance here is simply another way of expressing percentage non-correlateness, with 10% approximating to a distance of 3 lexical items. What this means, then, is that the lolo sublist, which is typically more changeable, shows considerably less distance between Quechua and Aymaran than the hihi items, which are generally more resistant to change.

This, on the face of it, is odd—at least if these two groups are related. Two comparisons may serve to show that it is certainly not the norm for related groups. In the same graphs in Figure 6.15 above we see that within the Aymaran cluster the lexical distance from Kawki and Jaqaru to the Aymara root is 14.9% for the lolo graph on the left but 9%, rather lower, for the hihi graph on the right. We find similar results in the case of Greek and a sample of Romance languages from the Dyen, Kruskal, and Black database, which represent two Indo-European groups of comparable sizes and overall lexical distance from each other. Here, the comparable distances are 52% for the lolo sublist and 32% for the hihi group. The figures are different, clearly, but the pattern is the same: for the two Aymaran groups, and the two Indo-European ones, we find greater distance for the lolo sublist, and greater similarity for the hihi meanings. This is precisely the opposite of the pattern shown in Figure 6.15 for Quechua compared with Aymaran.

What the Aymaran-internal and Indo-European calculations have in common, of course, is that they involve languages which are known to belong to a single group, whether at the subfamily or family level. In the case of Quechua compared to Aymaran, this is not necessarily the case: and indeed our figures would seem to argue against common ancestry, and for a relationship of contact. Common ancestry would appear to correspond regularly to calculations of greater distance for the lolo subgroup than for the hihi one, simply because the lolo items, by definition, are more likely to change. The opposite trend, as in the striking figures for Quechua as compared with Aymaran, where three times as much distance is apparent in the hihi as in the lolo items, favours an argument of contact rather than common ancestry. If two groups show greater affinities in the sublist which is more prone to contact, then contact seems, to put it bluntly, the most appropriate explanation. The fact that this is precisely the opposite balance to those cases where we can be much more confident that we do have common ancestry strengthens this conclusion; at this stage it may be accidental that the threefold additional distance between Quechua and Aymaran hihi sublists matches the threefold additional Spanish loans we found on average in the Andean lolo sublists, but the parallel is at least indicative and worthy of further investigation. None of this proves that Quechua and Aymaran never shared a common ancestor; but it does suggest a very significant influence of contact as the main determinant of the lexical similarities between the two groups.

6. 4 The Uses of Computational and Quantitative Methods

The computational and quantitative techniques we have illustrated here are intended to identify, represent, and elucidate problems in linguistic classification. We have shown that it is possible to test different programs and applications against cases of known language histories, whether these involve common ancestry or contact or both. We have argued that network approaches in general are more flexible and insightful than those based only on trees, and that these allow us access to a means of representing the whole history of languages, not only those aspects which derive by descent with modification from a single ancestral state. Nonetheless, each of the models we have illustrated has its advantages and disadvantages: for example, Network generates an extremely helpful list of those items incompatible with a tree structure, which can then be checked individually by linguists who know the languages involved well; on the other hand, it is suitable only for character-based data. NeighbourNet, which works on distance data and seems optimal for discerning the effects of contact in lexical lists, cannot by its nature list the problem characters, since it is based on figures derived from a composite character list. The data we have, and the way we wish to analyse them, will therefore determine which program we decide to use.

It is worth reiterating that the first and essential stage of working with these programs and representations involves helping linguists to demonstrate that the insights already achieved through purely linguistic methods are sound, and to test and perhaps refute less likely hypotheses. At the same time, increased awareness of the benefits of such computational techniques in known cases may convince more historical linguists that they can also be generalized into the unknown. Most of this chapter has been devoted to demonstrating that new quantificational and computational methods can affirm what linguists feel they already know, and for this we make no apology. It is only when such methods are accepted in these standard cases, tested and affirmed by simulations based on what linguistic methods have already established, that linguists are likely to trust them in resolving other and more complex cases where linguistic opinion persistently differs, and the data do not allow a purely linguistic resolution. Our own illustrations of the merits of these methods for such unclear cases are tentative and preliminary, but we hope they indicate the possible benefits of quantitative and computational approaches in future research.

However, one potential problem remains with the methods we have used so far: all are based on second-order data coding, whether this involves assessments of likely cognacy, or degree of intelligibility for correlates. Ideally, we might wish to introduce alternative methods for first-order comparison of linguistic data (which will require sophisticated measures of similarity), and also to explore the possibilities for quantitative work outside the lexicon; we return to these issues in Chapter 8. First, however, we turn to another pressing question. Our trees and networks contain nodes and reticulations: can we use linguistic data to suggest dates for these, and if so, are those dates likely to be accurate?

7

Dating

7. 1 Lexicostatistics and Glottochronology

7. 1. 1 Troublesome Terms

Embleton (2000: 143) provides an admirably concise summary of the goals of mathematical approaches to classification, and it is certainly worth quoting the relevant paragraph in full here:

Since at least the 1930s, linguists have been seriously and practically interested in the development of mathematical techniques for assessing the closeness of the relationship between a pair of languages, using only information from the contemporary languages themselves. Applied pairwise, this leads to the reconstruction of a family tree for a group of genetically related languages, without the use of any actual historical information about the languages or language family. If one can either determine a rate of linguistic change, or calibrate one of the branch lengths of the putative tree against some external information, one can then assign dates to the splits in the family tree.

The first two of these three sentences have to do with the usual historical-linguistic practices of classification. The description, admittedly, does not cover the comparative method itself, since this is not inherently mathematical; but with one further more specific restriction to lexical data it would certainly be applicable to lexicostatistics. The third sentence, however, moves beyond both lexicostatistics and classification to the further and secondary issue of dating. And the 'If' beginning that sentence is, in our opinion, one of the biggest 'ifs' anywhere in historical linguistics.

From the previous chapters, which involved various applications, tests, updatings, and computerizations of lexicostatistics, it should be clearly apparent that we are enthusiastic adherents of that type of quantitative classificatory method. This does not mean there are no remaining questions: we would quibble with Embleton's apparent restriction, above, to pairwise applications, and have reported on areas of unclarity, where future work is needed, and on research in progress which promises a more sensitive and complex instantiation of lexicostatistics (Heggarty forthcoming). We have also proposed that the family tree should give way to network representations, which have the advantage of distinguishing common origin and divergence from contact, while recognizing and depicting both. Equally, as we shall see in the next chapter, we are not arguing that lexicostatistics alone is sufficient: it is essential that we continue to attempt to develop related mathematical classificatory methods using data from other levels of the grammar.

However, while we are happy to embrace and promote lexicostatistical methods as part of a set of complementary approaches to language classification, we have quite the opposite attitude to glottochronology. We believe that glottochronology has been tested and found not only wanting but entirely invalid. By extension, as we shall show below, there are reasons to be extremely sceptical at best of other supposed solutions to the dating problem in linguistics.

Before continuing to consider these other approaches to dating, however, we must first turn our attention to a terminological confusion. Since we are promoting lexicostatistics, at least as worthy of further testing and development, but suggesting that glottochronology is a blot on the historical-linguistic landscape, it might not be surprising that we do not welcome the frequent conflation of the labels for these two methods. Such conflation and confusion, however, is distressingly common. Campbell (1998: 177), for instance, heads his relevant section 'Glottochronology (Lexicostatistics)'. He notes that there may in principle be a difference between lexicostatistics as 'the statistical manipulation of lexical material for historical inferences (not necessarily associated with dates)', and glottochronology as 'a method with a goal of assigning a date to the split-up of some language into daughter languages'; however, Campbell suggests that 'in actual practice, this distinction is almost never made; both names are used interchangeably' (ibid.). Likewise, Fox (1995: 279–80) notes that 'Though potentially different in scope, these two terms are used virtually synonymously by most scholars, as they designate what is, in effect, a single method.' However, as noted initially in Chapter 1 above, we follow instead the lead of Trask (1996: 362), who points out the tendency to conflate the two terms but considers this 'not good practice', and of

Embleton (2000: 145) who proposes that lexicostatistics should be applied only to quantitative analyses of vocabulary without the further step of dating, for which the term glottochronology should be retained: 'This . . . is the usage . . . which I would strongly advise, to prevent further confusion.'

7. 1. 2 Glottochronology: Practice and Problems

If we are to understand why lexicostatistics and glottochronology should be seen as different, we must first be able to define glottochronology. We propose to differentiate the two terminologically because glottochronology is a further step, an application of lexicostatistics. It is true that both methods rely on the notion of basic vocabulary; but glottochronology takes the calculations of lexicostatistics and uses these for a separate purpose, namely dating. It is possible to use lexicostatistics without ever proceeding to do glottochronology; but it is not possible to do glottochronology without first doing lexicostatistics.

Glottochronology was proposed by Swadesh (1955, 1971), and the main equation used in dating is derived in Swadesh (1950) and discussed further by Lees (1953). In the 1950s linguists were becoming aware of and intrigued by the possibilities offered in archaeology by the development of carbon-14 dating—an early equivalent of the current 'new synthesis' between historical disciplines. Carbon-14 is radioactive, and is present in the atmosphere in a constant ratio relative to ordinary carbon. When plants take in air and nutrients they trap carbon, and therefore obtain both carbon and carbon-14. In turn, when animals eat plants, they will also come to contain both carbon and carbon-14 in that same, constant ratio. When these animals and plants die carbon-14 in the remaining organic material then decays at a constant rate over time, so that a certain fixed proportion will disappear for every unit of time. In consequence, organic material can be dated by finding the present ratio of carbon to carbon-14 in the specimen, then calculating the difference between this and the atmospheric ratio, and finally calibrating and converting this difference into units of time.

The attraction of these ideas for historical linguists is immediately obvious. Although we can tell a good deal from family trees (and more, as we have argued, from networks), there are certain things we cannot read off these diagrams, the most obvious being the dates assigned to nodes and splits. Even in some of our computational approaches where branch lengths may be meaningful, they can only be relative: if one branch is longer than another, this may mean more change, or a longer period of development, or both, but we cannot make direct translations into units of time. Nor can we extrapolate to say that two branches with the same length in different trees must mean the same time since the respective common ancestors. There is also, more generally, a perennial human fascination with where we come from, and this extends to when we as a group or a species were living in certain areas, and how long we spent there.

As Swadesh (1952: 452) put it, 'prehistory represents a great obscure depth which science seeks to penetrate'. But to answer these questions or contribute to these debates linguistically, by developing an equivalent of carbon-14 dating for language, it would first be necessary to identify some element of language that changed at a constant rate, a linguistic analogue for carbon-14 decay.

The obvious candidate, given the activities of historical and comparative linguists at the time, was of course basic vocabulary. Swadesh and Lees argued that given lexicostatistical scores for pairs of languages, only one further step was necessary for dating, and this involved the application of the formula in (1); for further details and a full derivation, see Embleton (1986)—though beware that Embleton's version of the formula is for the rate of loss, R, rather than the rate of retention, r, as here.

(1) The glottochronological formula

$$t = \frac{\log c}{2 \log r}$$

t = time depth in millennia

c = percentage of cognates

r = 'glottochronological constant'

This formula tells us that we can calculate the time depth since separation (which is t), by taking the logarithm of the percentage of cognates shared between the two languages we are comparing (which is c), and dividing that by twice the log of r, r being the glottochronological constant. The whole point of using basic vocabulary, remember, is that it is hypothesized to change at a constant rate; and if that is the case then we need to find the rate at which it does change, to allow us to apply the formula.

Lees (1953) approached this problem by identifying 13 pairs of control languages: the members of each pair are related, either as earlier and later stages of the same language, or as mother and daughter. The 13 pairs Lees selected are listed in (2).

(2) Value for the rate constant: Lees (1953); 13 pairs of control languages
    1. Old English (AD 900–1000) and Modern English
    2. Plautine Latin (200 BC) and Early Modern Spanish (AD 1600)
    3. Plautine Latin and French of AD 1650
    4. Old High German (AD 800–900) and Modern German
    5. Middle Egyptian (2100–1700 BC) and Coptic (AD 300)
    6. Koine Greek (250 BC) and Modern Athenian Greek
    7. Koine Greek and Modern Cypriot
    8. Ancient Classical Chinese (AD 950) and Modern Mandarin
    9. Old Norse (AD 800–1050) and Modern Swedish
   10. Classical Latin (200 BC) and Modern Tuscan Italian
   11. Classical Latin and Modern Portuguese
   12. Classical Latin and Modern Romanian
   13. Classical Latin and Modern Catalan

In each case the qualification for inclusion was that recorded evidence of both earlier and later members of each pair was available, allowing a lexicostatistical calculation of percentage cognates to be made in the usual way. The similarity measures calculated by Lees are given in (3), where c is the percentage of cognates shared by the two members of the particular pair for the 215-item Swadesh list he used; the 'time' (t) column lists the known period between the earlier and later languages in the pair, expressed in millennia; and r is the percentage of cognates retained per millennium, based on the previous two columns.

(3)

	c (%)	t	r (%)
1. English	76.6	1.0	76.6
2. Spanish	65.5	1.8	79.1
3. French	62.5	1.85	77.6
4. German	84.1	1.1	85.4
5. Egyptian	53	2.2	74.9
6. Greek	69	2.07	83.6
7. Cypriot	67.8	2.07	82.9
8. Chinese	79.5	1.0	79.5
9. Swedish	85	1.02	85.3
10. Italian	68.6	2.15	83.9
11. Portuguese	62.9	2.15	80.6
12. Romanian	56	2.15	76.4
13. Catalan	60.6	2.15	79.2

When these values for r were averaged across the 13 language pairs, Lees derived a value of 81%, which we can then take as the glottochronological constant, allowing us to solve the equation in (1) for any language pair. In fact, Swadesh later modified this value to 86%, based on the 100-item list; this in itself might raise initial doubts over the method, since we are meant to be dealing with a constant, which turns out to be a variable. Mathematically speaking, we might argue that the range of variation is still not extensive, and that we should be working with calculated errors and confidence intervals in any case, meaning that minor deviations from the core value of the constant will be lost in the noise. Given the topics of previous chapters in this book, an explanation of this variation is not hard to find either: we have already demonstrated that different items in basic vocabulary lists do change at different rates, and the 200-meaning list contains overall a slightly higher proportion of less conservative items than the shorter list. Accepting this, however, already challenges one of the assumptions of glottochronology, since it demonstrates that basic vocabulary certainly does not change at an absolutely constant rate. Nonetheless, taking Swadesh's revised value as more accurate, we would calculate that two related languages should on average retain 86% of common vocabulary over 1,000 years, 70% after 1,180 years, 50% after 2,290 years, and 20% after 5,560 years. According to Kroeber (1955), the method hits its outer limit at 11,720 years, at which point we would predict 8% shared vocabulary, a figure he claims would be indistinguishable from the level of chance resemblance.

There is a vast literature on glottochronology, expressing views for and against (for some examples see Kroeber 1955; Gudschinsky 1956; Hoijer 1956; Rea 1958, 1973, 1990; Arndt 1959; Gleason 1959; Hymes 1960; Bergsland and Vogt 1962; Teeter 1963; Dyen 1964, 1973; Sankoff 1970); there are also textbook accounts in, for instance, Fox (1995), Trask (1996), and Campbell (1998). What follows here can only summarize this extensive discussion and exemplification of the method. However, the main point is clear enough. The methodology of glottochronology seems both straightforward and transparent; the problems lie with the results, and with the underlying assumptions. The dates achieved by following the steps set out above and applying the formula simply do not equate to known historical events. Thus, we can calculate split dates of AD 1586 for Italian and French; AD 874 for Romanian and Spanish (the first split within Romance); AD 860 for English and Dutch; and AD 1575 for German and Dutch. In all these cases the dates are vastly too late: by the 1500s the Romance languages had demonstrably been separate and diverging for upwards of a thousand years, with even some recorded literature for evidence. On the other hand, we also find the opposite difficulty, with considerable overestimates of the time depth between Tok Pisin and English, for instance: the formula generates a split date upwards of 2,000 years ago, although Tok Pisin is only at most 200 years old. Some dates derived from the formula, then, are too late, and others are too early.

Part of the blame for these anomalous results has tended to be placed on the whole notion of basic vocabulary and Swadesh-type meaning lists. We do not propose to pursue this line of argument here, however. It has already been established, certainly, that there are difficulties in completing basic meaning lists and in calculating percentages of cognates. As we saw in the last chapter, modified lists have been suggested for different language groups (as in Alpher and Nash's list (1999) for Australia, Matisoff's CALMSEA (1978, 2000) and Heggarty's CALMA (forthcoming) lists): this would scarcely be necessary if we were really dealing with completely universal senses. We have already noted that there is no very clear protocol for collecting lists (see Slaska forthcoming, in preparation), or for deciding between apparently equivalent possible entries: Gudschinsky (1956), rather alarmingly, suggests tossing a coin in such cases, and while this is a perfectly valid approach statistically, it is clearly unacceptable linguistically. However, all these are issues for lexicostatistics, which is concerned with deciding and completing the lists, and calculating similarity scores; they are not in any direct way the concern of glottochronology, which is a possible, optional way of using those similarity scores once we have them. Much of our discussion over the past few chapters has involved the ways we might refine or change our lexicostatistical methodology to make it more sensitive, more appropriate for different languages and situations, and more suited to quantitative and computational testing. However, even if we resolved all these issues, this would still not begin to tackle the problems specific to glottochronology. Nothing we can do to assist lexicostatistics will directly affect the applicability of dating algorithms to language splits.

The real challenges to glottochronology do not involve the lists themselves, or the cognacy scores we derive from them. They involve the assumption that we can apply a glottochronological constant (which in itself asserts that change happens at a constant rate in some domain at least) to these figures to convert them into time depths. The rate constant is already an average across a range of language pairs, but as (2) shows, 11 out of the 13 pairs that Lees (1953) used are Indo-European, and 6 of these are Romance. Perhaps, then, the range of languages on which the calculations of the constant were based should be broadened, as far as possible, to include other families. However, this might not help much, since it is particularly worrying that the dates the formula produces for Indo-European, and specifically for Romance languages, are among those that vary significantly from the likely actual dates of separation.

The real difficulty is the assumption of anything like a constant rate of change. As we have seen, basic meanings are relatively resistant to borrowing; but that does not mean they are immune to its effects. Similarly, they may change, all other things being equal, at a slower rate than the lexical semantics of a language taken as a whole. But all other things are often not equal; and if the whole language and the community speaking it are affected by a particular set of social circumstances that make change faster or slower, these factors cannot be expected to bypass the basic vocabulary and affect everything else. Indeed, we can demonstrate that they do not. Bergsland and Vogt (1962), in a damning indictment of glottochronology, have shown that Old Norse and Modern Icelandic share 96% cognates, which would produce a glottochronological time depth of 258 years; likewise, Old Armenian and Modern Armenian share 97%, giving a split date of 211 years. Both, of course, are massive underestimates, suggesting that conservative societies inhibit vocabulary loss. On the other hand, languages like East Greenlandic Eskimo have productive and far-reaching systems of taboo, which accelerate vocabulary loss and will depress similarity scores and inflate time depths. The same will apply to languages which have had histories particularly affected by contact: as Trask (1996: 364) observes, 'there was until recently a Gypsy variety of Armenian which, in spite of preserving the Armenian grammatical system almost intact, had virtually no Armenian words left in it'. Factoring out the effects of contact may help in some of these cases, but not all: social factors including the degree of isolation, the extent of literacy, and population density may all affect rates of change in ways we do not fully understand, and certainly cannot algorithmically correct.

There have been attempts (see Sankoff 1970, 1973; Embleton 1986) to work more parametrically within glottochronology, allowing replacement rates to vary, and attempting to filter out loans; and the accuracy of such revised models does improve when tested on cases where the real dates and histories are well known. However, the mathematics of these revised models is much more complex, and, as we have already seen for Embleton's approach to loans (in Ch. 3 above), they do not generalize readily to unclear and controversial situations. Any attempt to calculate likely errors for cases where we do not have any obvious way of corroborating the dates achieved is likely to produce extremely high confidence intervals. If we can only say that dates are likely to be right, assuming no unusual social situations, within several millennia, then we might wonder whether this kind of calculation is a productive use of linguists' time at all.

7. 2 Dating and Time Depth in Linguistics and Biology

In the rest of this book we have turned frequently to biology as a source of methodological insights and cousinly comparisons with a cognate discipline. There have often been helpful parallels, especially with population genetics, since here we find the same core concerns with systems descending and differentiating from single common ancestors, alongside possible interference from other populations. It may then be worth examining the issues of time depth and dating in biology, to see whether we can again learn anything from practice and assumptions there. This section is derived from the much more extensive discussion in McMahon and McMahon (2000), to which readers are referred for further details and references.

Our initial expectation might be that the parallels are less helpful here than in other areas, since biologists typically do include split dates on branching points in family trees, and are known to calibrate their dates according to a 'molecular clock'. On closer inspection, however, it is obvious that many similar problems arise in both disciplines. On the one hand, certain groups of cyanobacteria have survived apparently unchanged for 2,000 million years (Schopf 1994); on the other, Weiner (1994) reports evolutionary changes in Darwin's finches which were observed taking place by a single researcher. The idea of a constant rate of change seems equally mythical in biology; Simpson (1949, cited in Ridley 1997: 239) suggested that 'the question "How fast has evolution occurred?" is meaningless unless we add, "The evolution of what group of organisms, of which of their structures, and at what time in their history?".' It is possible to invoke factors like natural selection, which will operate at different intensities in different situations, to explain such variation in rate: cyanobacteria seem to be occupying much the same niche as their distant ancestors, whereas Boag and Grant (1981) attribute rapid changes in Darwin's finches to extreme weather conditions which dramatically altered the island vegetation. However, like the social factors which shape the course and speed of language change, selection pressures and the factors underlying them are unpredictable, and not always generalizable. If we were to find traces of similarly fast evolutionary developments in the fossil record to those we find for Darwin's finches, we might be inclined to invoke climatological factors; but we could not confirm this hypothesis directly.

Likewise, biologists do have estimates of rates of change, but they also recognize that these are rates, plural. Haldane (1949) proposed that the variable rate of change could be expressed in units called darwins; technically, if a measurement changes from x_1 to x_2 in n million years (note the rather larger time periods characteristic of work in evolution), then we measure the rate of evolution as $(ln\ x_2 - ln\ x_1)/n$ darwins. Crucially, however, the rate in darwins can be derived only from a known amount of change in a known period of time; we cannot reverse the relationship and work from darwins to dates.

These factors do not, however, argue against the molecular clock, since issues of variability and selection arise at the phenotypic level (on the physical surface, where genetic instructions are put into action), whereas the molecular clock is a feature of evolution in the genes themselves. But even here the complexity is that there are many different molecular clocks, since every protein changes at its own distinctive rate. For example, fibrinopeptides change at a rate of 8.3×10^{-9} per amino-acid site per year, while at the other extreme histone H4 changes at only 0.01×10^{-9}. Essentially, this reflects the fact that changes in the fibrinopeptides do not have any radical structural consequences for the phenotype, so they can accumulate mutations neutrally; changes in the histones, on the other hand, will tend to be lethal, so a higher proportion of the mutations will be removed by selection. However, the rate of change within each protein will tend to be constant, since the consequences of change in that protein will tend to be the same, and this has been tested using rate tests across species. This largely follows from the fact that most protein and DNA variation occurs in an environment sheltered from the natural selection which applies to phenotypes (Kimura 1983), meaning that the variability per protein should be substantially reduced. It would appear, then, that each molecular clock ticks at a different rate, but they all keep pretty good time.

Calculations of rates of change in biology are frequently used to establish dates of species split. In time-honoured scientific fashion, they will first be assessed against known split dates, which are themselves arrived at using corroborative fossil evidence; they can then be generalized from the known into the unknown, to propose dates where no fossil evidence is available. Confidence intervals for relatively low time depths (and remember that a low time depth for biology will seem stratospherically high for linguistic evidence) will be fairly large, though they can be reduced to some extent if we include a large number of characters: thus, Nei (1985: 42) calculates the time of separation for human 'Caucasoid' and 'Negroid' populations as 113,000 years, though even using 85 different genetic measures this still carries a confidence interval of plus or minus 34,000 years. When we work over shorter time depths it is also possible to use systems like mitochondrial DNA, which mutates approximately 20 times faster than normal, autosomal DNA (Cann et al. 1987); however, the greater resolution this offers must be balanced against the greater likelihood that the faster mutation rate will produce parallel developments in different populations.

From these specific examples in biology, and others, we abstracted (in McMahon and McMahon 2000: 68, from which we paraphrase loosely below) five general requirements for successful dating. First, the system must change, and that change must be inherited or otherwise passed on reliably from generation to generation. Second, we must understand the mechanisms by which these changes occur and are transmitted. Third, the rate of change must be relatively constant, or at least normally distributed around a constant; or if there is bias, we must understand the reasons for the bias and its direction. Fourth, changes should be random, or if they are directional we must be able to predict or recover the factors determining that directionality. Finally, the rate of change must be relatively low over the timescale in which we are interested. If the rate is too high, there will be too much noise from variation, and we will not be able to discern the signal that indicates common ancestry; and if it is too low, we will only be able to work over extremely long time depths. If we take these five factors into account, it is obvious why phenotypic dating, based on superficial characters, has not been successful: 'we do not understand exactly how a face comes to look like a face, or a tooth like a tooth' (ibid.). These surface systems are too complex, affected by too many different interacting influences, to be modelled and dated as wholes, although we can use them for classification and grouping. However, molecular dating has been reasonably successful, since the elements mutating are small, self-contained, and measurable, and are moreover insulated to a great extent from the selection pressures that rage around phenotypic features.

How, then, does linguistic evidence perform on our five criteria for successful dating? It is certainly true that mutation and inheritance are involved: the inheritance of surface patterns is not direct, of course, but once changes are established in a population, they shape the acquisition and usage of the next generation. The problem, however, is that although mutation might be spontaneous and stochastic, as it is in biology, the transmission of changes, and their success or failure, seems to be under quite active selection pressure: we may not be conscious of activating or inhibiting particular changes, but our subconscious desire to identify with some groups rather than others may have the same effect. This causes a problem, equally, for the second criterion, since we may understand the mechanisms underlying change to some extent, but we certainly cannot predict them. This clearly places linguistic change closer to phenotypic than to molecular change, with obvious consequences for dating; and this conclusion is reinforced when we turn to the third and fourth criteria, since we have already seen that the rate of linguistic change does not appear to be constant, even in the carefully selected basic vocabulary, and that change can be directional, with the factors determining that directionality not yet clearly understood. Finally, since the rate of change is so plainly variable, and since this variability depends so much on unpredictable and contingent social issues, notably involving contact, we cannot guarantee that the rate of change will always be kept within the required bounds, or that we can tell when social factors reach the necessary pitch to take it outside them.

These issues contribute to three central problems, which together seriously compromise the prospects for successful dating in the case of language. On the one hand, change is not random; but on the other, although we may understand some of the factors responsible for selection pressure (such as prestige), we cannot quantify or predict them. Furthermore, individual mutations in biology are typically independent, while in linguistics this is not the case: one change can create the conditions for another, again causing difficulties for quantification. Finally, in biology a change will either apply neutrally or under selection; it will not change category halfway (unless, unusually, the environment changes first). But in language we seem to be dealing with two distinct phases during the life cycle of a change, since the stage of initiation may be analogous to random mutation, but later the variants generated by that initial development may gain social significance and hence come under selection pressure. Just as change gets interesting from the linguist's point of view, then, the analogies with molecular genetic change break down. The theoretical parallels and methodological solutions from biology which have been so productive elsewhere in this book desert us in terms of dating at the point where essentially random mutation becomes directed, selected change.

7. 3 Dating Brought Up to Date

The lively debates over glottochronology in the 1960s and 1970s seemed to end in an approximate consensus that the method had been exhaustively tested and found not to be successful. Of course, some linguists continued to work towards refinements (Sankoff 1970, 1973; Embleton 1986; Starostin 2000); but in general glottochronology has been rejected. The papers collected in Renfrew, McMahon, and Trask (2000) do in some few cases discuss prospects for dating, but for the most part they serve to suggest that by the late 1990s historical-linguistic concern in this area had shifted very substantially towards the question of whether the comparative method is time-limited as to the period over which it can successfully be applied. Clearly, if the method were applicable only up to, say, 8,000 or 10,000 years, simply because the available data would be expected to deteriorate over such a period until the small remaining number of cognates would be indistinguishable from chance, this would affect the possibility of correlating linguistic and archaeological or genetic results in a meaningful way over the kinds of time depths of interest for those other disciplines. Although this is an important issue, it is not one we can discuss in any detail here. Our own view, as readers might expect given our emphasis on variation and variability, is that talk of a fixed ceiling in millennia on the operation of the comparative method is incoherent. This position follows naturally from our rejection of any single, constant or near-constant, rate of change: the issue here is the amount of change which has to happen before relationships become unreconstructable, and that will take longer for some languages, at some periods, and in some areas of the grammar, than for others.

However, dating language splits and proto-languages has recently again hit the headlines—quite literally, since two recent papers on the topic, Forster and Toth (2003) and Gray and Atkinson (2003), have appeared in high-profile general-science journals, followed by considerable media attention and debate. Forster and Toth (2003) is an application of Network to the history of the Insular and Continental Celtic languages, with a particular emphasis on the calculation of branching order and split dates. Gray and Atkinson (2003) also focuses on Indo-European, attempting to calculate a most likely date for Proto-Indo-European, and thereby to choose between two competing hypotheses on the origins of this language family. As we shall see, both approaches are essentially glottochronological, and, perhaps inevitably, both are problematic, to different degrees.

Forster and Toth (2003) are primarily concerned with the history of Insular as opposed to Continental Celtic, and the long-standing question of whether Insular Celtic arrived in Britain in a single wave, subsequently differentiating into Brythonic and Goidelic branches, or whether these branches were transmitted independently to Britain and Ireland respectively. These different options, however, have clear temporal implications, so that Forster and Toth equally aim to date the introduction of Insular Celtic (as well as, less directly, the initial split within Indo-European). In doing so, it is particularly important for them to include data from Continental as well as Insular Celtic: any attempt to ascertain the most likely relationship between the branches of Celtic must necessarily include comparison of both. However, the surviving evidence of Continental Celtic is both meagre and often unclear, meaning that a method is required which will work tolerably well on a small number of data points, and on data which are inherently messy. For these reasons, Forster and Toth (ibid.) elected to use Network.

Forster and Toth (ibid.) base their analysis on 35 items in 13 Indo-European languages (with Basque as an outlier): the list of languages and characters is given in (4).

(4) Languages and characters from Forster and Toth (2003)

    (*a*) Languages:

Continental Celtic:	Gaulish
Insular Celtic:	Old Irish, Modern Irish, Modern Scots Gaelic, Modern Welsh, Modern Breton
Other Indo-European:	Latin, Classical Greek; Modern English, French, Occitan, Italian, Spanish
Non-Indo-European:	Basque

    (*b*) Characters:

Grammatical:	SV or VS syntax; nominative singular masculine suffix; genitive singular masculine suffix; dative singular masculine suffix; nominative singular feminine suffix; genitive singular feminine suffix; [ps] > [ks]
Lexical:	'to gods', 'and to men', 'has offered', 'son of' (patronymic suffix), 'bull', 'three', 'crane', 'oven', 'loaded', 'grand total', 'thing', 'and' (used in lists, e.g. 'person and person and person' in a list of names), 'has made', 'first', 'second', 'third', 'fourth', 'fifth', 'sixth', 'seventh', 'eighth', 'ninth', 'tenth', 'month', 'day', 'mother', 'daughter'

The selection of characters used, and the mixture of grammatical, lexical, basic, and not-so-basic items, reflects inherent restrictions following from the inclusion of Gaulish, which is attested only in a range of inscriptions.

Forster and Toth (ibid.) in fact proceeded to discount 7 of these characters ('has offered', 'oven', 'grand total', 'thing', 'person', 'and', and 'has made'), since these have more than five states, and therefore 'contribute disproportionately to network complexity' (ibid. 2); this reduces the list to 28 items. They proceed to process first binary and then

multi-state characters, producing an eventual network with the expected
branches (English; Greek; Romance, with Latin closer to the root; Goidelic Celtic; Brythonic Celtic; and Gaulish), along with a list of characters
along each branch showing which have contributed to the specific split.
As one might anticipate, the network is predominantly tree-like, suggesting relatively low levels of contact and replacement for these characters.
Forster and Toth (ibid.) make the point, apparently contra Ringe, Warnow, and Taylor (2002), that the lexical characters appear more robust
than the grammatical ones in establishing these branchings: 'it is interesting that the first five ordinal numbers... are sufficient to subdivide the
languages into known relationships... whereas the grammatical suffixes
are less informative because they are frequently lost along independent
branches of the tree' (2003: 3). Much depends, of course, on the specific
lexical and grammatical characters selected.

Their next step is to date the branching points in the tree, and here
Forster and Toth (ibid) argue robustly that 'uniformity in the retention
rates of items is not required when average mutation rates are used... nor
need all branches mutate at the same speed... as long as there are enough
branches at an ancestral node to provide a reliable average'. Their time
estimates are based only on their lexical data (reducing the data points
used further from 28 to 21), and their calculations rely on calibrating
from known split dates. Thus, Latin and Romance are split by 2 lexical
characters, and have been separated for 2,000 years; Old and Modern
Irish are divided by 1 lexical character and 1,000 years; and Old Irish and
Scots Gaelic are separated by 2 lexical items and 1,500 years, for instance.
On this basis, Forster and Toth arrive at an average of 1 lexical mutation
per 1,350 years, allowing dating of the various split points in the tree
according to the number of lexical states that differ between each splitting
pair. From these assumptions and calculations follows, first, support for a
single Common Celtic branch, which then diverges into Continental and
Insular branches: in other words, Forster and Toth (ibid.) argue for the
introduction of a single branch of Celtic into Britain, with a subsequent
split *in situ* into Goidelic and Brythonic. Forster and Toth (ibid.) then
arrive at a date of 3200 BC for the split of Continental and Insular Celtic,
and 8100 BC for the initial divergence of Indo-European. These dates are
clearly extremely early, suggesting both that Celtic arrived in Britain and
that Indo-European began diversifying into its daughter subgroups considerably sooner than has generally been supposed. This has a particular

significance for the Indo-European date, since there are two main current hypotheses on the homeland and divergence pattern of this group. Marija Gimbutas (1973) argued for an identification of the Indo-Europeans with the Kurgan people, and hence a homeland in the Russian steppes, requiring a date for the proto-language of around 4000 BC. However, Renfrew (1987) has proposed an association between the spread of Indo-European and the spread of agriculture through Europe, from a putative homeland in Anatolia (around the area of modern Turkey); since agriculture was introduced to Europe from around 6000 BC, it follows that Forster and Toth's proposed date is more in keeping with Renfrew's hypothesis than with Gimbutas's. For further discussion of these alternatives see Bellwood and Renfrew (2002).

There are, however, various difficulties with Forster and Toth's methods and proposals, which have been roundly criticized by, for example, Larry Trask (2003). First, while it is encouraging that Network can achieve sensible branchings in the tree on the basis of such a small number of data points, we must recall just how small that data set is, especially for the dating applications: results based on such lightly populated databases cannot be more than extremely tentative. To an extent, this is unavoidable for Celtic if we are to include languages like Gaulish, with their inevitable problems of attestation; but dating Indo-European using methods of this kind could and should involve a much larger number of characters and languages. To an extent, the tentative nature of these results is, of course, reflected in Forster and Toth's calculation of ranges of error for their dates: the Indo-European date of 8100 is accompanied by an error of $\pm$ 1,900 years, while the Insular and Continental Celtic divergence date of 3200 is stated as $\pm$ 1,500. In other words, while the break-up of the two branches of Celtic, and the arrival of Celtic in Britain, could have happened around 3200 BC, it could equally have happened around 4700 BC on the one hand, or 1700 BC on the other. These dates, of course, depend completely on the mutation rate, or range of rates, assumed (and Forster and Toth do not appear to include any error in the estimated calibrated mutation rate, which could be at least as big again). As we have seen, Forster and Toth (2003: 5) argue for 1 change per 1,350 years. However, our own calculation, based on our hihi list (the most conservative meanings) from the Dyen, Kruskal, and Black (1992) database, suggests 1 lexical substitution per 470 years $\pm$ 50 years. Forster and Toth's rate is so surprisingly low because of their exclusion of the

7 (from the original 35) characters with most states. This exclusion prioritizes those characters which have changed relatively little, though not by any objective or generalizable prior criteria. However, prioritizing those characters with very low mutation rates will also increase the negative effect of individual coding errors, with each such error potentially contributing 1,000 years to the dating estimates. As we have seen in earlier chapters, we cannot be sure, even for the best understood, most carefully collected, and most thoroughly analysed linguistic data, that no such errors have crept in; and Forster and Toth are dealing with relatively recent splits. Post-selection prioritization of the apparently most conservative (and hence binary rather than multi-state) data in this way may seem to be an obvious way to improve the tree-ness of a network. However, this will not necessarily provide a better depiction of the real relationships at issue, since the multi-state characters might reflect recent events more accurately. Evidence from work on Polynesian languages (Grace 1967) indicates that the most conservative lexical data may give very poor results in terms of recent splits, presumably because the processes of change affecting these are not the same as for rapidly mutating, contact-prone items. This hypothesis requires further testing, but highly mutable items (especially where the contact situation involves closely related languages or dialects) might turn out to provide better results for recently separated languages, up to 2–3,000 years, while more conservative and less borrowable data might be more effective for the diagnosis of older genetic relationships.

These points might seem to suggest a need for further refinement and consideration of more data, while holding out some hope for the calculation of dates in this way. However, there is a much more serious difficulty to be considered, relating to the method of calculation itself. In fact, reading Forster and Toth (2003), including the supplementary material available online, gives very little information about an absolutely crucial factor, namely the method by which states are determined for characters. How did Forster and Toth reach their judgement that the character 'mother' is binary, 'first' is ternary, and 'daughter' multi-state? We are told that the calculations for the paper were done by hand, but there is remarkably little on how; and this is also true of Forster, Toth, and Bandelt (1998), where these methods are first set out and tested on Alpine Romance languages, using a more extensive data set based on the

Swadesh 100-meaning list. No computational tools have been employed, and there is no indication at all of more than a surface inspection method in dividing characters into states, and assigning actual data to those states.

In quantitative work of this kind the quality of the linguistic data used is vitally important: errors or undiagnosed admixture may completely mask the phylogenetic signal, especially in small families or with small data sets. Forster and Toth's attempt at dating (2003), particularly in Celtic, may well fall into this problematic category. The central problem here is the lack of cognacy judgements or objective measurements of similarity. An accumulation of minor errors due to borrowing, misclassification, or poor selection of meanings could together make their estimated dates wholly unreliable and unrealistic. This is particularly problematic in Forster and Toth's work (ibid.), because there is clear evidence that Celtic has experienced significant interborrowing, as shown in Figure 7.1. Here, our Splitstree analysis of the Dyen, Kruskal, and Black (1992) database shows that the phylogenetic signal is strong, but that clear reticulations are generated within Celtic. This pattern strongly suggests interborrowing; and its effects may be disproportionately high because of Forster and Toth's focus on a single subfamily.

The picture is made even more complex by the likely interfering effects of external history. The paucity of the Gaulish data gives us very little information on the development of Continental Celtic. However, Continental Celtic may well have had more contacts with other languages than its Insular sister group, leading to different types of historical development. Not all of the languages and varieties with which Continental Celtic would have been in contact have survived; those that have are in some cases attested only as lightly as Gaulish. It follows that some historical contacts may be unknown, and perhaps unknowable; and this will have a considerable impact on the time depth of the family, artificially extending it, and potentially contributing to an unrealistically early date for the initial split of Celtic.

There are, then, serious problems with Forster and Toth's attempts (2003) to date the initial divergence of Celtic and Indo-European. Their methodology, in the crucial sense of assigning states, is completely unclear, and at best seems to be based on face-value similarity, raising the same doubts as for multilateral comparison and the like. Their

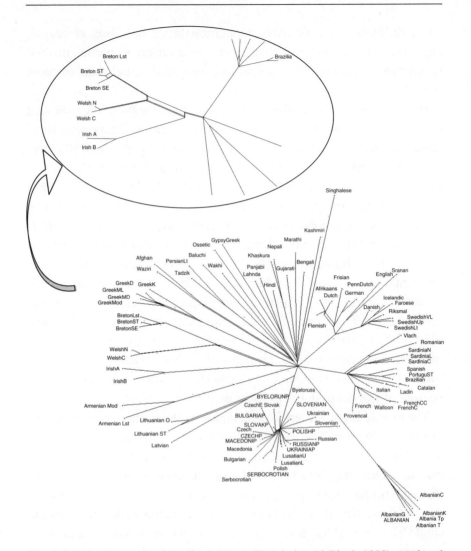

Fig. 7.1 Indo-European data (from Dyen, Kruskal, and Black 1992), analysed using Splitstree (Huson 1998); inset shows reticulations, and hence suspected borrowings, within Celtic

prioritization of less multi-state characters is prima facie reasonable, but might lead to rejection of precisely those data most likely to provide reliable information on more recent splits. The impact of borrowing, especially within groups, does not seem to be taken into consideration at all, though we have shown (see Ch. 4 above) that even one miscoding of a loan as a cognate can lead to dramatically different tree structures from sensitive, network-based programs. Perhaps most worryingly, Forster and Toth do not seem to understand the nature of their data sufficiently clearly, taking the parallels with genetics too seriously and literally. In particular, geneticists can usually assume independence in the mutational direction of different genetic loci; but this assumption is frequently violated with linguistic data. Neither the rate nor the direction of borrowing between languages will necessarily be independent over time, as can be seen from the multiple borrowings from Latin into French, or from French into English since the eleventh century. In addition, Trask (2003) has reported a range of serious errors in Forster and Toth's linguistic data, which make their findings less reliable. These factors together raise serious doubts over Forster and Toth's attempts at dating.

Whereas Forster and Toth (2003) base their arguments principally on Celtic, with their dating of Indo-European a secondary issue, Gray and Atkinson (2003) focus very clearly on attempting to determine the most likely split date for Indo-European. There are also considerable differences, however, between their approach and that of Forster and Toth (2003). Gray and Atkinson (2003) rely on the Dyen, Kruskal, and Black (1992) database, and are therefore clearly working with data based on linguists' best-informed judgements of cognacy; they are not applying their own, presumably similarity-based assessment of states. Furthermore, their use of a wide range of Indo-European languages should minimize the effects of contact on the dating of the whole tree, since individual contact events are likely to be localized to relatively few branches, and will therefore be smoothed out in the computational analysis, resulting only in a minor increase in the variance around the estimated maximum-likelihood dates. This is especially relevant since Gray and Atkinson have used a Bayesian Markov chain Monte-Carlo simulation method, which allows the estimation of uncertainty in the trees obtained by sampling across a range of trees with different probabilities. They dated 14 nodes in their trees using external information, then applied rate-smoothing algorithms, which accommodate the existence of variability in rates of change, while penalizing such rate changes across branches. The effect is to smoothe out variation in rates across the tree while simultaneously allowing a measure of rate variability.

Gray and Atkinson's consensus tree (2003) shows a branching structure completely compatible with more conventionally generated linguistic trees, with most major branches strongly supported in terms of probability. Those branches which are more weakly supported, moreover, are those which would equally be considered doubtful from a linguistic perspective, such as the composite branch composed of Albanian and Indo-Iranian, which has a probability of only 0.36. This composite tree, furthermore, clearly favours a time for Indo-European expansion which is compatible with Renfrew's farming-spread hypothesis and a homeland in Anatolia, rather than with Gimbutas's Kurgan hypothesis. Their date for the initial split of Hittite from the Indo-European lineage is around 8,700 years BP. On the other hand, 'The consensus tree also shows evidence of a period of rapid divergence giving rise to the Italic, Celtic, Balto-Slavic and perhaps Indo-Iranian families that is intriguingly close to the time suggested for a possible Kurgan expansion' (ibid. 438), perhaps holding out some hope of a rapprochement between these two homeland hypotheses. It should be noted, however, that although Gray and Atkinson provide a date for the overall family tree for Indo-European, their analysis in fact generates a wide range of possible dates, which include the figure of 8,700 years BP, but by no means only that date. True, their range on the face of it excludes the dates usually associated with the Kurgan hypothesis; but they cannot accurately date splits within the IE tree.

Gray and Atkinson, then, have used a substantial and essentially reliable database for a well-studied family, and have exercised extreme care in their use of these data. They have assessed potential problems for their phylogenetic approaches, and have wherever possible sought to check for their effects. For example, recognizing that errors in cognacy judgements (which are, after all, judgements even where based on extremely carefully collected and analysed data) may contribute to errors in dating, they have rerun their analysis excluding all cognate sets marked by Dyen, Kruskal, and Black (1992) as 'dubious'. If phylogenetic approaches to dating are to be adopted, they should follow this kind of pattern, working with linguists' existing analyses and seeking to incorporate methodological checks, and introducing computational approaches to sharpen our view and improve the reach of our methods. Surely this is better than overriding existing linguistic approaches and substituting methods which are quite likely to be poorer and more error-prone than those they seek to replace. However, although some approaches to dating may be better than others, we are not recommending acceptance or use of any of them, certainly not at this point; the reasons for this reticence are spelled out in the next section.

7. 4 General Problems for Dating

The key problem with approaches to dating linguistic 'events' is that even careful and judicious analyses of the sort seen in Gray and Atkinson (2003) are prone to essential and underlying difficulties, such that the results obtained there for Indo-European, for instance, cannot appropriately or confidently be generalized to other families. Crucially, we cannot assume independence in the rate and direction of change from language to language or from period to period; and yet we *must* make those assumptions to allow generalizable dating procedures to be developed. In contact languages, like pidgins, creoles, mixed languages, perhaps dying languages, and languages in convergence areas, these assumptions are arguably invalid all the way along the line.

To test the significance of these effects we return to the data from south-east Western Australian languages analysed and published by David Nash (2002), and considered as an illustration of network-based methods in the last chapter. Recall that the interrelationships of these languages are poorly understood, although the effects of contact and convergence in Australia are well known. Furthermore, available data are extremely restricted, consisting typically of an incomplete, modified Swadesh list, collected in most cases from a single speaker. Limited, unanalysed data of this kind arguably represent a worst-case test for phylogenetic methods, though they are certainly not atypical, and might in fact represent the norm—in terms of available data and prior, comparative-method analysis of cognacy—to a greater extent than does the exceptionally well-analysed Indo-European.

The resulting Splitstree diagram for these Australian data, shown in Figure 7.2, can be compared with the much more strongly tree-like picture for our Indo-European data shown in Figure 7.1 above.

If all the Australian data are included, contact-induced similarities dominate any discernible tree-like pattern, so that in Figure 7.2, 20 of the 26 languages are collapsed as a single node. Since Splitstree is a network-based phylogenetic method, it can at least in principle accommodate contact phenomena as well as indicators of common ancestry. If the order of splitting cannot be determined using a relatively sensitive phylogenetic method of this kind, there is clearly no prospect at all of generating reasonable dates, or indeed any dates at all, for the divergence of these sister systems.

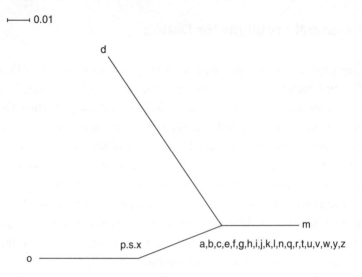

Fig. 7.2 Australian data from Nash (2002) analysed using Splitstree (Huson 1998) (for key see Nash 2002, table 1)

There are two possible ways of generating a marginally more tree-like diagram. If we include only a subset of languages, rejecting any list with fewer than 70 items, and including only one list from each region to minimize the effects of contact between adjacent languages and groups, some phylogenetic signals do emerge. However, as we have already seen, the effects of borrowing between closely related languages and dialects can contribute to more accurate dating for relatively recent splits; and since we do not know how recent these splits were, we might be excluding the most useful data. Alternatively (or additionally), we can change the method we use, favouring a more sensitive network-based approach like NeighbourNet (Bryant and Moulton 2004). As we argued in the previous chapter, NeighbourNet seems to operate at a resolution well suited to complex linguistic data sets, while Splitstree is more prone to becoming confused in these circumstances, leading to prioritization of any signal of tree-ness at the expense of other connections, or indeed to the total collapse of structure observed in Figure 7.2. NeighbourNet provides a marginally more tree-like structure, shown in Figure 7.3, but with very considerable reticulations, reflecting the existence of many different and incompatible signals of similarity, and in turn again suggesting that contact has been a very major factor in producing these linguistic links.

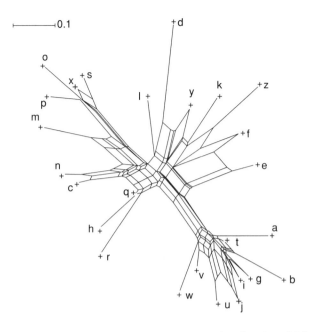

Fig. 7.3 Australian data from Nash (2002) analysed using NeighbourNet
(Bryant and Moulton 2004) (for key see Nash 2002, table 1)

On this basis we might simply decide that excluding particularly contact-prone languages is the right way forward. However, even if we could
exclude such languages from consideration (and diagnosis of contact, as
we have seen, is not always straightforward), we would find that most if
not all languages go through periods in their histories where they are
under particular influence from a particular source. This equally invalidates any assumption of constancy in rate, albeit locally, for those languages, rather than globally. And rate-smoothing and penalization of
variation on the Gray and Atkinson (2003) pattern relies on a knowledge
of external history for calibration which is not always available—not to
mention a quantitative grasp of the extent of variation, from period to
period and family to family, which we currently do not have and may
never achieve. Even if we succeeded in calculating the total, global,
possible range of variation in rate, integrating a factor of this magnitude
into our calculations without any clear understanding of how it might
apply to a given group or time period would undoubtedly vastly increase
our errors, making calculated dates laughably imprecise.

On the contrary, it seems that the success of any phylogenetic model in determining historical relatedness between languages and the timing of cultural events will depend critically on the balance between convergence and divergence; and even limited lexical borrowing can have a discernible and problematic influence, at least on the dating part of the equation. This makes the phylogenetics of language change, based for example on word-list data, comparable with phenotypic rather than molecular genetic evolution, because just as with phenotypic change there is selection pressure at work. Moreover, this selection pressure (and of course this need not mean conscious, deliberate decisions), which drives the fixation of initially random variation in lexical usage, will vary across speaker groups and across time, and depends partly on extralinguistic factors such as population contact and prestige. Again, we find here a challenge to assumptions of independence in the data, since at different periods there will, for example, be particular concentrations of loans in given semantic domains: thus, we find numerous religious borrowings from Greek and Latin into Old English. We might be able to estimate the time depth involved *post hoc* in such well-characterized cases, but this cannot be assumed in situations where the contact relationships are not fully understood. As we have shown in the simulation work reported in Chapters 4 and 6, even low levels of linguistic interchange can seriously disrupt trees, and therefore also any dates derived from these.

In short, then, dating in cases like the Australian one cannot conceivably succeed. Where contact-induced change has been sufficiently extensive, it will outweigh any signal of common ancestry, so that branching will be minimal or non-existent. Where there are no branching points to date, we cannot date them. Although NeighbourNet did provide a minimally tree-like signal for the Australian data, it must be remembered that it produces, by its distance-based nature, phenograms rather than phylograms. In other words, the graph gives an indication of relative similarity between systems, but assigning a historical interpretation in terms of contact or common ancestry is a separate stage of the enterprise. Yet even in cases where contact is known to have been less disruptive, dating divergence between languages will be inherently problematic. Culture, prestige, social influence, and chance will affect the direction but also the speed of change. There is also much more we can learn from phylogenetic methods and computer simulations before we begin the contentious secondary enterprise of dating. If we insist on attempting to estimate dates now, we can do so only for the few sufficiently well-researched cases where borrowing can be analysed out, and even here, as shown in the Indo-European cases, we will find error and unclarity. Incidentally, we will also require a restriction to a very specific set of data, including the most conservative and least borrowable meanings, though we have argued already that using a more extensive and variable data set can be more illuminating in establishing both families and contact patterns: choosing the optimal data set for dating therefore means restricting our chances of reaching interesting conclusions in other domains.

This does not, of course, mean relative chronologies can never be established: we do not need dates to say (indeed, to know) that in English, Breaking preceded the Great Vowel Shift, or that Old Irish existed earlier than Modern Irish. The order of events is not the same as their timing, and we can establish one without being able to say anything convincing about the other. As McMahon and McMahon (forthcoming *a*) point out, there is a relevant analogy here in informal human family trees, where we might be able to establish the relationships between individuals, but not necessarily to date earlier lives in the tree, without parish records or notes in family Bibles. We can reach approximate dates for previous generations because we know a good deal about human generation intervals, which also change in different geographical areas and periods, though this can only be approximate, and might for individual cases be quite wrong. For language, however, we know neither the average 'generation interval', if there is one, nor the range of variation we might expect to find; we cannot therefore generalize across families or across tree topographies.

Nor, at least in our opinion, does our view that dating is inadvisable and unproductive at this stage make us simply Luddites. One possible reaction to our call for attempts at dating to stop, at the very least temporarily, is that this is not a scientific approach to a problem. We are often directed to consider the history of carbon-14 dating in archaeology, which many archaeologists liken, in its early phases, to glottochronology now. The method did not always go right at first, and its practitioners did not always know why, but the most important thing was to continue trying until those problem parameters were worked out, and the method could be refined. The argument from this is that we should take the same approach for dating in linguistics, and keep trying until we have achieved an equally generalizable and robust model.

There are several crucial differences which make this hopeful outcome, in our view, utopian. Whereas for carbon-14 dating the initially erroneous results were derived from assumptions which were known to be measurably true, the assumptions underlying glottochronological dating are known to be false. In the case of carbon-14 dating, the factors disrupting the early attempts were not necessarily known, but could be identified and corrected through reanalysis and checking. In the case of glottochronology, we know the problematic factors responsible for the errors only too well: the difficulty is that they are contingent and situation-specific, so that we cannot correct for them in any generalizable way. Good science does result from the refinement of initially problematic results, but not from the persistent use of a method which is fundamentally flawed.

Until we have more and better data, more extensive and structured cross-linguistic databases available for quantitative study, more sophisticated models and simulations, and hence a clearer idea of the signals we can expect under particular social and linguistic circumstances, we believe that we cannot hope to provide accurate and generalizable dates. Persisting with attempts at dating under present circumstances threatens, in our view, to repeat the catastrophic history which equated lexicostatistics with glottochronology, leading to more than thirty years spent trying to disentangle the confusion between the two and rehabilitate and improve lexicostatistics. The last thing the emerging discipline of quantitative historical linguistics needs is to alienate our colleagues in more traditional historical linguistics by cheerfully repeating the errors of glottochronology, allowing legitimate methods to be tarred with the same brush as illegitimate ones, and encouraging the rejection of both. Instead, we can call a halt to attempts at dating now, until we have established what we can and cannot validly do with our phylogenetic methods, under assumptions which are reasonable for language rather than for any other, ostensibly similar, system. We can concentrate on getting the quality of the data as right as we can, and on formulating methods which help us discern and interpret different patterns. Jumping ahead to temporal interpretation of patterns we only half perceive is at best premature, and at worst threatens the whole enterprise.

8

Quantitative Methods Beyond the Lexicon

8. 1 Today the Lexicon, Tomorrow...

Our focus in this book so far has stayed rather firmly fixed on the lexicon, and on methods of comparison which apply to vocabulary or, more accurately, to cognacy judgements calculated over basic meaning lists. There are two reasons for this. First, lists of this kind are already well known in comparative linguistics, and we have been keen to demonstrate that it is possible to apply quantitative methods to familiar data: this is simply another case of starting from the known and moving subsequently into the unknown. Linked with this is the fact that methods for comparing meanings already exist, and are therefore available for testing and computerizing; but this is not the case, certainly not to the same extent, for other areas of the grammar. Working in areas other than the lexicon therefore means both developing methods for comparison and demonstrating that these can be quantified to good effect, and it did not seem to us a useful start to ask our readers to accept both simultaneously.

However, we have now shown that meaning-based comparison and quantification, allied with novel tree and network representations for visualizing their results, can work together to provide confirmation of known results. They can also allow us to reach testable hypotheses in cases where the picture is considerably hazier, as we saw for the Andean languages, although here there was also an element of novelty in the methods of comparison we employed. It now seems fitting, as the final step in our investigation, to assess the prospects for comparison beyond the lexicon. This is not just a question of completeness—languages, after all, are not the same as dictionaries—but also follows from questions raised earlier in the book about the inherent suitability of lexical or meaning-based data for comparative purposes. As we saw in Chapter 3, Ringe, Warnow, and Taylor (2002) have argued that phonological and morphosyntactic characters provide better coherence with accepted lineages than lexical ones; and if there is a chance that non-lexical data might provide a higher resolution, or more reliable results, then it would be completely improper not to investigate them. This time the tree and network diagrams and programs we use will be familiar from the previous chapters; but we face questions over the data to be collected, the techniques to be employed in quantification and comparison, and the interpretation of the results we find.

In this chapter we shall be concentrating in particular on comparison in the phonetics, and will have virtually nothing to say about morphosyntactic comparison. This is not intended as a prejudging of the issues, or an assumption that phonetic rather than morphosyntactic data will in the end prove optimal for comparison. It is partly an accident of expertise, and partly follows from our particular interest, as discussed in Section 8.5 below, in dialect comparison. While dialects may often have diverged too little in either lexicon or grammar to allow finely graded comparisons to be achieved, phonetic differences are frequently clear and salient, so that from this perspective phonetic comparison is an obvious and potentially highly productive route to follow.

Meanwhile, activity is certainly starting in the area of morphosyntactic comparison. Heggarty (forthcoming) presents an outline database and methodology for comparison of typologically different languages; this involves weighting and quantification of similarities and differences in marking a core sub-part of morphosyntax, notably including basic grammatical roles and relations, number, biological gender and lexical classes, animacy, humanness, and definiteness. Perhaps the best-known initial exploration of morphosyntactic comparison is Nichols (1992), which develops a typologically based proposal that certain grammatical features are particularly resistant to change and therefore signal family affiliation more effectively than other possible lexical or structural features. Nichols argues that this set of conservative features includes head marking versus dependent marking; dominant alignment; position on the cline from polysynthetic to isolating; and possession of an inclusive/exclusive distinction. These features tend to be deeply integrated into the grammar, and are the basis of language typologies; and Nichols argues that they can also be seen as markers of deep and otherwise potentially unrecoverable genetic relationships.

However, we find here a difficulty we have already encountered with Swadesh lists, in that even features or meanings or grammatical characteristics that change slowly and reluctantly, and that are relatively resistant to borrowing, will inevitably change and be borrowed sometimes. And, sure enough, Mithun (2004) has recently argued that features like those picked out by Johanna Nichols may help define linguistic areas; clearly, it is hard to reconcile this with their alleged genetic stability. One factor which might initially seem to weigh in favour of Nichols's proposed conservative features is that they are clearly rather abstract, and can be realized in different languages in radically different ways; this distinguishes them from the rather more concrete and necessarily more restricted characters included in Ringe, Warnow, and Taylor (2002). In other words, two languages may have an inclusive/exclusive distinction, but may mark it with etymologically totally independent affixes, or indeed one may not use affixes at all. In the cases reported by Mithun, direct material borrowing therefore cannot be invoked, because although we find parallel structures, we do not find borrowing of the substance that carries the structure. Nonetheless, Mithun (2004) has argued that in the Central Northwest Coast of the USA we find sharing, among genetically unrelated languages and groups, of features including core argument categories; morphological complexity; and head or dependent marking. She suggests that these shared features show the scope bilinguals may have for borrowing large, complex structures, including stylistic options, from one of their languages into another. Idioms, expressive stylistic devices, and rhetorical choices may be adopted, become more frequent, and then set the scene for subsequent structural changes in the borrowing language; something similar seems to lie behind Ross's concept of metatypy (2001) whereby speakers may borrow semantic structure and ways of expressing ideas before syntax.

To assess these claims and counterclaims fully, of course, we crucially need as much data as possible from a very wide range of languages, ideally covering many different families, geographical areas, and types. No matter how suitable certain characteristics might be for comparison in theoretical terms, they cannot be tested fully in the absence of appropriate data; and there is a crying need, if work in this area is to progress, for appropriately structured, wide-ranging databases to be constructed.

Clearly, this brings its own questions, most pressingly on the choice of features and languages to be included; and these are not wholly independent either, since it may not be obvious that a particular feature should be included unless we know in advance about the particular set of languages which manifest it. The good news is that these questions are being confronted, for example in the *World Atlas of Linguistic Structure* under development at the Max Planck Institute for Evolutionary Anthropology in Leipzig. The not-so-good news, perhaps inevitably, is that constructing a database of this kind is a Herculean task, so that the preliminary structure that exists so far is still very lightly populated with data, especially from some regions of the world. The work is beginning, then, and is both promising and much needed, but is still at too early a stage of development for us to comment on it more fully here.

8. 2 Key Questions for Phonetic Comparison

The discussion so far might suggest that measuring similarity in sounds is obviously much more straightforward than measuring similarity in morphosyntax; but, in fact, exactly the same questions of what we measure and how we measure it have to be addressed here, though the answers may have to be somewhat different. It is true that we are quite used, in phonetics and phonology, to discussing the notion of phonetic similarity; but phonologists and phoneticians discuss phonetic similarity so much precisely because it is so problematic. Take, for instance, one of the best-known conundrums in elementary English phonology, and a mainstay of beginners' classes in phoneme theory—namely the fact that, based on distribution alone, [h] and [ŋ] could be allophones of the same phoneme, since [h] is restricted to onsets, while [ŋ] is found only in codas. Of course, this purely technical argument bears no relation at all to speakers' intuitions, and we can justify maintaining /h/ and /ŋ/ as separate phonemes on the basis that they are so phonetically dissimilar: one is oral and the other nasal, one a fricative and the other a stop, one voiceless and the other voiced, and so on. True, both are pulmonic egressive consonants; but that is a pretty big natural class.

However, this apparently neat and conclusive argument brings us to the core of the difficulty with phonetic similarity. If these two sounds are not similar enough to count as allophones of a single phoneme, how similar do allophones have to be, and how do we measure degrees of similarity anyway? If we are allowed two or three features' difference, but find this rules out cases where there are other grounds for arguing that two sounds really do belong to the same phoneme, we might suggest that there is something wrong with the feature system; or that certain features have a close relationship elsewhere in the phonology and therefore some-how count as one. Lass (1984: 19), in a characteristically forthright assessment, notes that 'This is a tricky criterion; but we can accept it as intuitively plausible, and in practice workable, even if not formally defin-able.' We have met this kind of reliance on intuition before in work on language comparison and classification; but we have also argued else-where in this book that we urgently need to be able to formalize those intuitions; and this is true for phonetics just as for meaning lists and vocabulary.

In order to measure similarity in phonetics we have to address two key problems, which Heggarty, McMahon, and McMahon (forthcoming) refer to as the compatibility problem and the quantification problem respectively. First, we have to sort out parameters which are cross-lin-guistically viable, so that we can analyse and accommodate the differ-ences between individual languages within a single, unified model, and allow them to be compared against each other in a way that ensures we are comparing like with like. Second, we have to be able to measure these differences and fit them into a numerical system which we can then test against known relationships and potentially also against speakers' intu-itions on degrees of relatedness. It is certainly well worth attempting to establish appropriate, compatible and quantifiable features in phonetics, since a successful method of phonetic comparison would provide much finer-grained comparisons than an ostensibly similar volume of lexical data. We can see this simply by comparing the amount of data a conven-tional, 200-meaning Swadesh list would provide for a lexical-as opposed to a phonetic-comparison method. For each meaning slot in a binary comparison of language A with language B we can reach only an assess-ment that the words carrying this meaning are cognate between A and B, giving a score of 1 (or 100%), or that they are not, giving 0. There are no intermediate scores. True, there is an element of caricature here, since the all-or-nothingness of traditional lexicostatistics is somewhat diluted by the use of a list containing multiple items, providing an overall score which is between 100% and 0%. True, also, we saw in the previous chapter that Heggarty (forthcoming) has proposed certain developments of lexical comparison which permit a more nuanced approach, with potential cognates graded for plausibility. Nonetheless, when we consider the possibility of phonetic comparison of whole words as well as individual segments it immediately becomes apparent that however sophisticated our lexical comparisons might be, comparing phonetics should allow us to exploit many more data points for each entry in a meaning list.

Solving the compatibility and quantification problems appropriately will determine how good these comparisons are. In the next two sections we will outline two possible ways of solving these problems, and therefore of measuring phonetic similarity. The two methods have been developed independently and in parallel, the first within work on dialect comparison and the second primarily in historical and comparative linguistics, though, as we shall see, it also allows development into dialect comparison. For further information on other existing and possible approaches to phonetic comparison, and for general discussion, see Kessler (forthcoming).

8. 3 Nerbonne and Heeringa's Approach to Phonetic Similarity

Dialectometry, or the development of methods for measuring similarity among dialects, was pioneered by Goebl (1982, 1984), though his work has primarily involved lexical comparison. An extension of these quantitative, computational approaches to the phonetics was first proposed by Kessler (1995), working on dialects of Irish, and has subsequently been taken up and developed most intensively by John Nerbonne, Wilbert Heeringa, and their co-workers (see Nerbonne and Heeringa 1997, 2001; Nerbonne, Heeringa, and Kleiwig 1999; Heeringa, Nerbonne, and Kleiwig 2002; Nerbonne and Kretzschmar in press), primarily for dialects of Dutch.

It is easier to introduce Nerbonne et al.'s methods by beginning with the quantification problem. Nerbonne, Heeringa, et al. here calculate 'Levenshtein distances' (Levenshtein 1965; Sankoff and Kruskal 1983; Navarro and Raffinot 2002), also known as edit distances. These involve a range of algorithms, developed outside linguistics, which measure the distance between the elements in strings. One string will be converted into another by insertions, deletions, and substitutions, and the fewest operations necessary are counted to provide the edit distance between two strings. Edit distance, then, is the minimum number of operations required to get from one string to the other. Strings can, of course, be found in many domains, and early applications of Levenshtein distances were outside phonetics, for example in calculating differences between DNA sequences; aligning texts; and measuring and correcting errors in keyboard input.

Algorithms of this kind have the virtue of computational simplicity, but can produce results strikingly at odds with historical-linguistic developments and intuitive notions of linguistic similarity. In their earlier work Nerbonne et al. calculated edit distance in the simplest possible way, meaning that 'the pair [a,t] count as different to the same degree as [a, ɔ]' (Nerbonne and Heeringa 1997: 1). While on one level it is true that a single operation of substitution is involved here, and therefore that the edit distances for both strings are the same, it is not at all true that a linguistic substitution of [t] for [a] (put differently, a change of [a] to [t]) is as likely or natural as a substitution of [ɔ] for [a]. Sound changes far more commonly involve differences in phonetic quality than complete insertions or deletions of segments, or changes of linear order like metathesis. A framework of phonetic comparison based on edit distances is therefore based on change types which are relatively rare, and lumps together many quite different and differently motivated changes of quality: a minor degree of vowel raising would count as the same as an assimilation changing [m] to [n] or [b]. Arguably even worse, Nerbonne et al. count a substitution, or a segmental replacement (of either [t] or [ɔ] for [a]), as a sequence of one deletion and one insertion, and therefore assign changes like assimilations a cost of two, double the cost of the more unusual complete segment insertion or deletion.

In more recent work Nerbonne et al. do move towards a more nuanced quantitative technique: Nerbonne and Kretschmar (2003: 4) recognize explicitly that 'linguistic variation is gradual', while Nerbonne, Heeringa, and Kleiwig (1999: ix) accept that 'Replacement costs . . . vary depending on the basic sounds involved' (though unfortunately they do not illustrate these different replacement costs, opting to use distances which are 'simplified . . . for clarity' (ibid.)). It would appear that measures of feature overlap are being used in these more detailed calculations, but since the features referred to are different in different papers, some being binary and others scalar, it is difficult to replicate these calculations. We are told (ibid.) that the differences between the segments [i] versus [e], and [i] versus [u] are no longer rated as equal but as 1 and 5 respectively, but it is not clear how these figures are derived. There is an accompanying table showing that [i] and [e] are rated as 2 for advancement, and [u] as 6; while [i] and [u] are rated as 4 for high, with [e] as 3. Why, though, should the difference between a front and a back vowel be 4, while the difference between a high and high–mid vowel is 1? If these figures are intended to be universally applicable, they suggest that the average, or perhaps maximal, number of height contrasts should be 4, which seems about right, but that the average, or perhaps maximal, number of contrasts in frontness/backness should be 6, which is staggeringly high. The incorporation of features and gradience into the edit-distance measurements is therefore to be welcomed as potentially adding phonetic detail and contributing to a more nuanced quantification; but to understand and assess this fully the features used need to be spelled out fully and justified as part of a universally applicable model, where the numerical codes assigned are principled and recurrent.

   How, then, do Nerbonne et al. deal with the compatibility problem? This question has already been answered in part, albeit implicitly, since calculation of edit distances necessarily involves segment-by-segment matching through the strings under comparison. This might not be such a significant problem for comparisons between dialects, but would almost certainly compromise the method if it were extended to comparisons between languages or across considerable spans of time, since it would then be more likely that changes in the order of segments would have taken place. The most obvious of these would be metathesis, where two segments change places, as in Middle English *bridde, friste*, which become Modern English *bird, first*. However, elisions of vowels, changes of consonants to glides and subsequently to the second elements of diphthongs, lengthenings and shortenings of segments, and introductions of new segments will all create difficulties for straightforward, linear segment-matching algorithms. Initially, it might seem that the effect of such changes on Nerbonne et al's model would be relatively minor, since comparing the 'wrong' pair of segments etymologically can only give a score of 1 or 2, and even a minor change of quality, as we have seen, would in their earlier work be scored as a difference of 2 in any case. However, this will be much more problematic for any more sensitive, feature-based instantiation of their approach. Paradoxically, the more complex and gradient version of edit-distance calculations is likely to be compromised much more seriously by segment mismatches than the coarser-grained one.

The compatibility problem also includes one further issue: we have considered how the segments within two strings might be matched up, but how do Nerbonne et al. select the strings to compare in the first place? This does not seem to be discussed at any length in their work to date, perhaps suggesting that Nerbonne et al. see it as a non-issue, since they are working mainly with dialect data and, in the normal case, lexical divergence between dialects will take place mainly by partial shifts in sounds or meanings, rather than complete replacement with a non-cognate lexical item. Nonetheless, differences of historical source, contact patterns, or sociolinguistic preferences may indeed lead to dialect variation (think of Scots *beagie* as against English *turnip*, for example). It is not entirely clear what Nerbonne et al. do in cases where their strings are not true cognates.

Finally, any new method requires testing and validation, and Nerbonne et al. propose to calibrate their results by comparing the tree diagram produced from their distance matrices with a dialect map reflecting the opinions of 'expert dialectologists' (Nerbonne and Heeringa 1997: 15). These dialect maps were also, however, based in part on speakers' own judgements of the distance between varieties, introducing elements of perceptual dialectology. This is an intriguing application of perceptual findings, but since work in this area is also at a relatively early stage and is still to a great extent uncorroborated, using it to test a second developing method cannot be conclusive.

Nerbonne et al., then, are approaching phonetic dialect comparison from the perspective of segment matching within pairs of cognates. Their methodology relies on the calculation of edit distances, and this has the virtue of extreme computational simplicity, though at the expense of resolution and linguistic detail. The features used by Nerbonne and his colleagues are more phonological than phonetic, and the particular values used do not always seem to be derived in a principled way; moreover, their adoption of whole-word averaging of segmental differences means the same phonetic difference may end up counting for more or less in one comparison than in another. In terms of compatibility, linear matching of segments will be problematic in cases where segmental order has changed historically, and the process of validation against dialect maps derived in part from speaker intuitions can be only a starting point. This may be a helpful beginning, though whether it will generalize usefully from its original domain of dialect comparison to the language level remains to be tested.

8. 4 Heggarty (forthcoming); Heggarty, McMahon, and McMahon (forthcoming)

We turn now to a rather different approach to phonetic similarity. Both these methods are under development and investigation; neither is proven, and both require further testing and assessment. But the second method contrasts usefully with the first. Whereas the edit-distance approach is extremely simple, Heggarty's method requires rather complex assessment of phonetic features, which moreover are weighted. Whereas Nerbonne et al. are seeking to produce a classification of Dutch dialects, and therefore assess their results in terms of their match with consensus dialect maps, our approach has been to seek to quantify phonetic differences in as much detail as possible, and to consider both dialect and language differences. As we shall see, the results may not look like conventional, historical trees at all; but then a quantification of phonetic similarity may be interesting precisely because it does not map exactly on to a historical classification. Validation in our case, then, seeks to compare our results for phonetics with those for lexical meaning, and to assess whether the disparities we find correspond to real, explicable differences in patterning between phonetic and lexical change.

To understand Heggarty's method we must again turn to the central problems of quantification and compatibility. Here the approach to both is linked, and involves incorporating information we already know to be linguistically appropriate and meaningful. In the case of quantification, as we shall see, the method is built on our existing knowledge of articulatory features; and to ensure compatibility, segments in different languages or dialects are compared via a template corresponding to the common ancestral form for the lexical item in question.

In the case of quantification Heggarty proposes a system of essentially articulatory phonetic features, of the type familiar from IPA descriptions: a sound may be a voiceless alveolar fricative, or a high front unrounded short vowel, or a bilabial nasal stop, and we can use this information to compare and classify sounds—after all, that is what such descriptors are for in the first place. If we are comparing two consonants, we might isolate three initial parameters on which they might differ, namely location of stricture, degree of stricture, and voicing. If we take [t] and [d] as our sounds to be compared, we find that of course these do not differ for place or manner, since they are both alveolar stops, but that they have opposite values for voicing. If we then accepted that all these features were equally important, we would score the difference between [t] and [d] as one-third, or 33%.

However, Heggarty argues strongly that in quantifying phonetic difference, or similarity, we not only need to find something to measure, and then measure it; we also have to understand and incorporate in our calculations the fact that not all features or aspects of language structure are equal. In other words, Heggarty's approach crucially involves a weighted system of features. Nerbonne et al. do not consistently use weighting in their analyses, suggesting in one discussion that 'Weighting of features mostly improves the results' (Nerbonne and Heeringa 2001: 11) but elsewhere that 'Unweighted representations outperform representations to which weightings were added' (Nerbonne and Heeringa 1997: 13). Their notion of weighting is, however, specific to the dialect set under consideration, being based on information gain; Heggarty, on the contrary, proposes a universal system whereby features should be weighted on a universal basis.

Such weighting relies on a range of criteria. The first, and arguably the most straightforward, involves principles which follow from the organization of phonological systems. Taking our example of [t] versus [d], and the three features of location and degree of stricture and voicing which potentially distinguish them, we can see that cross-linguistically we commonly find only a two-way distinction for voicing, but at least three values for the two stricture features (these figures are supported by the UPSID database; see Maddieson 1984). That is, languages will usually have stops, fricatives, and approximants, and labials, alveolars, and velars (at least); but they will usually have only voiced and voiceless consonants. Clearly, this is a guiding principle, and we might find a language with six places of articulation, or an additional contrast involving creaky or breathy voice; but these are certainly in the minority, and, after all, guiding principles are what we are after if our system is to be universally applicable. Translated into numbers, all this means that

Heggarty grades a difference in either place or manner as more salient than a difference in voicing, assigning up to 2 nominal points for the most significant differences in location and degree of stricture and only 1 to voicing, so that [t] and [d] will be identical for 4 out of 5 possible points, and therefore count as 80% similar. Likewise, [d] and [g] will be the same for manner of articulation and for voicing, scoring 3, but will differ for place by 1 point, meaning they are also 80% similar; [b] and [g] are further apart for place, and therefore lose both place points, but are the same for manner and voicing, making them 60% similar; [b] and [s] are 1 apart for manner, 1 apart for place, and 1 apart for voice, and therefore only 40% similar; and likewise [b] and [ɣ] are 40% similar, though this time because they share voicing and lose 1 point for the difference in manner and both for place. Exactly the same process is followed in scoring vowel differences, and here again there are three core dimensions, namely height, back-ness, and lip-rounding. Cross-linguistically, there are generally more distinctions on the height dimension than on the other two, so we assume that there are 4–5 points of similarity for vowels. Simplifying somewhat, we can say that 3 come from the height dimension (scoring from high to high–mid to low–mid to low), and 1 from lip-rounding (rounded or not). For the backness dimension things are rather more complex, because (as is evident from the shape of the vowel quadrilateral, and phonemic uptake cross-linguistically of backness distinctions) there is more scope for phonetic difference in backness between high vowels than between low ones. Calculations are adjusted to reflect this phonetic reality, though in broad terms we can say that one point of difference on our vowel parameters also corresponds to losing 20% of similarity for a vowel comparison.

Of course, this is not the whole story (something much closer to it is set out in Heggarty forthcoming). There are more features, like nasality, differences in airstream mechanism, and lateral versus central, for instance, and all these have to be weighted internally and relative to the core parameters. Even within the core, there should ideally be a certain amount of weighting, to recognize the fact that, for example, the denti-alveolar region tends to support more potential distinctions than other areas of the vocal tract, at least for fricatives. In addition, there is an inherent limitation in the fact that the model is currently almost exclusively articulatory, while it is well known that auditory differences are also vitally important in segment distinctiveness. For vowel comparison in particular, but also to capture acoustic affinities of consonants like the well-known case of [f] and [x], for instance, the means of comparison clearly has to be developed further to incorporate non-articulatory information. Currently, comparisons between consonants do employ a certain number of ad hoc adjustments to recognize and take account in the calculations of known cases like [f] and [x], where acoustics and articulation mismatch sharply. Moreover, the vowel comparison is based around the cardinal vowel points, which in their initial formulation did already aspire to represent both articulatory and acoustically equal steps. In any case, this weighting does allow finer discrimination of sounds than any unweighted system, and this detail is achieved on the basis of universal, objective decisions on grading.

However, not all Heggarty's principles of weighting are derived from cross-linguistic patterning in sound systems: some are essentially logical, and are introduced where the relative significance of linguistic differences is clear but we might require some guidance on how to calculate the appropriate mathematical value. Thus, for instance, a stop like [k͡p] combines two articulations, and there are no linguistic arguments for seeing one element as more salient, or important, or higher-valued than the other. Heggarty would therefore assign the two elements within this doubly articulated sound a ratio of 1 : 1. On the other hand, in a stop with a secondary articulation like [pʲ] there are equally good reasons for prioritizing the primary articulation over the secondary palatalization. Where one element is more important than another, but there are no grounds for arguing for a more complex division, Heggarty's simplest-ratio principle would assign a ratio of 2 : 1. Although there is no space to develop the argument in detail here, Heggarty also applies the simplest-ratio principle to the problems of length and gemination, and to the appropriate quantification of the contribution each element makes to a diphthong or affricate.

It is all very well to be able to assign satisfactorily precise mathematical values to the differences between segments, but such comparisons are potentially jeopardized if we cannot be sure we are comparing the right segments in the first place. This brings us to the equally important compatibility problem. As we have already seen, changes like metathesis, coalescence, epenthesis, and segment loss, as well as the compensatory effects of some of these processes, can seriously disrupt a simple, segment-by-segment linear comparison. However, these problems are already familiar from the comparative method: there, they are resolved by comparing daughter languages with the hypothesized common ancestral form, to assess what segmental reorderings, insertions, and deletions might have taken place. It is possible to apply this kind of knowledge here, too. Just as Heggarty proposed to resolve the quantification problem by building on our existing knowledge of phonetic features, so he ensures compatibility by comparing daughter language or dialect forms through a template consisting of the appropriate proto-form.

That little preposition 'through', however, carries quite a lot of weight in the last sentence. It is absolutely vital that the forms under comparison are not compared **to** the common ancestral form; they are compared to one another, but **through** that common ancestor, which is included purely to ensure accurate segment matching. So, if we were comparing two daughter-language forms, both of which had lost a final consonant which we hypothesize on other grounds for the common ancestor, the daughter forms would be scored as identical in this respect, since both lack the final consonant; they would not be penalized in any sense for losing an element which is there in the node form. To take a slightly more complex case, if we were comparing two varieties of English, one of which had [hamstə] for *hamster* while the other had [hampstə] with an epenthetic [p], a linear analysis would be fine up to the fourth segment, but would then compare [s] with [p], [t] with [s], schwa with [t], and nothing with schwa, concluding that there is strikingly little resemblance between these words in their second halves, regardless of the identity we find at the beginning. We can avoid this by matching through the ancestral form, which here will correspond to the form without the epenthetic [p]. In this case, that will allow [m] to be compared with [m], [s] with [s], and the additional [p] with both [m] and [s], capturing the fact that it shares features with both. It is clear from this illustration that matching is also not fully segmental, but rather featural or gestural, with parts of segments in one language potentially corresponding to whole segments in another. We would find a similar pattern if one daughter had factored out a nasal vowel from the ancestral form, for example, into a sequence of oral vowel plus nasal consonant. Note that, because the common ancestral form provides only a node, or pivot, to allow accurate slot matching, the phonetic details of the ancestral segments are neither necessary nor particularly important: we do not have to have a perfect reconstruction, if such a thing were possible, for this kind of comparison to take place, but only an idea of vowel and consonant order, and major gestures like nasals. Arguments about the phonetic accuracy versus phonological abstractness of reconstructed forms therefore represent no obstacle to work of this kind; though, as Heggarty notes, in cases where we do have a reasonable grasp of the likely characteristics of the ancestor, as with Latin or Old English, for example, we can also enter those forms in the database in their own right, as an additional language for comparison which happens to have forms identical with those in the node representations. Finally, comparison through these node forms also allows Heggarty to compare whole words rather than just pairs of segments; the latter would obviously be at odds in any case with a method which is intended to move beyond the segment in comparing gestures and features.

Since there is space here for only an outline of the method, we do not propose to develop the details further, but turn to the question of validation, as we did for Nerbonne and Heeringa's method earlier. Some results from a very small corpus, namely the numerals 'one' to 'ten' for a selection of Romance varieties and languages, are given in Table 8.1.

One possible application of this kind of comparison technique, again not developed in detail here, is shown in Table 8.2 for a larger set of 100 Romance cognates: Heggarty's phonetic similarity program, which automatically carries out the steps outlined above over transcriptions entered into an Access database, can also generate phonological statistics relating to the overall structural characteristics of the languages being compared.

From Table 8.2 we can see, for instance, that French on average has the shortest words from this sample of Romance languages, while Italian has fewest consonants for each vowel; meanwhile, Italian has the most complex onsets but no codas, while French and Catalan have the most complex codas, and are also rather high in onset complexity. In a sense, this is not telling us anything we did not already know, or could not calculate by hand; but it is putting figures on our intuitions, and providing a quantitative confirmation of the fact that certain languages and varieties simply sound more similar. These comparative statistics are also a by-product of more complex comparative work, and could not be calculated so readily without the program and the design which lies behind it.

Table 8.1 Phonetic similarity of cognates of the numerals 'one' to 'ten' in a selection of Romance varieties (100 = identity)

	Italian	Spanish: Madrid	Spanish: Bogotá	Spanish: Venezuela	Portuguese: Lisbon	Portuguese: Rio	Portuguese: Salvador	Portuguese: São Paulo	French: Paris	French: Southern	Romanian	
Lat.	*59*	*54*	*54*	*52*	*49*	*48*	*50*	*52*	*40*	*40*	*54*	Classical Latin
	It.	68	69	66	57	61	60	60	43	43	61	Italian
		SpM.	**98**	**94**	66	69	70	69	47	47	54	Spanish: Madrid
			SpB.	**94**	66	69	70	69	47	47	54	Spanish: Bogotá
				SpV.	62	67	66	66	45	45	54	Spanish: Venezuela
					Pt.L	**89**	**88**	**94**	56	56	53	Portuguese: Lisbon
						Pt.R	**93**	**91**	54	54	53	Portuguese: Rio
							Pt.S.	**91**	54	54	54	Portuguese: Salvador
								Pt.SP.	54	54	55	Portuguese: São Paulo
									FrP.	**93**	45	French: Paris
										FrS.	45	French: Southern
											Rom.	Romanian

Note: In Table 8.1 Latin is entered as a variety in its own right, and figures involving comparisons with Latin are given in italics. Figures in bold indicate comparisons between dialects of the same language, which are typically over 80; scores for varieties of different languages range from 70 (Salvador Portuguese compared with Madrid Spanish or Bogotá) down to 40 for French and Latin, or, among present-day languages, the 43 for French and Italian.

However, these computational calculations also produce same initial surprises when we use them to produce a tree with PHYLIP (Felsenstein 2001). The tree in Figure 8.1 is the output of Fitch, based on the Romance data for the numerals 'one' to 'ten', and rooted using Latin.

On the face of it, the tree in Figure 8.1 has two immediately obvious problems. First, the two Iberian languages fail to appear together, and Portuguese instead clusters with French. Second, not all New World varieties of Spanish or of Portuguese cluster together either: the Spanish of Bogotá and the Portuguese of the interior of São Paolo State are closer to their European counterparts. This would, indeed, be a serious

Table 8.2 Sample phonological statistics from 100 Romance cognate sets (meanings used are listed in Heggarty, McMahon, and McMahon forthcoming)

Language Variety	Average word length (long segments weighted more)	Average number of syllables per word	Consonant to vowel ratio	Average onset complexity (in segments)	Average coda complexity (in segments)
Latin	5.89	2.26	1.31	0.97	0.88
Italian	5.08	2.17	1.06	0.96	0.00
Spanish Madrid	4.60	1.96	1.20	0.86	0.22
Spanish Venezuela	4.49	1.96	1.12	0.85	0.22
Portuguese Lisbon	4.03	1.92	1.28	0.89	0.15
Portuguese Brazil (Esperitu Santo)	4.27	1.92	1.08	0.91	0.08
Galician	4.51	1.95	1.16	0.90	0.21
Catalan	3.83	1.47	1.43	0.92	0.61
French	3.07	1.15	1.38	0.91	0.68
Romanian	4.30	1.68	1.41	1.00	0.55

challenge—if we expected phonetic comparisons necessarily to produce a historical, cladistic tree recapitulating the historical order of branching of these languages and varieties. We do naturally expect such a result when we are working with Swadesh lists—but remember that this is only because we know such lists are based on judgements of whether two items are likely to be descended from the same common ancestor or not; and this is obviously historically based information. In the case of phonetics we cannot have any such expectation, since sound changes of the same kind, affecting the same classes of segments, in similar contexts and indeed for the same reasons, are quite likely to happen in different languages and dialects by sheer chance. Homoplasy, or convergent development, is just more common in phonetics.

What this means is that different trees can tell different stories. Lexical data, at least when we are working with cognates, should produce a phylogram which incorporates cladistic, historical information. But it seems that phonetic comparison is much more likely to produce a phenogram, representing the degree of similarity between varieties in terms of

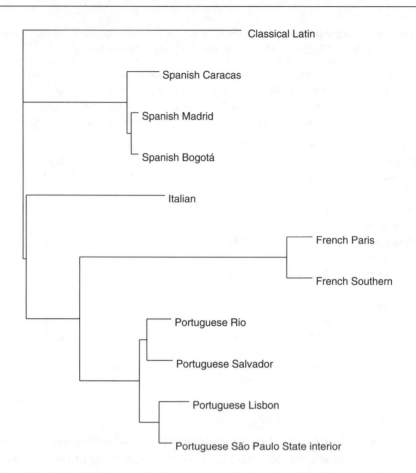

Fig. 8.1 Rooted Fitch tree for Romance varieties using the results for phonetic similarity for the numerals 'one' to 'ten' as shown in Table 8.1

phonetics, rather than showing the order of historical branching. Phonetic comparison gives phenetic trees. If this is so, we should anticipate that sometimes the two types of tree will not match. When that happens, we need to consider what the reasons might be, and if we cannot find any in the history or the synchronic structures of the languages concerned, then we have a problem indeed. In this case, Bogotá and Caracas Spanish, for instance, do share certain features that are taken as a common trait of Latin American Spanish, such as conflating as /s/ what in Madrid are still two distinct phonemes, /θ/ and /s/. But since the Latin American varieties split from their European sisters Colombian highland Spanish (Bogotá) has been highly conservative, remaining very similar to Madrid Spanish, while other Latin American varieties have undergone extensive phonetic change. Similarly, at the language level, the Fitch branch lengths in Figure 8.1 tell us that French is the language which has changed most extensively; but some of the changes it has experienced, like nasalization and devoicing or loss of certain final vowels, have also affected Portuguese, outweighing the 'Iberian' features common to Portuguese and Spanish. In turn, Spanish has undergone certain innovations, such as diphthongizations, which have not affected French or Portuguese.

If we can find good reasons for the discrepancies between phylograms based on lexical data and phenograms based on phonetic similarity, then we should not write off either. Instead, we should see them as informing us about distinct aspects of the structures and histories of languages, helping us to understand why languages or varieties which historical linguists assure us have much in common may today sound rather different. Prioritizing features which we **know** tell us about the histories of these systems might lead us to ignore other features which pull languages and varieties together today; conversely, highlighting those similarities may put the history in a different context. Some trees tell us about history, and others tell us about similarity. The truth may be neither pure nor simple; it seems not to be singular either.

Finally, Figure 8.2 shows a subset of the results for 100 Romance cognates displayed as a scatter plot using the statistics package SPSS, and comparing the change between Latin and Caracas Spanish on the one hand and Latin and Madrid Spanish on the other.

Forms in the top right-hand corner are identical to one another and to their Latin ancestor, while those in the bottom left-hand corner show most difference from Latin. If all words in the two Spanish varieties were now identical to one another, regardless of their distance from Latin, they would fall on a straight line; and deviations from this straight line in either direction show that the phonetic shape of the word in one variety is more different from Latin. Points below the line indicate a more conservative form in Madrid Spanish, or at least a form closer to the Latin one; conversely, points above the line show cases where Caracas Spanish is closer to Latin than Madrid Spanish is. If the rate of change in both varieties had been identical, then we would expect a roughly equal scatter of points above and below the line; in fact, there are more points below the line, indicating that Caracas Spanish has changed more than Madrid Spanish.

We can, then, derive some interesting results and patterns from our phonetic-similarity measures, again using a range of computer techniques

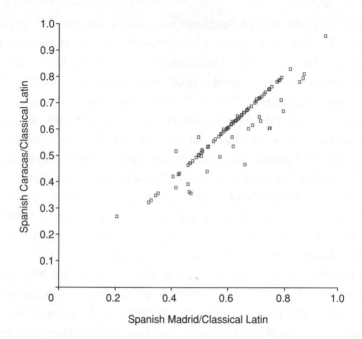

Fig. 8.2 Scatter plot of phonetic similarity between Latin and Caracas Spanish
plotted against the similarity between Latin and Madrid Spanish for the
100-cognate sample used in Table 8.2

to analyse and visualize the data. In addition, we can compare the trees we
obtain from phonetic comparison with those from lexical data: recognizing
that different data sets may give different results for perfectly respectable
reasons does not mean they cannot validly be compared, and indeed from
that comparison we may find explanations for the discrepancies. Again,
then, hunting for correlations can be productive, though we must bear in
mind that we will not always find them, and should not always expect to—
this was true for correlations between languages and genetics in populations, and it is true for lexical and phonetic change.

8. 5 Phonetic Similarity and Dialect Comparison
    for English

As we have seen already, Heggarty's method of phonetic comparison
produces some interesting initial results for Romance. It is, however,
intrinsically limited at present by the fact that the languages under

comparison must be demonstrably related, since the method absolutely requires the postulation of a node form composed of the common ancestral form, to resolve the compatibility problem and allow appropriate segment and gesture matching. In future work this requires the investigation of possible additional programming solutions, to assess whether the common ancestral node form can be replaced by a 'best-match' template intermediate between the transcriptions being compared. For the moment, however, there is one area of comparison where the limitation imposed by the requirement of relatedness is supremely irrelevant: this is the case of dialect comparison, since dialects of the same language are, of course, known to be related anyway.

If our phonetic method seems promising for dialect comparison and classification, this is exactly where lexical methods are least helpful. As Starostin (2000: 226–7) notes, 'Every comparativist who has worked with glottochronology knows that closely related dialects usually have a cognacy rate of 90% or more on Swadesh's 100-word list'. The window for lexical comparison is therefore not suitable for work on dialects, since they will all be too similar to allow appropriately graded assessments of relative similarity. However, dialects would therefore seem to be a promising testing ground for phonetic comparison; as we have seen, it is in the analysis of Dutch dialect differences that Nerbonne et al.'s method has been developed. We shall instead focus on varieties of English.

The current emphasis on variation in linguistics means it is scarcely necessary to justify a view that dialects are important for linguistics; and they are certainly important for historical linguistics, if we accept that variation may be the first step towards family-tree-type diversification. In fact, Kessler (1995: 60) goes so far as to claim that 'Defining dialects is one of the first tasks that linguists need to pursue when approaching a language.' However, he goes on to state the basic problem we face here: 'Unfortunately, dialect definition can be a time-consuming and ill-defined process.'

Certainly, if we could calculate the degree of similarity among dialects, we might be able to address a whole range of questions. First, we often hear (and use) terms like 'northern English'—but 'the North' is debatable land in more than one sense, as demonstrated by Wales (2002), and it is not clear at present how we might justify linguistically the inclusion or exclusion of a variety from the 'northern English' set. Second, and more abstractly, imagine we have two substantial dialect areas and a transitional variety: how would we work out whether the transitional dialect is really intermediate, or whether it might incline towards one or other of the areas it lies between? Finally, when we look at varieties which have been established relatively recently, like New Zealand English, or Englishes in the USA or Canada, for instance, how can we measure whether they still reflect the varieties from which they are descended? And how can we spot the particular features which are shared?

The most promising approach to these questions would involve adopting a dialectometrical approach: that is, quantifying the differences between dialects by measuring or counting features of some sort. For the lexicon at least, the problem we might encounter here, as illustrated in the Starostin quote above, is that classical lexicostatistics is a rather blunt, yes-or-no instrument which is unlikely to provide the fine resolution we need for differences below the language level. Even with a more nuanced approached to lexical analysis (Goebl 1982, 1984), the list we would require might be prohibitively large, since there would not be a great deal of movement in basic vocabulary over the timescale we might informally associate with dialect rather than language divergence. Alternatively, we could consider grammatical structures, but, at least in the case of English, these arguably show least differences between dialects, especially if we are comparing non-standard varieties with one another. In any case, as Miller (2003: 109) points out for Scots, there are many uninvestigated and underinvestigated areas of non-standard morphosyntax: 'There is a small army of questions; where is the small army of researchers?' Finally, we could consider perceptual dialectology as a method for grouping dialects. However, this is a technique still in its infancy, and again it would be begging the question—and maybe several questions—to assume the same results and classifications would follow from speakers' subjective judgments and from objective measurements. This comparison is an important target for the future—but we need the objective measurements first!

Our method for English dialect comparison is relatively rudimentary, and our results are therefore only preliminary. Because we are particularly keen that any method developed should work at both the dialect and language levels, we have included mainly English varieties, but also a small number of other Germanic languages. Consequently, when it comes to the compatibility problem and the selection of a node form through which to compare the different reflexes, we necessarily work with

Proto-Germanic, rather than a variety of Old English. Note that a form of present-day Standard English would not be appropriate for segment-matching purposes, even if we did restrict our comparisons to modern English varieties only, because it cannot be assumed that, say, Standard Southern British English represents anything like the ancestral form for other contemporary dialects. The obvious example would be post-vocalic /r/, which was clearly present in the ancestral form, and is still present in current rhotic varieties, but would be omitted from the node form if this were based on SSBE.

As for quantification, we used Heggarty's program (forthcoming) for phonetic comparison, but clearly this has to be applied to a set of equivalent forms. We asked a number of linguists, to whom we express particular thanks,[1] to transcribe 60 cognate words in 'their' varieties: where possible, the linguists we approached were also native speakers. To an extent, our choice of varieties, which are listed in (1), was driven by personal contacts and by the other demands on colleagues at a particular point in the academic year, and we recognize that there is nothing perfect about our sampling procedure. Clearly, fuller coverage of varieties would be a priority for the future.

(1)   Varieties of English and related Germanic languages used in initial phonetic comparisons:

Proto-Germanic	Standard Scottish English
Old Icelandic	Glasgow
Modern Icelandic	Buckie
German (*Hochdeutsch*)	Tyrone (traditional)
Old English (West Saxon)	Tyrone (standard)
General American	Standard Southern British English/RP
Australian (Victoria)	Middlesbrough
Sheffield	Tyneside (traditional)
Liverpool	Berwick
Wisbech	Derby

[1] We are most grateful to Gavan Breen, David Britain, Jayne Carroll, Karen Corrigan, Paul Foulkes, Patrick Honeybone, Mark Jones, Carmen Llamas, Warren Maguire, Kim Schulte, Jen Smith, Jane Stuart-Smith, and Dom Watt, who showed considerable patience and fortitude in the face of a complex and changing set of instructions for phonetic transcription. We appreciate not only their completed transcriptions, but, perhaps even more importantly for future work, their suggestions for changes and developments.

There are, of course, other potential pitfalls with this method. For instance, our 60 words, listed in (2), have to be cognates, because they are being matched through an ancestral node form, and there consequently has to be a plausible common ancestor. Earlier we noted that this restricts the applicability of the phonetic-comparison method to within families for the moment, pending the development of 'best-match' programming which would allow linear matching in strings through a best-compromise template form, rather than one based on a hypothesized common ancestor. This is not the problem, clearly, when it comes to the comparison of dialects and closely related languages, as here within Germanic, where no one's credulity is strained by the proposal of a common ancestral form. However, the requirement for cognates necessarily restricts the set of eligible forms, raising a question of whether our list is fully representative in terms of coverage of sounds and environments.

(2) 60 Germanic cognates for phonetic comparison

beech	give	new	sun
blood	good	night	ten
bloom	grass	nine	thou (you sing.)
brother	green	nose	three
daughter	hand	one	tongue
day	hold	salt	tooth
ear	horn	say	two
eight	hot	see	water
eye	hundred	seven	what
father	I	sing	wind
fire	knee	sister	wolf
five	moon	six	wool
foot	mother	snow	worm
four	mouse	son	year
full	name	star	young

There are also obvious issues of transcription practice. It is true that our instructions, issued in a hefty document to those intrepid colleagues volunteering (the verb here is sometimes passive rather than active) to take part in our pilot study, were fairly authoritarian, making it absolutely clear that we were looking for phonetic rather than phonemic transcription, and placing particular emphasis on issues like vowel length, for instance. Nonetheless, even the best instructions will leave some scope for variation, and some people naturally transcribe with more diacritics than others. In particular, there may be a tendency for transcriptions of standard varieties to be broader and closer to phonemic; and, conversely, sometimes transcribing non-standard varieties leads to a maximization of differences as transcribers understandably wish to mark those features they see as particularly diagnostic of 'their' variety. Including historical varieties, here West Saxon Old English, increases the chances that we are not comparing like with like when it comes to the relative breadth and detail of our transcriptions. Finally, Heggarty's method was initially calibrated on Romance languages and dialects, as shown in the previous section, so that certain improvements to sensitivity for Germanic (specially in the area of vowel differences) remain to be incorporated fully into the system.

Given these caveats, the results presented below must be seen as preliminary, but still provide some indication of how data of this kind can be used in dialect comparison. Figure 8.3 shows a Fitch tree for the varieties

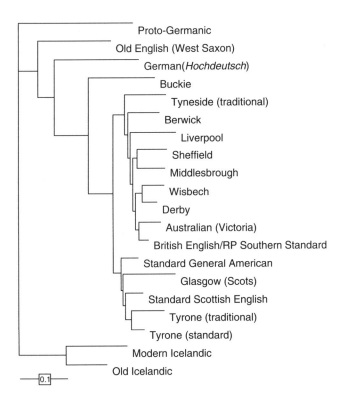

Fig. 8.3 Fitch tree (PHYLIP: Felsenstein 2001) based on phonetic difference between English and Germanic varieties

in (1), using phonetic-similarity measures for the 60 cognates in (2). Since Fitch has meaningful branch lengths, shorter branches indicate less phonetic difference from the common ancestor, here Proto-Germanic. As usual, this is one of many possible trees, and ideally bootstrapping would be required to sample the tree space and indicate the confidence we may have in different clusterings within the tree; for the moment, this tree is purely illustrative of the potential of the method.

There are several general points worth noting from this tree. First, and closest to the root, we find Old English West Saxon suitably positioned as a sister of the common ancestor of the English varieties. It is somewhat disconcerting, perhaps, to find *Hochdeutsch* also within the English group; this is likely to reflect shared sound changes between Standard German and some of the English varieties, a possibility we shall test below using NeighbourNet. The data then split into three groups. One consists only of Buckie, a northern Scots variety which on these data appears as particularly conservative; we return to this below. The two more substantial groupings essentially include English English versus Scottish and Irish varieties. For this tree at least, Victoria Australian patterns definitively with the English English varieties, as indeed does Berwick. On the other hand, General American is grouped with the Scots and Irish varieties, though it also appears as the variety closest to the English English branch, suggesting that our methods are detecting similarities with both major groups. However, here as elsewhere in the tree, notably within the English English branch, where the structure is very flat indeed, we find extremely short branch lengths, suggesting that there may be limited confidence in the order of some of these splits; put slightly differently, the program is experiencing difficulties in drawing a tree at all, and a number of other structures would be almost equally compatible with the data. As we have seen in earlier chapters, situations like this, where there may be conflicting signals in the data, are more appropriately analysed using network methods.

The most suitable of the various options available would seem to be NeighbourNet (Bryant and Moulton 2004): as we have established in earlier chapters, the resolution provided by this program seems well suited to linguistic data, and it is also designed for distance data of the type generated by our phonetic comparisons. The use of distance data effectively rules out currently available versions of Network; and, similarly, the number of varieties and groupings is too large to be accommodated comfortably in Splitstree. Figure 8.4 therefore shows a NeighbourNet diagram for our English and Germanic varieties, highlighted to indicate one particularly major split in the data.

It is immediately obvious from Figure 8.4 that there are many reticulations, again reinforcing the impression from the short branch lengths in our earlier Fitch diagram that the structure is not wholly tree-like. Nonetheless, the NeighbourNet diagram also shows the English English varieties plus Victoria Australian on one side, and the Scottish and Irish varieties on the other. Buckie again is pulled back towards the root, near West Saxon Old English. And this time the position of General American is even more clearly intermediate between the Scots and Irish varieties on one hand and the English ones on the other.

However, the added value we obtain from NeighbourNet which is particularly helpful in cases like this is the possibility of highlighting individual splits, and asking why the groups fall on either side of that split: in other words, we can ask what splits mean. If we were using Network we might be able to make the relevant inferences from the list of non-tree-like items generated automatically by the program; those items not present in such lists can be taken as supporting the tree structure. In earlier chapters we identified the absence of such a list as a minor shortcoming of NeighbourNet compared with Network. However, it is possible to remedy this by carrying out a subsequent statistical analysis of the data underlying the distance matrix, using a standard statistical package (here, SPSS). This involves asking which cognates have closer scores for two languages on the same side of the relevant split, compared to the distances between one of those languages, and another language on the other side of the split. In this case we have compared Glasgow and General American, which both fall on one side of this particular split, with Glasgow and RP, or Standard Southern British English, where RP falls on the opposite side of the split. We can then show which cognates are primarily responsible for the split, by examining those which are furthest from the line bisecting the diagram in Figure 8.5: points on the line show cognates which are equidistant in both pairwise comparisons, and which are therefore either identical in all three varieties, or are different in both comparisons in the same way.

In Figure 8.5, there are few cognates substantially below the line, meaning that most similarities between Glasgow and RP are also found between Glasgow and General American. On the other hand, quite a

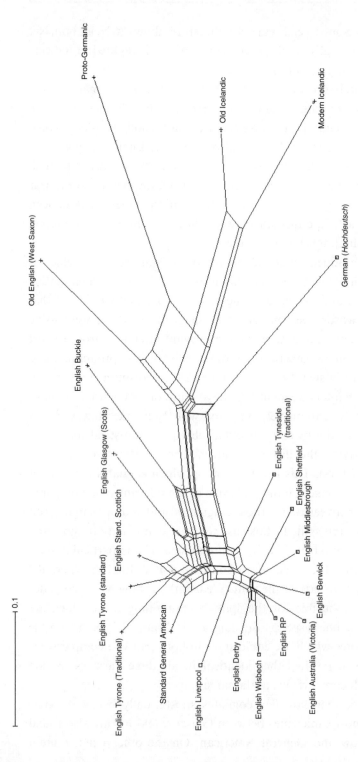

Fig. 8.4 NeighbourNet of English and Germanic varieties, phonetic-similarity data for 60 Germanic cognates

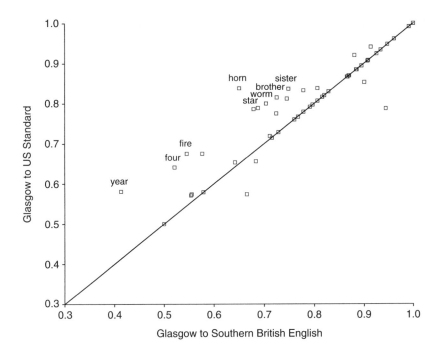

Fig. 8.5 A closer look at the cognates responsible for the major split

number of cognates fall a fair way above the line, showing they are more strongly similar between Glasgow and General American than between Glasgow and RP. In addition, the particular cognates we find make good phonetic sense: the labels reveal that a significant proportion of these share the particularly salient feature of rhoticity. This, then, provides a further partial validation of these methods, since the cognates contributing most to the major split in the data do share features which are traditionally acknowledged as useful classifiers for English varieties. Interestingly, this feature of rhoticity may in part account for the attraction of *Hochdeutsch*, which is also non-rhotic, towards the English English varieties in the Fitch tree in Figure 8.3. Of course, it might not always be the case that splits in the data are due to commonly recognized, traditional shibboleth features of this kind; one attractive prospect for a method of this kind is that it may reveal shared or contrasting constellations of features of which we might not be immediately aware. As we have suggested on various occasions above, one hallmark of a promising

Table 8.1 (repeated) Phonetic similarity of cognates of the numerals 'one' to 'ten' in a selection of Romance varieties (100 = identity)

	Italian	Spanish: Madrid	Spanish: Bogotá	Spanish: Venezuela	Portuguese: Lisbon	Portuguese: Rio	Portuguese: Salvador	Portuguese: São Paulo	French: Paris	French: Southern	Romanian	
Lat.	*59*	*54*	*54*	*52*	*49*	*48*	*50*	*52*	*40*	*40*	*54*	Classical Latin
It.		68	69	66	57	61	60	60	43	43	61	Italian
SpM.			**98**	**94**	66	69	70	69	47	47	54	Spanish: Madrid
SpB.				**94**	66	69	70	69	47	47	54	Spanish: Bogotá
SpV.					62	67	66	66	45	45	54	Spanish: Venezuela
Pt.L						**89**	**88**	**94**	56	56	53	Portuguese: Lisbon
Pt.R							**93**	**91**	54	54	53	Portuguese: Rio
Pt.S.								**91**	54	54	54	Portuguese: Salvador
Pt.SP.									54	54	55	Portuguese: São Paulo
FrP.										**93**	45	French: Paris
FrS.											45	French: Southern
Rom.												Romanian

Note: In Table 8.1 Latin is entered as a variety in its own right, and figures involving comparisons with Latin are given in italics. Figures in bold indicate comparisons between dialects of the same language, which are typically over 80; scores for varieties of different languages range from 70 (Salvador Portuguese compared with Madrid Spanish or Bogotá) down to 40 for French and Latin, or, among present-day languages, the 43 for French and Italian.

method is its ability both to confirm what we know and to generate and strengthen hypotheses in cases where we may not know very much.

It is possible to use similar statistical techniques to identify the cognates and features which are distinctive for particular varieties. An obvious candidate for further analysis here is Buckie, which appeared in Figure 8.3 closest to the baseline, and in Figure 8.4 closest to the root, of all the modern English varieties. It is also separated from the two major groupings in both diagrams by a relatively long, and therefore relatively well-supported, branch. Closer examination of our phonetic-comparison data can help us quantify how different Buckie is from other varieties, as shown in Figure 8.6, and pinpoint the cognates which are contributing to that difference, as shown in Figure 8.7.

Figure 8.6 contrasts Buckie with Sheffield. Our tree in Figure 8.3 already suggested that there are many more similarities between Sheffield and RP than between Buckie and RP (as any naive listener would immediately agree); this was also consistent with the location of Buckie on one side of the major split in Figure 8.4, and Sheffield and RP on the other. The graphs in Figure 8.6 in turn show that all Sheffield words are more than 50% similar to their RP counterparts, with a mean of 89% similarity, while for Buckie some words are less than 30% similar to the RP equivalents, with a mean of 72%. The Romance data shown in Table 8.1, repeated above for convenience, provide a context for these figures. Bold figures show similarity scores for dialects of the same language; the range includes the 89% for Sheffield and RP. On the other hand, the closest figures to our 72% for Buckie versus RP are found in the italic figures, which are values for comparisons of different Romance languages, notably Spanish versus Portuguese and Spanish versus Italian.

Finally, we can again use standard scatter plots to show which items are more conservative in particular varieties, by comparing two varieties with the ancestral form: sticking with the same varieties for the moment, Figure 8.7 shows Proto-Germanic versus Sheffield, and Proto-Germanic versus Buckie.

The items above the line are more conservative in Sheffield, or have changed more in Buckie, or both; and the points below the line show items that are more conservative in Buckie, or have changed more in Sheffield, or both. It is straightforward to identify which point equates to which cognate; again, this represents something of a checking mechanism, since we can then establish whether our phonetic comparisons are based on recognized, or at least understandable, differences. Outliers above and below the line are again labelled in Figure 8.7; for the most part, those below the line are conservative in Buckie in retaining the velar fricative [x] or post-vocalic [r], or are innovative in Sheffield because of [h]-dropping. Points above the line variously indicate innovations in Buckie, involving loss of [v] in *give* and [d] in *wind*, or vowel changes, as in *father* and *wind*.

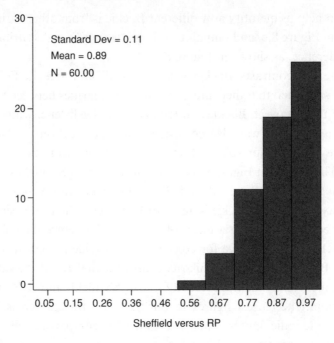

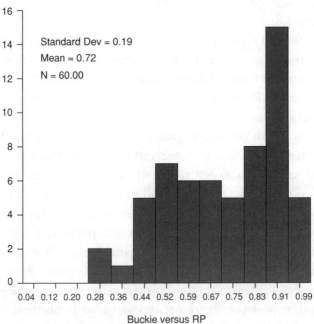

Fig. 8.6 Distribution of phonetic differences across cognates: Sheffield versus RP (top), Buckie versus RP (bottom). X-axis shows frequency; y-axis shows similarity scores per word

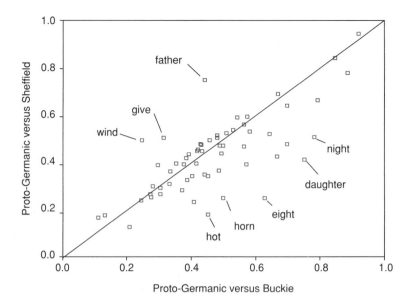

Fig. 8.7 Phonetic distances from Proto-Germanic to Sheffield and Buckie
plotted against each other

8. 6 Summing Up

The message of this chapter is in many ways the same as the message of
the whole book. We have been presenting a range of methods, some
designed by biologists, some by linguists, but all at least potentially
applicable to language data. Clearly, these methods need further refinement: for the phonetic-comparison work, that means more varieties,
more items, and more sophisticated matching techniques. All these
methods also produce figures and representations that require interpretation if we are to cast light on different aspects of the histories of the
languages and varieties we are comparing. The outputs of computer
programs are not the end of the story by any means: as in other quantitative areas of linguistics, like sociolinguistics or corpus linguistics, the
point is not just getting the numbers. It's what you do with them afterwards in terms of interpretation that counts. But the figures themselves
can confirm our insights and hypotheses, and can also reveal differences
that might not be visible, as it were, to the naked eye.

Our aim in this book, then, has been to demonstrate that historical
linguists now have a range of quantitative and computational methods at

our disposal which might improve our prospects in dealing with classification, contact, and variation. Partly, these methods can help us to
provide representations for situations we understand perfectly well. Approaches based on network structures have the advantage of drawing
trees but interrupting those trees with reticulations and connections to
represent contact events and their consequences. In analyses based on
lexical lists, undiagnosed or misdiagnosed loans seem to give a consistent
signal in network diagrams, so that we can also develop ways of testing
for contact-induced changes in cases where we cannot otherwise be sure if
they have happened or not. This can help us, potentially, to work out
what the more plausible answer might be in cases where either contact or
common ancestry might be at issue; in other words, we are not only
investigating new ways of representing linguistic affinities, but new ways
of reconstructing the most likely histories that brought those affinities
about, too. And, finally, there are cases where we know we have relatedness, for instance when we are dealing with dialects of the same language
or very closely and transparently related languages; but quantitative
methods can still make a contribution in calculating relative distances
between varieties, and establishing which particular features are responsible for that distance.

This all sounds hopeful, and it is meant to; but there is a long way to go
in testing and designing methods. Most programs are only now being
applied to language data, having been developed for something else; and
there tend to be several alternative ways of gathering or coding the data to
feed into the programs in the first place, few of which are agreed, and
none watertight. The more cases we can apply these methods to now, the
more we will learn about the signals they provide under different circumstances, and the more we may learn to trust and to use them; and our data
need not always be from real languages, but can sometimes validly and
valuably involve computer simulations. These results can then be used in
interactions between historical linguistics and related disciplines too,
making the prospect of the 'new synthesis', and the possibility that
linguistic data can make real contributions to our understanding of
population histories, a realistic and exciting one.

We must remember, though, that these methods are additions to the
historical linguist's and dialectologist's tool kit. They are not replacements for linguistic knowledge, experience, and insight. They need sensitive handling to make sure that the right programs are applied to the right

kinds of data, and that the underlying assumptions of models are not violated. It is undeniably true that you can get rubbish out of a bad program, or a good program used badly. Then again, you can get rubbish out of some of our colleagues too, with no computational aids whatsoever. The point is for us all to work together, not to be constantly trying to demonstrate that the programs and coding methods can be applied without linguistic insight and advice, or that linguists can get to the right answer without an objective and repeatable computational approach. Sometimes they can; but our point is that, without that objectivity and repeatability, it is not possible a priori to distinguish those cases from others where the answer looks plausible but is just plain wrong. At the same time, our computational approaches should ideally be feeding further linguistic hypothesis making, not just confirming what is already known, though that is valuable in itself. If a model generates data, or isolates particular features, or comes up with a set of numbers or a network or a tree which looks odd, or doesn't immediately make sense, this does not necessarily mean that the program has been misused, or badly designed, or that the whole idea of applying computer programs to linguistic data is misguided. We have to be open-minded enough to accept that the programs might be detecting a signal that is really there, but has not yet been noticed, and see how our linguistic theories and classifications might look if we modified them to accommodate the new results. On the other hand, quantitative historical linguists also have to accept that our programs might sometimes run away with us, and that some results might be artefactual or misleading. There are plenty of opportunities, if so, to explore different approaches to coding, or new programs, or to become more rigorous in the checks and balances we apply. We are, after all, at the beginning of the enterprise.

References

ADELAAR, WILLEM F. H. (1989), review of Greenberg (1987), *Lingua*, 78: 249–55.

ALPHER, BARRY, and NASH, DAVID (1999), 'Lexical replacement and cognate equilibrium in Australia', *Australian Journal of Linguistics*, 19: 5–56.

ARENDS, JACQUES, MUYSKEN, PIETER, and SMITH, NORVAL (1995). (eds.), *Pidgins and Creoles: An Introduction* (Amsterdam: Benjamins).

ARNDT, WALTER W. (1959), 'The performance of glottochronology in Germanic', *Language*, 35: 180–92.

BAEHRENS, W. A. (1922), *Sprachlicher Kommentar zur vulgärlateinischen Appendix Probi* (Halle).

BAKKER, PETER (1997), *'A Language of Our Own': The Genesis of Michif—the Mixed Cree–French Language of the Canadian Métis* (New York: Oxford University Press).

—— (2000), 'Rapid language change: Creolization, intertwining, convergence', in Renfrew, McMahon, and Trask (2000), 585–620.

—— and MAARTEN MOUS (1994) (eds.), *Mixed Languages: Fifteen Case Studies in Language Intertwining* (Amsterdam: IFOTT).

BANDELT, HANS-JÜRGEN, and DRESS, A. W. M. (1992), 'Split decomposition: a new and useful approach to phylogenetic analysis of distance data', *Molecular Phylogenetics and Evolution*, 1: 242–52.

BANDELT, HANS-JÜRGEN, FORSTER, PETER, and RÖHL, A. (1999), 'Median-joining networks for inferring intraspecific phylogenies', *Molecular Biology and Evolution*, 16: 37–48.

—— —— SYKES, BRYAN C., and RICHARDS, MARTIN B. (1995), 'Mitochondrial portraits of human populations using median networks', *Genetics*, 141: 743–53.

BARBUJANI, GUIDO (1997), 'DNA variation and language affinities', *American Journal of Human Genetics*, 61: 1011–14.

BATEMAN, RICHARD, GODDARD, IVES, O'GRADY, RICHARD, FUNK, V. A. MOOI, RICH, KRESS, W. JOHN, and CANNELL, PETER (1990), 'Speaking of forked tongues: the feasibility of reconciling human phylogeny and the history of language', *Current Anthropology*, 31: 1–24, 177–83.

BAXTER, WILLIAM H., and MANASTER RAMER, ALEXIS (1996), review of Ringe (1992), *Diachronica*, 13: 371–84.

—— (2000), 'Beyond lumping and splitting: probabilistic issues in historical linguistics', in Renfrew, McMahon and Trask (2000), 167–88.

BELLWOOD, PETER, and RENFREW, COLIN (2002) (eds.), *Examining the Farming/Language Dispersal Hypothesis* (Cambridge: McDonald Institute for Archaeological Research).

BENDER, MARVIN L. (1969), 'Chance CVC correspondences in unrelated languages', *Language*, 45: 519–31.

BENGTSON, JOHN D., and RUHLEN, MERRITT (1994), 'Global etymologies', in Ruhlen (1994), 277–336.

BERGSLAND, K., and VOGT, H. (1962), 'On the validity of glottochronology', *Current Anthropology*, 3: 115–53.

BLACK, PAUL (n.d.), 'Lexicostatistical lists: Kokaper (with Kok-Babonk)', (unpublished MS).

BLOOMFIELD, LEONARD (1933), *Language* (New York: Holt, Rinehart and Winston).

BOAG, PETER, and GRANT, PETER (1981), 'Intense natural selection in a population of Darwin's Finches (*Geospizinae*) in the Galápagos', *Science*, 214: 82–5.

BOWERN, CLAIRE, and KOCH, HAROLD (2004) (eds.), *Australian Languages: Classification and the Comparative Method* (Amsterdam: Benjamins).

BRYANT, DAVID (2004), 'Radiation and network breaking in Polynesian linguistics', paper presented at the 'Phylogenetic Methods and the Prehistory of Languages' meeting, Cambridge, July 2004.

—— and MOULTON, V. (2004), 'Neighbornet: an agglomerative algorithm for the construction of planar phylogenetic networks', *Molecular Biology and Evolution*, 21: 255–65.

—— FILIMON, FLAVIA, and GRAY, RUSSELL (in preparation), 'Untangling our past: languages, trees, splits and networks', to appear in R. Mace, C. J. Holden, and S. Shennan (eds.), *The Evolution of Cultural Diversity: A Phylogenetic Approach* (forthcoming).

BUCK, C. D. (1949), *A Dictionary of Selected Synonyms in the Principal Indo-European Languages: A contribution to the history of ideas* (Chicago, Ill.: University of Chicago Press).

CAMPBELL, LYLE (1988), review of Greenberg (1987), *Language*, 64: 591–615.

—— (1998), *Historical Linguistics* (Edinburgh: Edinburgh University Press).

—— (2003), 'How to show languages are related: methods for distant genetic relationship', in Brian Joseph and Richard Janda (eds.), *The Handbook of Historical Linguistics* (Oxford: Blackwell), 262–82.

—— (2004), *Historical Linguistics*, 2nd edn. (Edinburgh: Edinburgh University Press).

—— (forthcoming), 'Areal linguistics: the problem to the answer', to appear in Yaron Matras, April McMahon, and Nigel Vincent (eds.), *Linguistic Areas* (London: Palgrave Macmillan).

—— and MITHUN, MARIANNE (1979*a*). 'Introduction: North American Indian historical linguistics in current perspective', in Campbell and Mithun (1979*b*), 3–69.

—— —— (1979*b*) (eds.) *The Languages of Native America* (Austin, Texas: University of Texas Press).

CANN, REBECCA (2000), 'Talking trees tell tales', *Nature*, 405: 1008–9.

—— STONEKING, MARK, and WILSON, ALLAN (1987), 'Mitochondrial DNA and human evolution', *Nature*, 325: 31–6.

CAVALLI-SFORZA, LUIGI LUCA (2000), *Genes, Peoples and Languages* (London: Allen Lane/Penguin).

—— MENOZZI, P., and PIAZZA, A. (1994), *The History and Geography of Human Genes*, (Princeton, NJ: Princeton University Press).

—— —— —— and MOUNTAIN, J. (1988), 'Reconstruction of human evolution: bringing together genetic, archaeological and linguistic data', *Proceedings of the National Academy of Sciences USA*, 85: 6002–6.

CERRÓN-PALOMINO, RODOLFO (2000), *Lingüística Aimara* (Peru: Centro Bartolomé de las Casas).

CHADWICK, JOHN (1990), *The Decipherment of Linear B* (Cambridge: Cambridge University Press).

CHEN, MATTHEW, and WANG, WILLIAM (1975), 'Sound change: actuation and implementation', *Language*, 51: 255–81.

CLACKSON, JAMES (1994), *The Linguistic Relationship Between Armenian and Greek* (Oxford: Blackwell; Publications of the Philological Society).

CYSOUW, MICHAEL (2000), Message posted to the HISTLING discussion list, HISTLING@VM.SC.EDU.

DARWIN, CHARLES (1996) [1859], *The Origin of Species* (Oxford: Oxford University Press).

DIXON, R. M. W. (1980), *The Languages of Australia* (Cambridge: Cambridge University Press).

—— (1997), *The Rise and Fall of Languages* (Cambridge: Cambridge University Press).

—— (2001), 'The Australian linguistic area', in A. Aikhenvald and R. M. W. Dixon (eds.), *Areal Diffusion and Genetic Linguistics* (Cambridge: Cambridge University Press), 64–103.

—— (2002), *Australian Languages* (Cambridge: Cambridge University Press).

DORIAN, NANCY (1978), 'The fate of morphological complexity in language death', *Language*, 54: 590–609.

DURIE, MARK, and ROSS, MALCOLM (1996) (eds.), *The Comparative Method Reviewed* (Oxford: Oxford University Press).

DYEN, ISIDORE (1964), 'On the validity of comparative lexicostatistics', in Lunt (1964b), 238–52.

—— (1973), 'The validity of the mathematical model of glottochronology', in Isidore Dyen (ed.), *Lexicostatistics in Genetic Linguistics: Proceedings of the Yale Conference* (The Hague: Mouton), 11–29.

—— KRUSKAL, JOSEPH B. and BLACK, PAUL (1992), 'An Indoeuropean classification: a lexicostatistical experiment', *Transactions of the American Philosophical Society*, 82/5 (data available at <http://www.ldc.upenn.edu>).

EHRET, CHRISTOPHER (1995), *Reconstructing Proto-Afroasiatic (Proto-Afrasian): vowels, tone, consonants and vocabulary* (Berkeley, Calif.: University of California Press).

EMBLETON, SHEILA M. (1986), *Statistics in Historical Linguistics* (Bochum: Brockmeyer).

—— (2000), 'Lexicostatistics/glottochronology: from Swadesh to Sankoff to Starostin to future horizons', in Renfrew, McMahon, and Trask (2000), 143–66.

EVANS, NICHOLAS (2004) (ed.), *The Non-Pama-Nyungan Languages of Northern Australia: Comparative Studies of the Continent's Most Linguistically Complex Region* (Canberra: Pacific Linguistics).

FELSENSTEIN, J. (2001), *PHYLIP: Phylogeny Inference Package: Version 3.6*, Department of Genetics, University of Washington.

FORSTER, PETER, and TOTH, ALFRED (2003), 'Toward a phylogenetic chronology of ancient Gaulish, Celtic, and Indo-European', *Proceedings of the National Academy of Sciences*, 100: 9079–84.

—— —— and BANDELT, HANS-JURGEN (1998), 'Evolutionary network analysis of word lists: visualising the relationship between Alpine Romance languages', *Journal of Quantitative Linguistics*, 3: 174–87.

—— POLZIN, TOBIAS, and RÖHL, ARNE (in press), 'Evolution of English basic vocabulary within the network of Germanic Languages', in Jeremy Clackson, Peter Forster, and Colin Renfrew (eds.), *Phylogenetic Methods and the Prehistory of Languages* (Cambridge: McDonald Institute for Archaeological Research).

FOULKES, PAUL (1993), 'Theoretical implications of the /p/ > /f/ > /h/ change' Ph.D thesis (University of Cambridge).

FOX, ANTHONY (1995), *Linguistic Reconstruction: An Introduction to Theory and Method* (Oxford: Oxford University Press).

GAMKRELIDZE, THIOMAS, and IVANOV, VJAČESLAV (1995), *Indo-Europeans: A Reconstruction and Historical Analysis of a Proto-language and Proto-culture* (Berlin: Mouton de Gruyter).

GIMBUTAS, MARIJA (1973), 'The beginning of the Bronze Age in Europe and the Indo-Europeans 3500–2500 B.C.', *Journal of Indo-European Studies*, 1: 1–20.

GLEASON, H. A. (1959), 'Counting and calculating for historical reconstruction', *Anthropological Linguistics*, 1: 22–32.

GODDARD, IVES (1987), review of Greenberg (1987), *Current Anthropology*, 28: 656–7.

GOEBL, HANS (1982), 'Dialektometrie, Prinzipien und Methoden des Einsatzes der Numerischen Taxonomie im Bereich der Dialektgeographie', *Denkschriften der Österreichischen Akademie der Wissenschaften, philosophisch-historische Klasse*, 157 (Vienna: Verlag der Österreichischen Akademie der Wissenschaften), 1–123.

—— (1984), *Dialektometrische Studien: Anhand italoromanischer, rätoromanischer und galloromanischer Sprachmaterialien aus AIS and ALF*, 3 vols. (Tübingen: Niemeyer).

GRACE, GEORGE (1967), 'Effect of heterogeneity in the lexicostatistical test list: the case of Rotuman', in Genevieve A. Highland, Roland W. Force, Alan Howard, Marion Kelly, and Yoshihiko H. Sinoto, *Polynesian Culture History: Essays in Honor of Kenneth P. Emory* (Honolulu: Bishop Museum Press), 289–302.

GRAY, RUSSELL, and ATKINSON, QUENTIN (2003), 'Language-tree divergence times support the Anatolian theory of Indo-European origin', *Nature*, 426: 435–9.

—— and JORDAN, FIONA (2000), 'Language trees support the express-train sequence of Austronesian expansion', *Nature*, 405: 1052–5.

GREENBERG, JOSEPH H. (1987), *Language in the Americas* (Stanford, Calif.: Stanford University Press).

—— (1993), 'Observations concerning Ringe's *Calculating the Factor of Chance in Language Comparison*', *Proceedings of the American Philosophical Society*, 137/1: 79–90.

GUDSCHINSKY, SARAH (1956), 'Three disturbing questions concerning lexicostatistics', *International Journal of American Linguistics*, 22: 212–13.

HALDANE, J. B. S. (1949), 'Suggestions as to quantitative measurement of rates of evolution', *Evolution*, 3: 51–6.

HALL, ROBERT (1950), 'The reconstruction of Proto-Romance', *Language*, 26: 63–85.

—— (1960), 'On realism in reconstruction', *Language*, 36: 203–6.

—— (1976), *Proto-Romance Phonology* (New York: Elsevier).

HARRISON, S. P. (2003), 'On the limits of the comparative method', in Joseph and Janda (2003): 213–43.

HEERINGA, WILBERT, NERBONNE, JOHN, and KLEIWIG, P. (2002), 'Validating dialect comparison methods' in W. Gaul and G. Ritter (eds.), *Classification, Automation, and New Media: Proceedings of the 24th Annual Conference of the Gesellschaft für Klassifikation, University of Passau, March 15–17 2000* (Berlin: Springer), 445–52.

HEGGARTY, PAUL (forthcoming), *Measured Language* (Oxford: Blackwell; Publications of the Philological Society).

—— McMAHON, APRIL, and McMAHON, ROBERT (forthcoming), 'Dialect classification by phonetic similarity: a computational approach', to appear in Nicole Delbecque, Johan van der Auwera, and Dirk Geeraerts (eds.), *Perspectives in Variation* (Amsterdam: Mouton de Gruyter).

—— —— —— and SLASKA, NATALIA (2003), 'Lexicostatistics: the flaws and the fixes' paper presented at the International Conference on Historical Linguistics, Copenhagen.

HOENIGSWALD, H. M. (1960), *Language Change and Linguistic Reconstruction* (Chicago, Ill.: University of Chicago Press).

HOIJER, H. (1956), 'Lexicostatistics: a critique', *Language*, 32: 49–60.

HOLDEN, CLARE, and GRAY, RUSSELL (2004), 'Exploring Bantu linguistic relationships using trees and networks', paper presented at the 'Phylogenetic Methods and the Prehistory of Languages' meeting, Cambridge, July 2004.

HOLM, JOHN (1988), *Pidgins and Creoles, i. Theory and Structure* (Cambridge: Cambridge University Press).

—— (1989), *Pidgins and Creoles, ii. Reference Survey* (Cambridge: Cambridge University Press).

HOPPER, PAUL (1973), 'Glottalized and murmured occlusives in IE', *Glossa*, 7: 141–66.

HUSON, D. H. (1998), 'Splitstree: a program for analysing and visualizing evolutionary data' *Bioinformatics*, 14: 68–73.

HYMES, DELL (1960), 'Lexicostatistics: a critique', *Language*, 32: 49–60.

JOSEPH, B. and JANDA, R. (2003) (eds.), *The Handbook of Historical Linguistics* (Oxford: Blackwell).

KESSLER, BRETT (1995), 'Computational dialectology in Irish Gaelic', in *Proceedings of the 7th Conference of the European Chapter of the Association for Computational Linguistics* (Dublin: European Chapter of the Association for Computational Linguistics), 60–7.

—— (2001), *The Significance of Word Lists* (Stanford, Calif.: CSLI Publications).

—— (forthcoming), 'Phonetic comparison algorithms', to appear in *Transactions of the Philological Society*, 2005.

KIMURA, M. (1983), *The Neutral Theory of Molecular Evolution* (Cambridge: Cambridge University Press).

KOCH, HAROLD (1997), 'Comparative linguistics and Australian prehistory', in Patrick McConvell and Nicholas Evans (eds.), *Archaeology and Linguistics: Aboriginal Australia in global perspective* (Oxford: Oxford University Press), 27–44.

KROEBER, A. L. (1955), 'Linguistic time depth results so far and their meaning', *International Journal of American Linguistics*, 21: 91–104.

—— and CHRÉTIEN, C. D. (1937), 'Quantitative classification of Indo-European languages', *Language*, 13: 83–103.

KRUSKAL, JOSEPH, DYEN, ISIDORE, and BLACK, PAUL (1971), 'The vocabulary method of reconstructing language trees: innovations and large-scale applications', in F. R. Hodson, D. G. Kendall, and P. Tautu (eds.), *Anglo-Romanian Conference on Mathematics in the Archaeological and Historical Sciences, Mamaia, Romania, 1970* (Edinburgh: Edinburgh University Press), 361–80.

LABOV, WILLIAM (1994), *Principles of Linguistic Change, i. Internal Factors* (Oxford: Blackwell).

—— (2001), *Principles of Linguistic Change, ii. Social Factors* (Oxford: Blackwell).

LADEFOGED, PETER, and MADDIESON, IAN (1996), *The Sounds of the World's Languages* (Oxford: Blackwell).

LASS, ROGER (1984), *Phonology* (Cambridge: Cambridge University Press).

—— (1993), 'How real(ist) are reconstructions?', in Charles Jones (ed.), *Historical Linguistics: Problems and Perspectives* (London: Longman), 156–89.

LEES, ROBERT B. (1953), 'The basis of glottochronology', *Language*, 29: 113–27.

LEVENSHTEIN, V. I. (1965), 'Binary codes capable of correcting spurious insertions and deletions of ones', *Problems of Information Transmission*, 1: 8–17.

LIGHTFORT, DAVID (2002), 'Myths and the prehistory of grammars', *Journal of Linguistics*, 38: 113–36.

LOHR, MARISA (1999), *Methods for the Genetic Classification of Languages*, Ph.D. thesis (University of Cambridge).

LUCE, G. H. (1981), *A Comparative Word-List of Old Burmese, Chinese and Tibetan* (London: School of Oriental and African Studies).

LUNT, HORACE (1964*a*), discussion of I. Dyen, 'On the validity of comparative lexicostatistics', in Lunt (1964*b*), 247–52.

—— (1964*b*) (ed.), *Proceedings of the Ninth International Congress of Linguists* (The Hague: Mouton).

LURIA, SALVADOR E, GOULD, STEPHEN J., and SINGER, SAM (1981), *A View of Life* (Menlo Park, California: Benjamin/Cummins).

MACEACHERN, S. (2000), 'Genes, Tribes and African History', *Current Anthropology*, 41: 357–84.

MCMAHON, APRIL (1994), *Understanding Language Change* (Cambridge: Cambridge University Press).

—— HEGGARTY, PAUL, MCMAHON, ROBERT, and SLASKA, NATALIA (forthcoming), 'Swadesh sublists and the benefits of borrowing: an Andean case study', *Transactions of the Philological Society*, 103.

MCMAHON, APRIL, and MCMAHON, ROBERT (1995), 'Linguistics, genetics and archaeology: internal and external evidence in the Amerind controversy', *Transactions of the Philological Society*, 93: 125–225.

—— —— (2000), 'Problems of dating and time depth in linguistics and biology', in Renfrew, McMahon, and Trask (2000), 59–74.

—— —— (2003), 'Finding families: quantitative methods in language classification', *Transactions of the Philological Society*, 101: 7–55.

—— —— (2004), 'Family values', in Christian Kay, Simon Horobin, and Jeremy Smith (eds.), *New Perspectives on English Historical Linguistics, i. Syntax and Morphology* (Amsterdam: Benjamins), 103–23.

—— —— (forthcoming *a*). 'Keeping contact in the family: approaches to language classification and contact-induced change', to appear in Yaron Matras,

April McMahon, and Nigel Vincent (eds.), *Linguistic Areas* (London: Palgrave Macmillan).

McMAHON, APRIL, and McMAHON, ROBERT (forthcoming *b*) 'Cladistics', in Keith Brown (ed.) *The Encyclopedia of Language and Linguistics*, 2nd edn. (Elsevier).

McMAHON, ROBERT (2004), 'Genes and languages', *Community Genetics*, 7/1: 1–13.

MADDIESON, IAN (1984), *Patterns of Sounds* (Cambridge: Cambridge University Press).

MARTINET, ANDRÉ (1953), 'Remarques sur le consonantisme sémitique', *Bulletin de la Société de linguistique de Paris*, 49: 67–78.

MATISOFF, JAMES (1978), *Variational Semantics in Tibeto-Burman* (Philadelphia: Institute for the Study of Human Issues).

—— (1990), 'On megalocomparison', *Language*, 66: 106–20.

—— (2000), 'On the uselessness of glottochronology for the subgrouping of Tibeto-Burman', in Renfrew, McMahon, and Trask (2000), 333–72.

MATRAS, YARON (2000), 'How predictable is contact-induced change in grammar?', in Renfrew, McMahon, and Trask (2000), 563–83.

—— McMAHON, APRIL, and VINCENT, NIGEL (in press) (eds.), *Linguistic Areas: Convergence in Historical and Typological Perspective* (Palgrave).

MERRIWEATHER, D. A., KEMP, B. M., CREWS, D. E., and NEEL, J. V. (2000), 'Gene flow and genetic variation in the Yanomama as revealed by mitochondrial DNA', in Colin Renfrew (ed.), *America Past, America Present: Genes and Languages in the Americas and Beyond* (Cambridge: McDonald Institute for Archaeological Research), 89–124.

MILLER, JIM (2003), 'Syntax and discourse in Modern Scots', in John Corbett, J. Derrick McClure, and Jane Stuart-Smith (eds.), *The Edinburgh Companion to Scots* (Edinburgh: Edinburgh University Press), 72–109.

MITHUN, MARIANNE (2004), '"Unborrowable" areal traits', paper presented at the Linguistics Association of Great Britain annual meeting, London, September 2004.

MOORE J. H. (1994), 'Putting anthropology back together again: the ethnogenetic critique of cladistic theory', *American Anthropologist*, 96: 925–48.

MORELL, VIRGINIA (1990), 'Confusion in earliest America', *Science* (Apr. 1990), 439–41.

MUYSKEN, PIETER (1997), 'Media Lengua', in Sarah Grey Thomason (ed.), *Contact Languages: A Wider Perspective* (Amsterdam: Benjamins), 365–426.

NASH, DAVID (2002), 'Historical linguistic geography of South-East Western Australia', in John Henderson and David Nash (eds.), *Language in Native Title* (Canberra: Aboriginal Studies Press), 205–30.

NAVARRO, G., and RAFFINOT, N. (2002), *Flexible Pattern Matching in Strings: Practical Online Search Algorithms for Texts and Biological Sequences* (Cambridge: Cambridge University Press).

NEI, MASATOSHI (1985), 'Human evolution at the molecular level', in T. Ohta and K. Aoki (eds.), *Population Genetics and Molecular Evolution* (Tokyo: Japan Scientific Societies Press), 41–64.

—— (1987), *Molecular Evolutionary Genetics* (New York: Columbia University Press).

NERBONNE, JOHN, and HEERINGA, WILBERT (1997), 'Measuring dialect difference phonetically', in J. Coleman (ed.), *Workshop on Computational Phonology* (Madrid: Special Interest Group of the Association for Computational Linguistics), 11–18.

—— —— (2001), 'Dialect areas and dialect continua', *Language Variation and Change*, 13: 375–400.

—— —— and KLEIWIG, P. (1999), 'Edit distance and dialect proximity', in D. Sankoff and J. Kruskal (eds.), *Time Warps, String Edits and Macromolecules: The Theory and Practice of Sequence Comparison* (Stanford: CSLI), pp. v–xv.

NERBONNE, JOHN, and KRETZSCHMAR, W. (2003), 'Introducing computational methods in dialectometry', in Nerbonne and Kretzschmen (eds.), *Computational Methods in Dialectometry*; special issue of *Computers and the Humanities*, 37: 245–55.

NETTLE, DANIEL, and ROMAINE, SUZANNE (2000), *Vanishing Voices: The Extinction of the World's Languages* (Oxford: Oxford University Press).

NICHOLS, JOHANNA (1992), *Linguistic Diversity in Space and Time* (Chicago, Ill.: University of Chicago Press).

—— (1996), 'The comparative method as heuristic', in Durie and Ross (1996), 39–71.

O'GRADY, G. N. (1960), 'More on lexicostatistics', *Current Anthropology*, 1: 338–9.

OGURA, MIEKO, and WANG, WILLIAM (1998), 'Evolution theory and lexical diffusion', in Jacek Fisiak and Marcin Krygier (eds.), *Advances in English Historical Linguistics (1996)* (Berlin: Mouton de Gruyter), 315–44.

OSTHOFF, HERMANN, and BRUGMANN, KARL (1878), *Morphologische Untersuchungen auf dem Gebiete der indogermanischen Sprachen* (Leipzig: Hirzel).

OSWALT, ROBERT L. (1970), 'The detection of remote linguistic relationships', *Computer Studies in the Humanities and Verbal Behaviour*, 3: 117–29.

PAGE, RODERIC D. M. (1996), 'TREEVIEW: an application to display phylogenetic trees on personal computers', *Computer Applications in the Biosciences*, 12: 357–8.

—— and HOLMES, EDWARD (1998), *Molecular Evolution: A Phylogenetic Approach* (Oxford: Blackwell).

PAGEL, MARK (2000), 'Maximum-likelihood models for glottochronology and for reconstructing linguistic phylogenies', in Renfrew, McMahon, and Trask (2000), 413–39.

PATRICK, PETER (2002), 'The speech community', in J. K. Chambers, Peter Trudgill, and Natalie Schilling-Estes (eds.), *The Handbook of Language Variation and Change* (Oxford: Blackwell), 573–600.

POLONI E. S., SEMINO, O., PASSARINO, G., SANTACHIARA-BENERECETTI, A. S., DUPANLOUP, L., LANGANEY, A., and EXCOFFIER, L. (1997), 'Human genetic affinities for Y-chromosome P49a,f: *Taq*I haplotypes show strong correspondence with linguistics', *American Journal of Human Genetics*, 61: 1015–35.

PULGRAM, ERNST (1958), *The Tongues of Italy: Prehistory and History* (Cambridge, Mass.: Harvard University Press).

—— (1959), 'Proto-Indo-European reality and reconstruction', *Language*, 35: 421–6.

—— (1961), 'The nature and use of protolanguages', *Lingua*, 10: 18–37.

RANKIN, ROBERT L. (2003), 'The comparative method', in Joseph and Janda (2003), 183–212.

REA, JOHN A. (1958), 'Concerning the validity of lexicostatistics', *International Journal of American Linguistics*, 24: 145–50.

—— (1973), 'The Romance data of the pilot studies for glottochronology', in T. A. Sebeok (ed.), *Diachronic, Areal and Typological Linguistics* (The Hague: Mouton; Current Trends in Linguistics 11), 355–67.

—— (1990), 'Lexicostatistics', in Edgar Polomé (ed.), *Research Guide on Language Change* (Berlin: Mouton de Gruyter), 217–22.

RENFREW, COLIN (1987), *Archaeology and Language: The Puzzle of Indo-European Origins* (London: Cape).

—— (1999), 'Reflections on the archaeology of linguistic diversity', in Bryan Sykes (ed.), *The Human Inheritance: Genes, Language, and Evolution* (Oxford: Oxford University Press), 1–32.

—— and BOYLE, KATIE (2000), *Archaeogenetics: DNA and the population prehistory of Europe* (Cambridge: McDonald Institute for Archaeological Research).

RENFREW COLIN, MCMAHON, APRIL, and TRASK, LARRY (2000), *Time Depth in Historical Linguistics*, 2 vols. *(Cambridge: McDonald Institute for Archaeological Research)*.

RIDLEY, M. (1986), *Evolution and Classification: The Reformation of Cladism* (Longman: London).

—— (1997), *Evolution* (Oxford: Oxford University Press).

RINGE, DON (1992), *On Calculating the Factor of Chance in Language Comparison*, Transactions of the American Philosophical Society, 82 (Philadelphia: American Philosophical Society).

—— (1996), 'The mathematics of "Amerind"', *Diachronica*, 13: 135–54.

—— (1999), 'How hard is it to match CVC roots?', *Transactions of the Philological Society*, 97: 213–44.

—— WARNOW, TANDY, and TAYLOR, ANN (2002), 'Indo-European and computational cladistics', *Transactions of the Philological Society*, 100: 59–129.

ROSS, ALAN S. C. (1950), 'Philological probability problems', *Journal of the Royal Statistical Society Series B*, 12: 19–59.

ROSS, MALCOLM (2001), 'Contact-induced change in Oceanic languages in North West Melanesia', in Alexandra Aikhenvald and R. M. W. Dixon (eds.), *Areal Diffusion and Genetic Inheritance: Problems in Comparative Linguistics* (Oxford: Oxford University Press), 134–66.

ROSS, PHILIP (1991), 'Hard words', *Scientific American* (Apr. 1991), 71–9.

ROSSER, ZOE, et al. (2000), 'Y-Chromosomal diversity in Europe is clinal and influenced primarily by geography, rather than by language', *American Journal of Human Genetics*, 67: 1526–43.

RUHLEN, MERRITT (1991), *A Guide to the World's Languages, i. Classification* (London: Edward Arnold).

—— (1994), *On the Origin of Languages* (Stanford, Calif.: Stanford University Press).

SAITOU, N., and NEI, M. (1987), 'The neighbor-joining, method: a new method for reconstructing phylogenetic trees', *Molecular Biology and Evolution*, 4: 406–25.

SANKOFF, DAVID (1970), 'On the rate of replacement of word-meaning relationships', *Language*, 46: 564–9.

—— (1973), 'Mathematical developments in lexicostatistical theory', in T. A. Sebeok (ed.), *Diachronic, Areal and Typological Linguistics* (The Hague: Mouton; Current Trends in Linguistics 11), 93–114.

—— and KRUSKAL, JOSEPH (1983) (eds.), *Time Warps, String Edits and Macromolecules: The Theory and Practice of Sequence Comparison* (Stanford, Calif.: CSLI).

SAPIR, EDWARD (1916), *Time Perspective in Aboriginal American Culture: A Study in Method*, Memoir 90, Anthropological Series No. 13 (Ottawa: Geological Survey, Department of Mines).

SCHLEICHER, AUGUST (1863), *Die Darwinische Theorie und die Sprachwissenschaft: Offenes Sendschreiben an Herrn Dr. Ernst Haeckel* (Weimar: Böhlau).

SCHMIDT, JOHANNES (1872), *Die Verwantschaftsverhältnisse der indogermanischen Sprachen* (Weimar: Böhlau).

SCHOPF, J. W. (1992), 'Disparate rates, differing fates: tempo and mode of evolution changed from Precambrian to the Phanerozoic', in J. W. Schopf and C. Klein (eds.), *The Proterozoic Biosphere* (New York: Cambridge University Press).

SEBBA, MARK (1997), *Contact Languages: Pidgins and Creoles* (London: Macmillan).

SIMPSON, G. G. (1949), *The Meaning of Evolution* (New York: Yale University Press).

SIMS-WILLIAMS, PATRICK (1998), 'Genetics, linguistics, and prehistory: thinking big and thinking straight', *Antiquity*, 72: 505–27.

SINGH, ISHTLA (2000), *Pidgins and Creoles: An Introduction* (London: Arnold).

SKELTON, PETER, and SMITH, ANDREW (2002), *Cladistics: A Practical Primer on CD-Rom* (Cambridge: Cambridge University Press).

SLASKA, NATALIA (forthcoming), 'Lexicostatistics away from the armchair: handling people, props, and problems', to appear in *Transactions of the Philological Society*, 2005.

—— (in preparation), 'Meaning Lists in Historical Linguistics—A Critical Appraisal and Case Study', Ph.D. thesis (University of Sheffield).

SMITH, NEIL (1989), *The Twitter Machine* (Oxford: Blackwell).

SOKAL, ROBERT R. (1988), 'Genetic, geographic, and linguistic distances in Europe', *Proceedings of the National Academy of Sciences USA*, 85: 1722–6.

STAROSTIN, SERGEI (2000), 'Comparative-historical linguistics and lexicostatistics', in Renfrew, McMahon, and Trask (eds.), *Time Depth in Historical Linguistics* (Cambridge: McDonald Institute for Archaeological Research), 223–66.

SWADESH, MORRIS (1950), 'Salish internal relationships', *International Journal of American Lingusitics*, 16: 157–67.

—— (1951), 'Diffusional cumulation and archaic residue as historical explanations', *Southwestern Journal of Anthropology*, 7: 1–21.

—— (1952), 'Lexico-statistic dating of prehistoric ethnic contacts', *Proceedings of the American Philosophical Society*, 96: 453–63.

—— (1954), 'Perspectives and problems of Amerindian comparative linguistics', *Word*, 10: 306–32.

—— (1955), 'Towards greater accuracy in lexicostatistic dating', *International Journal of American Linguistics*, 21: 121–37.

—— (1971), *The Origin and Diversification of Language*, collected papers, ed. Joel Sherzer (London: Routledge).

TEETER, KARL (1963), 'Lexicostatistics and genetic relationship', *Language*, 39: 638–48.

THOMASON, SARAH GREY (1997), *Contact Languages: A Wider Perspective* (Amsterdam: Benjamins).

—— (2001), *An Introduction to Language Contact* (Edinburgh: Edinburgh University Press).

—— and KAUFMAN, TERRENCE, (1988), *Language Contact, Creolization, and Genetic Linguistics*, (Berkeley, Calif.: University of California Press).

TOVAR, ANTONIO, BOUDA, KARL, LAFON, RENÉ, MICHELENA, LUIS, SWADESH, MORRIS, and VYCICHL, W. (1961), 'El método léxico-estadístico y su aplicación a las relaciones del vascuence', *Boletín de la Real Sociedad Vascongada de los Amigos del País*, 17: 249–81.

TRASK, R. L. (Larry) (1996), *Historical Linguistics* (London: Arnold).

VAN DER MERWE, N. J. (1966), 'New mathematics for glotto chronology', *Current Anthropology*, 7: 485–500.

—— (2003), review of Forster and Toth (2003), Linguist List (<http://linguistlist org/issues/14/14–1876.html>, accessed March 2005).

WALES, KATIE (2002), ' "North of Watford Gap": A cultural history of Northern English (from 1700)', in Richard Watts and Peter Trudgill (eds.), *Alternative Histories of English* (London: Routledge), 45–66.

WANG, WILLIAM (1969), 'Competing changes as a cause of residue', *Language*, 45: 9–25.

WARNOW, TANDY, RINGE, DON, and TAYLOR, ANN (1996), 'Reconstructing the evolutionary history of natural languages', *Proceedings of the ACM-SIAM Symposium on Discrete Algorithms*, 314–22.

WATKINS, CALVERT (1976), 'Toward Proto-Indo-European syntax: problems and pseudo-problems', in Sanford B. Steever, Carol A. Walker, and Salikoko S. Mufwene (eds.), *Proceedings of the Chicago Linguistics Society: Papers from the Parasession on Diachronic Syntax* (Chicago, Ill.: Chicago *Linguistics Society*), 805–26.

WEINER, JONATHAN (1994), *The Beak of the Finch: Evolution in Real Time* (London: Cape).

WRIGHT, ROBERT (1991), 'Quest for the mother tongue', *Atlantic Monthly* (Apr. 1991), 39–68.

ZERJAL, T., DASHNYAM, B., PANDYA, A., KAYSER, M., ROEWER, L., SANTOS, F. R., SCHIEFENHOVEL, W., FRETWELL, N., JOBLING, M. A., HARIHARA, S., SHIMIZU, K., SEMJIDMAA, D., SAJANTILA, A., SALO, P., CRAWFORD, M. H., GINTER, E. K., EVGRAFOV, O. V., and TYLER-SMITH, C. (1997), 'Genetic relationships of Asians and Northern Europeans, revealed by Y-chromosomal DNA analysis', *American Journal of Human Genetics*, 60: 1174–83.

ZORC, R. D. (1995), 'A glossary of Austronesian reconstructions', in D. T. Tryon (ed.), *Comparative Austronesian Dictionary: An Introduction to Austronesian Studies* (Berlin: Mouton de Gruyter), 1105–97.

Index